VOCATIONAL STUDIES, LIFELONG LEARNING AND SOCIAL VALUES

For Pat, Paul and Sue, who are all members
of the lifelong learning community -
whether they know it or not

Monitoring Change in Education
Series Editor: Cedric Cullingford

Vocational Studies, Lifelong Learning and Social Values

Investigating education, training and NVQs under the New Deal

TERRY HYLAND
Lecturer in Continuing Education at the University of Warwick

Ashgate
ARENA

Aldershot • Brookfield USA • Singapore • Sydney

Published by
Ashgate Publishing Ltd
Gower House
Croft Road
Aldershot
Hants GU11 3HR
England

Ashgate Publishing Company
Old Post Road
Brookfield
Vermont 05036
USA

Ashgate website: http://www.ashgate.com

British Library Cataloguing in Publication Data
Hyland, Terry
  Vocational studies, lifelong learning and social values :
  investigating education, training and NVQs under the new
  deal. - (Monitoring change in education)
  1. Continuing education - Great Britain 2. Continuing
  education - Government policy - Great Britain 3. Vocational
  education - Great Britain 4. Vocational education -
  Government policy - Great Britain 5. Continuing education -
  Social aspects - Great Britain 6. Vocational education -
  Social aspects - Great Britain
  I. Title
  374'.0941

Library of Congress Catalog Card Number: 99-72977

ISBN 1 84014 847 0

Printed in Great Britain by
Antony Rowe Ltd, Chippenham, Wiltshire

Contents

List of Figures

List of Abbreviations

ALBSU	Adult Literacy and Basic Skills Unit
BCC	British Chambers of Commerce
BTEC	Business and Technology Educational Council
CAL	Computer-Assisted Learning
CBET	Competence-Based Education and Training
CBI	Confederation of British Industry
C&G	City and Guilds
CPVE	Certificate of Pre-Vocational Education
DES	Department of Education and Science
DfEE	Department of Education and Employment
DTI	Department of Trade and Industry
EDAP	Employment Development and Assistance Programme
FE	Further Education
FEDA	Further Education Development Agency
FEFC	Further Education Funding Council
FEU	Further Education Unit
GNVQ	General National Vocational Qualification
HCT	Human Capital Theory
HE	Higher Education
HEC	Higher Education for Capability
HMI	Her Majesty's Inspectorate
HRD	Human Resource Development
HRM	Human Resource Management
ICT	Information and Communications Technology
IiP	Investors in People
MA	Modern Apprenticeship
MSC	Manpower Services Commission
NACETT	National Advisory Council for Education and Training Targets
NCC	National Curriculum Council
NCVQ	National Council for Vocational Qualifications
NIACE	National Institute of Adult Continuing Education
NTETs	National Training and Education Targets
NTOs	National Training Organisations
NVQ	National Vocational Qualification

OFSTED	Office for Standards in Education
PCET	Post-Compulsory Education and Training
QCA	Qualifications and Curriculum Authority
RSA	Royal Society of Arts
SMEs	Small and Medium-Sized Enterprises
SVQ	Scottish Vocational Qualification
TEC	Training and Enterprise Council
TVEI	Technical and Vocational Education Initiative
UfI	University for Industry
VET	Vocational Education and Training
WTW	Welfare to Work
YTS	Youth Training Scheme

1 Lifelong Learning and Post-School Education and Training

Introduction

Lifelong learning is the slogan chosen by the Labour government to summarise, publicise and popularise its values and policies for education and training under the new administration. The government's National Advisory Group was appointed specifically to address issues of lifelong learning (Fryer, 1997), the concept features prominently in the Kennedy report on further education (Kennedy, 1997) and the Dearing report on higher education (Dearing, 1997), and lifelong learning assumptions dominate and dictate all the key policies in the government Green Paper *The Learning Age* (DfEE, 1998a). The concept of lifelong learning is, however, by no means a new one. Like its predecessor, the 'learning society', it has been appropriated from the adult education tradition (Hyland, 1994a; Edwards, 1997; Duke, 1992; Barnett, 1998) in order to prescribe a conception of learning, from the 'cradle to the grave' or, as Henry Morris put it, with the aim of 'raising the school leaving age to 90' (Kellner, 1998, p.15), to replace the mainstream and dominant school-centred, so-called 'front-loading' model of education. It might be worth examining these earlier manifestations in a little more depth before looking at the reconstructed model and the current policies being subsumed under the lifelong learning banner.

Learning, Life and Society

In a recent editorial celebrating its seventeenth year of publication, the *International Journal of Lifelong Education* rejoiced in the fact that 'lifelong education' has really come to the fore in the educational vocabulary in recent years' (IJLE, 1998, p.69). The editors go on, however, to complain that the concept is:

> increasingly being equated with continuing education and related rather specifically to vocational updating for which academic qualifications are awarded...we are certainly not here opposing the growth of academic and vocational qualifications that are emerging, but, if we are not careful, education which does not result in a qualification will not be regarded as 'real' education or 'real' learning (ibid.).

At various stages in the chapters which follow I will be criticising this excessively 'economistic' (Avis et al., 1996) conception of learning and the obsession with qualifications, awards and credit (Hyland, 1996a,c). For the moment it is worth taking note of the way in which the original meaning of lifelong learning has been mutated and employed to support objectives and policies which are quite some way from the philosophy of adult education espoused by mainstream practitioners.

Lifelong *education* (as opposed to lifelong *learning*, a shift which, as will be noted later, has important implications for practice) has its roots in the adult education tradition of 'recurrent education' (Houghton & Richardson, 1974) and *'education permanente'* (Schuller & McGarry, 1979) which seek to challenge the stereotypical school-centred, front-loading model of education.   The central perspective is of an education that is:

> planned as something which will be experienced by people in an individually ongoing, though discontinuous way, over the whole of their lives - and which will correspond with their emerging vocational, social and cultural aspirations (Legge, 1982, p.7).

Lawson (1975, pp.10-11) saw recurrent or lifelong education as a 'revolution...a shift in the current constellation of beliefs, values and technologies' of education; it is a reconstruction and reinterpretation of the educational task which:

> includes formal, non-formal and informal patterns of learning throughout the life cycle of an individual for the conscious and continuous enhancement of the quality of life, his own and that of his society (Dave, 1976, p.11).

Similarly, Lengrand (1975) asserts that the project of lifelong education is 'to be judged not in relation to other people or to a given body of knowledge external to the pupil, but in relation to the personal development of the particular individual' (p.51).

Contemporary versions of lifelong education, though retaining the learning throughout life connotations, tend to view the nature and purpose of learning primarily in terms of skills updating and the 'training and development needs' (Stephens, 1990, p.51) of employees. Tight (1998a) offers the view that the concept has become part of a trinity – lifelong learning, the learning organisation and the learning society – aimed at 'articulating the importance of continuing learning for survival and development at the levels of the individual, the organisation and society as a whole' (p.254). This provides interesting insights though it seems more accurate to say that, whereas the notion of the learning organisation applied to firms and businesses does have a legitimately vocationalist/economic thrust, we still need to account for the way in which the other two items of the trinity have also come to be interpreted in this circumscribed way. Lifelong learning, increasingly linked in government policy documents (DfEE, 1998a,c,e) with the 'Learning Age' in which learning is the key to success in the global market, does not, as Strain (1998) points out, naturally carry such instrumental and economistic connotations, and it is worth marking the re-programming of these new educational shibboleths. The policy slogan which immediately preceded lifelong learning, the 'learning society', serves to illustrate how the process of 'vocationalisation' (a *leitmotif* of recent trends; see Halliday, 1990; Avis et al.,1996; Hyland, 1991, 1992, 1998c) has transformed the whole system of post-compulsory education and training (PCET).

Visions of the Learning Society

Barnett (1998, pp.14-15) examines four different conceptions of the learning society in his critical evaluation of the 1997 Dearing report on higher education:

i) the continuing replenishment of human capital so as to maintain and strengthen society's economic capital;
ii) the maintenance of cultural capital and the quality of life of individuals and the collective;

iii) the inculcation of democratic citizenship;
iv) an emancipatory conception aimed at fostering self-reflexive learners who can respond to change in a rational and creative manner.

Barnett concludes that the:

> Dearing conception of the learning society is the *economic* conception...but with a human face. Individual learning and development are to be welcomed but principally for their contribution to the growth of economic capital (ibid., p.15; original italics).

Moreover, this conception is based on the 'belief that it is individuals who must shoulder the burden of their own continuing regeneration' (ibid.).

Dearing's preference for an economistic model of the learning society, on the grounds that 'in the future, competitive advantage for advanced economies will lie in the quality, effectiveness and relevance of their provision for education and training' (Dearing, 1997, para.34), though some way short of the most extreme vocationalised conceptions of the learning society, reflects the culture shift in educational values and aims that has occurred in Britain over the last twenty years or so (Tight, 1998b, makes some interesting comparisons which highlight commonalities in this respect between the Dearing, Fryer and Kennedy reports). The report on higher education by the Robbins committee (1963), though alluding to vocational preparation, was concerned principally with the intellectual, cultural and social aims of education, a perspective shared by the authors of the 1973 Russell Report (DES,1973) on adult education. All this is a long way from current conceptions of lifelong learning neatly summed up in the Secretary of State's comments on the 1998 government Green Paper. Mr Blunkett observed that:

> the ability to manage and use information is becoming the key to the competitive strength of advanced economies. With increasing globalisation, the best way of getting and keeping a job will be to have the skills needed by employers...For individuals who want security in employment and a nation that must compete worldwide, learning is the key (Blunkett, 1998, p.18).

Recent policy analyses of conceptions of the learning society have provided more detailed and finely nuanced models within which to locate and explain contemporary developments in lifelong learning. The first point of note in this sphere is that, in addition to the debate about whether the learning society is simply a 'myth' which has 'no real prospect of coming into existence in the forseeable future' (Hughes & Tight, 1998, p.188) or, alternatively, a project which 'redefines educational needs and refurbishes the institutional forms by which these are provided within the polity' (Strain & Field, 1998, p.239), there is a diverse and complex array of learning society models on offer.

Using the work of Gallie (1964) on 'essentially contested concepts' (Gallie gives the examples of freedom, religion and democracy to illustrate the idea), Young (1998) rightly chooses to characterise conceptions of the learning society as being:

> essentially contested, in which the different meanings given to it not only reflect different interests but imply different visions of the future and different strategies for getting there (p.193).

This observation is worth noting since, in examining recent and current policy and practice on post-compulsory education and training, it will be important to mark the difference between those that are merely 'mythical' or 'visionary' which, though not actually existing at present, provide prescriptions for future theory and practice, and those which are actually operating or, at least, are emerging from the contemporary welter of policy documents on lifelong learning. Rikowski (1998a) also makes a valuable contribution to the debate in pointing out that most (if not all) of the current conceptions of the learning society are essentially examples of 'idealist educationalist discourse' (p.223), often incorporating a strong 'utopian element' which renders them 'unhistorical', 'survivalist' and 'indeterminate' (pp.226-228). Against these constructions, which are underpinned by a 'general reluctance to see the learning society, in materialist, historical, form-determined ways', Rikowski recommends a 'materialist theory of the learning society [which] at least holds out the promise of a new form of society emerging out of existing capitalist society'(p.229).

Rikowki's trenchant critiques (1998b,c,d, 1999) of policy and practice in post-compulsory VET provide valuable insights into current trends in education and training (particularly with reference to employment-related skills and modern apprenticeships) and will be referred to again in later chapters of the book. At this stage, it is worth examining in more detail three elaborated typologies of the 'learning society' concept which supplement those offered by Barnett and others already referred to and which have the potential for providing a coherent, analytic framework for identifying and explaining current trends in the field.

Edwards (1997) identifies three 'senses' of a learning society distilled from the 'multiple discourses' (p.175) which have characterised debate in this field over the last quarter century (pp.184ff.):

1. Based on the adult lifelong education tradition discussed above, the learning society can be characterised as an 'educated society committed to active citizenship, liberal education and equal opportunities'. This conception 'supports lifelong learning within the social policy frameworks of post-Second World War social democracies'.

2. A learning society is a 'learning market enabling institutions to provide services for individuals as a condition for supporting the competitiveness of the economy'. This perspective 'supports the "economic policy framework adopted by many governments since the middle of the 1970s" with the aim of establishing "a market in learning opportunities…to meet the demands of individuals and employers for the updating of skills and competences"'.

3. A learning society is 'one in which learners adopt a learning approach to life, drawing on a wide range of resources to enable them to support their lifestyle practices'. In this version the 'normative goals of a liberal democratic society – an educated society – and an economically competitive society – a learning market – are displaced by a conception of participation in learning as an activity in and through which individuals and groups pursue their heterogeneous goals'.

On the basis of what has been discussed thus far about contemporary policy and practice on PCET, we can state fairly confidently that conception (1) was an early adult education vision which has never been fully realised, and versions of (3) are held by a number of contemporary commentators on post-school and adult education but, as yet, do not substantially influence policy and practice. Conception (2), on the other hand, seems to match perfectly current government policy on lifelong learning set out in the various DfEE *Learning Age* documents. In short, the prevailing model is the economistic model which Barnett identified in Dearing's vision for higher education though, as will be discussed in later chapters, this tends to be supplemented under New Labour with certain broader social and educational goals which were markedly absent from policy documents issued under their Conservative predecessors.

Young's (1998) analysis of the basic conceptions begins with the chilling observation that in 'all countries of Western Europe post-compulsory education is either...in a crisis, or, as in the Nordic countries and Germany, the subject of increasing questioning and critique' (p.189). The analysis goes on to to explain that:

> Post-compulsory education in the UK, however...also suffers from a crisis of its own history. The UK faces the economic and cultural challenges shared by all European countries that I have referred to. However, it also inherits a weak system of compulsory education...and low levels of participation and attainment (except in the private sector) in a post-compulsory sector that is over-specialized, sharply divided and with vocational provision that carries little credibility (p.190).

Against the background of this gloomy picture, Young outlines three models of the learning society which, in their own way, attempt to grapple with the post-school crisis:

1. *The schooling model*: stresses 'high participation in post-compulsory schooling as a way of ensuring that the maximum proportion of the population reach as far beyond a minimum level of education as possible' (ibid., p.194). Both strong (Nordic and S.E.Asian countries) and weak (UK, France) versions suffer from the flaw of conceptualising education as an end in itself, thus unduly perpetuating academic as against general or vocational culture. Schooling is also expensive (so not really affordable by poorer and developing nations) and does not fully connect with other forms of learning in communities, at work and in the diversity of non-formal settings.

2. *The credentialist model*: gives 'priority to ensuring that the vast majority of the population have qualifications or certificated skills and knowledge and that the qualifications people achieve are related to their future employment' (p.195). Germany provides a paradigm example of this model and aspects of the German approach were unsuccessfully attempted in Britain with the new vocationalist initiatives of the 1980s. Its main, and fatal, weakness is its concentration on credentials and certificates rather than skills and knowledge. At its worst it leads to the 'diploma disease' described by Dore (1976, 1997, and discussed in

greater depth in Chapter 3) resulting in chronic and wasteful qualification inflation.

3. *The access model*: represents a 'vision of a learning society of the future in which learning, after the phase of compulsory schooling, is increasingly freed from its ties with specialized educational institutions such as schools, colleges and universities' (p.197). It has connections with neo-liberal notions which seek to remove state control of education (Tooley, 1995) and, in an earlier version, can be linked to the de-schooling literature of the 1970s (Buckman, 1973). Its key weakness is that it rests on a utopian vision of self-motivated learners taking responsibility for their own learning bydrawing upon a wide range of resources and networks with the aim of building up an ever-expanding portfolio of knowledge and skills. Its main weakness is just this idealist rhetoric which is divorced from the real world of post- school learning in which, to take Britain as an example, there is a large cohort of under-achievers with around 7 million people lacking basic literacy and numeracy skills (DfEE, 1998a, p.12). Young asserts that the 'access model's focus on learner choice, access to IT, and credit transfer can only lead to low-level pracical skills, which all the trends suggest are less and less demanded by enployers' (p.199). In spite of all this (though I should stress that Young does not make these points, and that the following are part of my own analysis) this model, arguably, underpins much of what is currently developing in UK education, from school to university, that the model directly informs most of post-compulosry practice (especially in the FE sector), that it provides the rationale for most of the lifelong learning policies of the Learning Age documents and that it is, clearly and unequivocally, the model which provides the theoretical foundation for the development of contemporary schemes under the University for Industry (UfI) umbrella (see Hillman, 1997, discussed in later chapters).

From the critical remains of these models, Young then offers a preferred fourth strategy, the *educative model*, which 'starts with a recognition that all social life involves learning,whether conscious and planned or not' (p.203). It is further informed by Engestrom's work (1994) outlining three orders of learning: rote learning, learning by doing and expansive learning. Defined as a model within which the 'learner questions and begins to transform the context or community of practice in which the learning takes place', this idea of 'expansive learning' is recommended by Young who suggests that 'following through its implications can enable schools, colleges or training programmes to help students, teachers and people in the community to design and implement their own futures, as their prevailing practices show symptoms of crisis' (ibid., pp.203-4; I would connect this idea of expansive learning with, both the notions of 'deep' learning referred to in Chapter 2, and also with the main features of the 'studentship' strategies discussed in Chapter 7).

A third typology of the learning society is constructed by Ranson (1998a) who, drawing on a formidable range of theoretical and practical literature concerned with ways of linking learning with societal change and transformation, identifies four interrelated versions of learning societies:

1. *A society which learns about itself and how it is changing*: Drawing on the work of Schon (1971), this conception is concerned essentially with coping with structural change, economic, political, and cultural, by means of modifying approaches to learning. Within this framework, learning is used to temper the 'dynamic conservatism' of many societies so that they 'become capable of transforming themselves without intolerable disruption' (p.3).

2. *A society which needs to change the way it learns*: Using frameworks developed by Husen (1974), this society is informed by the attempt to reform educational/learning structures and modes to keep pace with technological, communication and epistemological change. In order to provide young people with general education, vocational education and 'general citizenship', reformed schooling/education systems will be required to accommodate 'first, a massive expansion in participation in education, second, the appropriate technology to support the knowledge explosion...third, the need to individualize instruction so that each student develops a programme of learning that suits them best' (Ranson, 1998a, p.4).

3. *A society in which all its members are learning*: A learning society is also 'one which recognizes that learning cannot be separated from society and is not just for the young but for all, throughout their lives' (ibid., p.5). Using ideas from radical writers on schoolling such as Holt (1977) and Illich (1973), Ranson further characterises the development of such a society in terms of its reflection upon the 'conditions for...continuing lifelong learning' which leads to the conclusion that

'diversity, accessibility, transferability, partnership and accountability become the defining characteristics of a comprehensive system of continuing education' (ibid., p.7).

4. *A society which learns to democratically change the conditions of learning*: This final societal stage is shaped by the idea that 'a learning society must be a learning democracy'. The task of 'reforming education from an elite (selective) to a socially just (comprehensive) system can never be a purely educational or pedagogical problem, but has to be conceived as a social and political one' (ibid.). In this sphere, the much-quoted Habermasian notion of 'communicative rationality' is utilised to explain how 'open public discourse' is required to bring about the optimal conditions of the learning society. The 'process of reasoning in public discourse helps to uncover common ends and thus to transform different groups into sharing a sense of the community, to become a public' (ibid., p.9).

Thus, Ranson offers us a form of stage-development model of how a learning society might operate in theory and practice; until the conditions of one stage are satisfied, it is not feasible to try to deal with the requirements of the subsequent stage. This highly nuanced and many-layered account of the learning society is completed – by drawing on a complexity of traditions such as Deweyan epistemology, Kolb's experiential theories and ideas surrounding the learning organisation and the learning city (community) – by Ranson through the description of how the polity, the learning democracy might address the urgent task of learning how to act together more effectively. If this task is to be realised:

> then a polity is needed for our time which expresses a new vision of the public domain, in which the public are conceived neither as passive clients, nor as competing consumers, but as active citizens encouraged to contribute to and take a shared responsibility for the development of their society – a learning society which grasps the value of opening itself to reflective understanding of the diversity of culture within as much as to the issues which press in upon it from without. The role of this democractic polity is to develop the conditions for such a learning society to unfold (ibid., p.24).

There is something in each of these typologies which can help us to characterise, explain and understand the contemporary debate about lifelong learning and the current policy trends and practical schemes being implemented in the post-compulsory sector. Indeed, Ranson's developmental model in many ways provides the ethico-political rationale for elements contained in the models offered by Young and Edwards, and there are clear connections between the key features of all three principal models. The analytic frameworks provided by these and other models will be referred to in later chapters, particularly in Chapter 8 which attempts to identify current New Labour education and training policies against the background of different conceptions of lifelong learning and the learning society. At this stage, it would be worth looking in more detail at the recent history of policy developments in education and training which led to the contemporary, contested, complex and often polarised, debate about the nature and function of learning and, more particularly, at the challenge to the old liberal ideal from utilitarian and economistic conceptions of the educational task.

The McDonaldisation of Education and Training

How can we explain the shift from broad social and cultural educational objectives, a consensus about which held until the mid 1970s, to the essentially utilitarian, economistic model of education and training which receives widespread endorsement and approval in the late 1990s? Policy analysts have pointed to a number of global trends which have characterised educational developments in industrial nations in the quarter century since the oil crisis of the early 1970s (Ball, 1990; Avis et al., 1996; Hutton, 1995; Halpin & Troyna, 1994).

Firstly, there has been a centralisation of state control over both education systems and social life in general (Jenkins, 1995), reflected in Britain in the 1980s 'New Right' challenge to the educational establishment through the introduction of a national curriculum and testing system (Maclure, 1989; Lawton, 1989), the erosion of local authority power, the application of market principles to education, and the attack on teachers' professional autonomy (Maclure, 1998; Hyland, 1998a). During the first half of 1998 prescriptions and detailed specifications for literacy and numeracy in the school curriculum issued by the Secretary of State for Education and Employment have demonstrated that the new Labour administration is no less inclined to centralised control over education than its Conservative predecessor (Wragg, 1998). In the further education (FE) sector, highly prescriptive schemes based on National Vocational Qualifications (NVQs) and, to a lesser extent, GNVQs provide a form of centralised control and post-school national curriculum, and the attempt to extend the NVQ schemes to higher education (Hyland, 1996b; Barnett, 1994) completes the process for all levels of the system. Most recently the Dearing report on HE with its emphasis on standard programme specifications for all degree programmes has reinforced state control over university curricula (Barnett, 1998), and Earl Russell has warned that the Teaching and Higher Education Bill will give the Secretary of State the 'power to kill universities altogether' (1997, p.16).

These developments in the HE sector, though occurring much later than the centralising control of school and FE curricula, provide an interesting example of the cascading of the 1980s New Right philosophy (now, of course, tempered, mediated and reconstructed as a 'third way' by the New Labour administration, Labour Party 1997; Brivati, 1998; Giddens, 1998) throughout the whole system. Alongside the growth of state regulation of education there has been (as was briefly referred to earlier) a parallel vocationalisation of the curriculum at all levels in line with what Barnett (1990) has described as the 'growing clamour from industry for the graduates it employs to have more work-related skills' (p.158). In fact, Barnett's systematic analysis of HE trends over the last decade or so provides a microcosm of the changes in the British educational system as a whole over the last few decades.

In recent times the modern university has experienced what Aviram (1992) has called an 'identity crisis' which, externally, 'stems from growing pressures on the university to prove its pragmatic utility' and, internally, 'from a lack of firm and shared belief within the university concerning the nature of its educational mission' (p.183). In similar terms, Barnett has written of the current 'undermining of the value background of higher education' (1990, p.8), epistemologically, through relativistic theories of knowledge and, sociologically, through the loss of academic freedom and autonomy as a result of the increasing influence of the state, industry and other agencies over what goes on in universities.   Similar developments have characterised continental HE systems in recent years. Neave (1992), for instance, has noted the 'strengthening of the vocational element in the higher education systems of Western Europe' (p.23) resulting in a tension between 'training in the mastery of techniques specifically geared to one precise occupation' and 'general study and the acquisition of understanding' (pp.5-6).   Broadly parallel movements towards a 'more vocationally or professionally oriented conception of advanced learning in the German HE system have been reported by Gellert & Rau (1992) and echoed in observations on university studies in France (Lamoure & Rontopoulou, 1992) and Norway (Berg, 1992).   Indeed, as Esland (1996) has commented, this 'globalisation' of vocational trends can be seen to match the globalisation of capital and industry in the current post-Fordist world economic climate.

In the school sector the vocationalisation of British education can be traced back to the 1970s when the 'Fordist industrial development model and its accompanying tripartite divison of schooling broke down when the end of the post-war, long boom in the 1973 oil crisis removed its economic underpinning of full employment' (Gokulsing, Ainley & Tysome, 1996, p.13).   However, rather than attending to the obvious causes of economic recession and decline – the dominance of finance capital, the erosion of the industrial base and the failure of investment policies – politicians initiated a concerted campaign aimed at the 'displacement of responsibility for economic failure and decline from political and economic arenas to the educational and training institutions' (Esland, 1990, p.v).

The end of the liberal consensus on the purpose of schooling is typically dated from the period of the Great debate following Callaghan's Ruskin College speech in 1976 (Whitty, 1985).   In the years that followed, the role of education in helping to boost economic and industrial performance was taken up by public figures and politicians and subsequently reflected in Department for Education and Science (DES) publications.   As Esland (1996b) has observed, between '1977 and the late 1980s countless conferences heard countless industrialists restate the Wiener (1981) thesis that Britain's economic problems stemmed from the fact that it was a nation of anti-industrial values' (p.46).   In the struggle for the curriculum in the late 1970s and early 1980s the vocational lobby, especially with the activities of the Manpower Services Commission (MSC) from the mid-1970s (Evans, 1992), gained a noticeable edge as the (as it was to turn out, short-lived) Certificate of Pre-Vocational Education (CPVE) was introduced into schools to parallel the growth of Youth Training Schemes (YTS) in the post-school sector (Sharp, 1997).

By 1984 Sir Keith Joseph, in his North of England Conference speech, was urging the adoption of a curriculum with a 'practical element' which was 'relevant to the real world'; the 'technical and vocational aspect of school learning should have its proper place' (Joseph, 1984, p.4).   The Green Paper *Education in Schools* (DES, 1977) had emphasised the role of education in aiding British economic recovery through the improvement of manufacturing industry, and the change of ethos is clearly reflected in the policy document *Better Schools* which recommended a 5 to 16 curriculum designed to foster:

> the qualities, attitudes , knowledge, understanding and competences which are necessary to equip pupils for working life.   With this aim in view the Government has established the Technical and Vocational Education Initiative (TVEI) which explores how best to fit work-related skills within full-time education (DES, 1985a, p.6).

From the outset, TVEI schemes were guided by the MSC definition of VET as that in 'which students are concerned to acquire generic or specific skills with a view to employment' and TVEI was designed ultimately to influence 'the whole curriculum including such areas as mathematics and English' (Pickard, 1985, p.23).

TVEI schemes became an integral part of the so-called 'new vocationalism'(Esland, 1990) of the 1980s, having a major impact on the 14-16 curriculum in particular since 'schools and local education authorities (LEAs) found it impossible in the long term to ignore the considerable cash incentives' (Sharp, 1997, p.11) supplied to support and popularise the schemes.   Both the spending power (the chief vehicle of manipulation and control) and the political authority of the MSC increased apace, particularly so in the post-school sector in which, at a stroke, the MSC took control of around 25% of work-related non-advanced further education in 1985/86 (Statham et al., 1989, p.177).   In subsequent years the Training Agency and later the Training, Enterprise and Education Directorate (TEED), a branch of the Employment Department (ED which is normally cited as the Department of Employment (DOE) prior to the 1990s), and the regional Training and Enterprise Councils (TECs) were effectively to restructure VET policy and practice around a New Right economic agenda under the umbrella of NCVQ activity (Hyland, 1994a; Avis et al., 1996; Marks, 1996).

Accounts of the most recent stages of this vocationalising process, particularly the development of NVQs and their impact on education and training, will be taken up again in later chapters, particularly in relation to the policies of the post-1997 New Labour agenda for VET.   At this point it is worth pointing to the hegemony of the New Right's attempts to re-engineer VET and also the relentless manner in which the principal objectives were imposed on the system. The New Right monetarist policies of the 1980s went hand in hand with the Treasury view 'that education should serve the economic needs of the country' (Ranson, 1984, p.223) and such a perspective has been maintained, with only slight changes of emphasis, right down to the policy papers on Competitiveness in the 1990s (DTI, 1994, 1995). Esland (1996a) articulates clearly the nature and purpose of such policies in his argument that:

> For the past two decades British education policy has been drawn increasingly into the national game-plan for Britain's participation in the global economy. Education's traditional liberal humanistic values have been derided and abandoned by the New Right and replaced by a totalizing and unreflexive business-oriented ideology expressed through a discourse based on markets, targets, audits, 'quality performance', and human resource management. Opportunities to influence future policy have been extended increasingly to employers, both as individuals on boards of governors and collectively on numerous quangos, at the same time as they have been withdrawn from educational professionals (p.20).

As a response to the official rhetoric about the need to equip all students with the high-level, technological skills for a new age, Esland reminds us that:

> as job opportunities for young people have declined, priority has been attached to preparing them for low-cost, 'flexible' labour markets capable of attracting inward investment and of undercutting the higher labour costs of those countries which British governments insist on calling their 'competitors'. In short, the acquiescence of educational institutions in what are seen as the demands of global capitalism is regarded by political and business leaders as axiomatic (ibid.).

Esland's powerful and coruscating critique of two decades of reform and restructuring of VET in Britain (approximately from 1975 to 1995) provides a conceptual and ideological framework within which to locate some of the central topics and issues to be discussed throughout the rest of this book. To conclude this section, it would be useful to examine another valuable explanatory framework, in the form of Ritzer's concept of 'McDonaldisation' which provides a powerfully imaginative way of articulating, understanding and explaining the economic/educational conflation which underpins the globalisation project described by Esland.

Ritzer (1993) originally used the term 'McDonaldisation' in the construction of a model to describe and explain the increasing technical rationalisation of more and more aspects of social life. It has been used to good effect by Hartley (1995) to describe the standardisation of university curricula and teaching/learning strategies, and provides a powerful metaphorical and heuristic tool (Hyland, 1998a; Alfino, Caputo & Wynyard, 1998) for mapping the sort of educational developments referred to above. The key features of the McDonaldisation of education and training in recent years can be presented in terms of the following categories:

- *efficiency*: of overriding importance - both to policy-makers and, through the manipulation of funding mechanisms by quangos such as the Teacher Training Agency (TTA), the Further Education Funding Council (FEFC) or the Higher Education Funding Council (HEFC), to educational institutions from schools to universities - is the 'efficient' delivery of products (in the form of achievement of approved qualifications or completion of courses) measured against national targets (NACETT, 1995, 1998). In practice, efficiency has been constructed to mean the achievement of the maximum in output terms with the minimum in input terms (length of courses, teaching/learning costs). One of the consequences of this input/output approach has been the modularisation of curricula, the atomisation of programmes into conveniently-sized individualised pre-packaged units for 'efficient' delivery to students. Institutions in both the further (Reeves, 1995) and higher education (Hyland, 1998a; Barnett, 1994) sectors become 'black boxes', the inner workings of which are important only to the extent that they succeed in converting inputs to outputs as efficiently as possible.

- *quantification and calculability*: in order to achieve the efficiency targets, outputs have to be easily identifiable and measurable, hence the overriding concern with outcomes (see Jessup, 1991) at the expense of everything else. The obsession with the outcomes of learning - at the expense of aims, purposes, knowledge,values and learning processes - is without question the *leitmotif* of developments in education and training over the last two decades and exemplified in perhaps its purest form in the rise of the NCVQ and the popularisation of CBET (Hyland, 1994a, 1997; Bates, 1998). In addition to an obsession with achieving end products in the form of approved outputs (national targets dominated by NVQs/GNVQs, or those approved for funding purposes under Schedule 2 of the 1992 Further & Higher Education Act; Great Britain Statutes, 1992, p.74), the certification of all forms of learning by attaching credit values to it (Hyland, 1996a,c) is a consequence of this 'commodification' and 'mercantilisation' (Lyotard, 1984) of knowledge and educational purpose.

* *predictability and control*: the quantification and commodification of education in this way results in a foreclosure of aims and puposes. The ends of education and training become fixed and pre-determined in terms of officially approved outputs in the form of national targets and predominantly couched in terms of precriptive NVQ/GNVQ specifications. In FE this process has been developing apace since the late 1980s with the result that the curriculum is now dominated by prescriptive programmes with little scope for anything other than what is officially accredited (to the detriment of many community, access or non-vocational 'leisure' type courses for adults, Burstall, 1996; Russell, 1997). Universities, as mentioned earlier, have been to some extent protected from such centralised encroachment until relatively recently but are now having to respond to an agenda defined by outside agencies. Dearing's report on the HE sector is leading to controls on both staff development and training and, in the form of a 'programme specification' which , for all degrees, gives the 'intended outcomes of the programme in terms of...key skills, cognitive skills, and subject-specific skills' (Dearing, 1997, Rec.21). The upshot of all this centralised prescription is to stifle student-teacher interaction and to inhibit the development of studentship (Bloomer, 1997) by severely restricting the scope for teachers and students to negotiate the curriculum.

* *fake fraternisation*: centralised control over the ends of education and training through highly prescriptive outputs raises the problem of satisfying the demands of consumers for choice and autonomy. It is a paradox that the growth of outcome- and competence-based programmes has been accompanied by a rhetoric of student-centredness and independent learning (see Jessup, 1991; Burke, 1995). The shallowness and sophistry of such developments, the idea of having closed ends but open means, has been demonstrated forcefully through the experiences of students and teachers charged with implementing, in particular, NCVQ-approved courses (Hyland, 1994b; Hodkinson, 1996; Wolf, 1995). There is a dynamic relationship and interaction between means and ends, process and product, learning and assessment, which precludes the possibility of simply bolting on behaviourist outcomes to programmes founded on cognitive/humanistic learning theories

The popularity and persuasiveness of student-centredness, however, has led CBET and outcomes-based learning proponents to seek to appropriate certain aspects of the progresssive tradition concerned with independent and self-directed learning (Edwards, 1993; Bates, 1998). Hence, the need for 'fake fraternisation' which, in the case of McDonald's customers consists in positively befriending a system designed essentially in the interests of maximum efficiency and profit-making (queuing to pay for meals, dutifully using disposable cutlery, etc.), in education and training is designed to persuade students, teachers and other end-users that they have autonomy and choice in a system in which highly prescriptive ouputs are all that matters.   In order to achieve such 'fraternisation', colleges have been re-engineered as providers of 'learner services'(FEU, 1992) and a whole battery of technicist innovations – needs analysis, modular options, learning contracts (Collins, 1991) – have been introduced to provide credibility for this 'humanising' enterprise.   In recent years the idea of providing 'flexibility' (Thomas, 1995) through computer-assisted learning (CAL) has moved centre stage for both schools (Cole, 1998) and FE/HE institutions (Armstrong, Thompson & Brown, 1997), and the use of such technology is a key element in New Labour's lifelong learning policies (see Hillman, 1997; DfEE, 1998a).   The links between CAL, learning networks and 'virtual' institutions (which might, after all, dispense with the need to employ quite so many teachers!) and the drive for greater efficiency in the future (doing yet more with even less) will be touched on in a number of places in subsequent chapters.

The McDonaldisation of education and training, involving standardisation, uniformity and centralised control of teaching and learning, has almost destroyed the idea of liberal education (Bailey, 1984; Collins, 1991) or, for that matter, any sort of education which is concerned with general educational goals relating to citizenship, social or personal development. The 'proliferation of centrally imposed policies and initiatives', observe Avis et al. (1996), has been powerful and coercive in its impact on the minds of practitioners and students' and the 'vocationalization of everyday life has functioned to disguise the complex and hugely problematic nature of the economizing of education' (pp.165-6). As an antidote to this it is worth examining what an alternative version of lifelong learning, informed by broad social values, might have to contribute to education and training.

Towards a Social Theory of Lifelong Learning

In contrast to the McDonaldised and excessively economistic conceptions of education and training, a 'social' theory of lifelong learning would be informed by the perspective, outlined by Ranson et al.(1996),which holds that:

> if society is seriously to address the problems facing education then the solution requires more than a quantitative expansion or more adaptation of existing systems. Rather it will need a reform of the organizing principles of learning: from an instrumental purpose, supporting the needs of the labour market and economic regeneration, to the moral and political purpose of cultural renewal; from learning for economic interest to learning for citizenship' (p.25).

In a more recent elaboration, Ranson & Stewart (1998) have described the 'learning society' as one which 'encourages individuals to value their active role of citizens and thus their shared responsibility for the common wealth' (p.270). As an inspirational statement, I would endorse the project outlined by Ranson with the following qualification. The instrumental nature of education can be applied just as well to, for example, education for citizenship (see, for instance, the citizenship document produced by the former National Curriculum Council, NCC, 1990) as it can to vocational preparation for work. In any case, if instrumental is interpreted in teleological terms as simply taking a means to an end, then what really matters is that both the means and ends satisfy the values and normative criteria built into the concept of education (Peters, 1966). Thus, if education is instrumental in bringing about 'cultural renewal' and 'learning for citizenship', then little more can be asked.

The distinction between 'instrumental' and 'non-instrumental' (or between 'general/vocational' or 'practical/theoretical') educational pursuits cannot be sharply drawn outside concrete and specific programmes since, as Peters (1978) has observed, both theoretical and practical activities can be engaged in 'for their own sakes' (p.9). As Dearden (1990) notes in examining the vexed questions surrounding the differences and relationships between education and training, there are no *a priori* reasons why, in certain contexts, they should not be perfectly compatible; a 'process of training could be liberally conceived in such a way as to explore relevant aspects of understanding, and in a way which satisfies the internal standards of truth and adequacy' (p.93; in this context see also Winch, 1995). Similar arguments are considered by Peters (1966) who, in proposing 'cognitive perspective' as one key feature of educational processes, would not 'deny value to activities which have a limited educational content'. Thus, although 'cooking...is obviously an activity which is necessary for the maintenance of a way of life', it can be done 'just as a tiresome chore, or it can be delighted in for the opportunities for skill and igenuity which it affords' (pp.176-7).

Building on the foundation established by Ranson, and on the older tradition of lifelong learning rooted in adult education theory and practice (Collins, 1991; Lawson, 1998; and referred to in Edwards, 1997), I want to offer a sketch of what a social theory of lifelong learning might look like. The key features of this model will inform my positive comments on alternatives to current conceptions of education and training, with particular application to a values-based vocational studies, and will be employed in subsequent chapters to interrogate New Deal and Learning Age initiatives and the lifelong learning policies which underpin them.

1) *Individual Autonomy within a Social/Community Context*

In terms of a general policy for education and training in Britain, there is a need to provide some sort of counter-balance to the forces which have created an education system which is 'deeply imbued with a culture of individualism' which serves to repudiate the 'nineteenth-century concerns with the social functions of education' (Hargreaves, 1982, pp.87,93). Since there is a sense in which a balanced and rational notion of individual autonomy is inseparable from learning and educational development, it will be important to show how related conceptions concerned with democratic citizenship (also principal objectives of current educational reform; Crick, 1998) require a 'public dimension' (Smith, 1997) in which autonomy is located within the framework of shared values that are a prerequisite of induction into any form of genuinely social practice (MacIntyre, 1981; Lawson, 1998). Individualistic conceptions of education and training divorced from the public and the social went hand in hand with the popularising of that particular brand of economic individualism which underpinned the triumphalist neo-liberal period of the 'enterprise culture' (Heelas & Morris, 1992) and, in a different form, they are still evident in New Labour policies (and also still prominent in assessment practices based on CBET linked to NVQs; see Hyland, 1997a, 1998d). As against this technicist, atomistic conception, the cultural revolution needed to achieve current lifelong learning objectives will need to reinforce the idea that 'learning is quintessentially social' (Coffield, 1998, p.26) and that, in the words of the National Commission on Education, 'expanding educational achievement and opportunity is a community issue' (NCE, 1993, p.334).

2) *Studentship and Learning Careers*

Notwithstanding the rhetoric on student-centredness and independent learning appropriated for propagandist reasons from the progressive and andragogic tradition (Collins, 1991; Edwards, 1997), the current McDonaldised system is informed by a powerful and stultifying technicism which militates against genuine choice and creative engagement on the part of learners (and also teachers). If the key objective of *The Learning Age* requiring 'putting learners first' and helping them to 'take charge of their own learning' (DfEE, 1998a, para.1.1) is to be achieved, some conception of 'careership' (Hodkinson, 1996) which stresses learner empowerment needs to be built into the system, particularly within the 14-19 age range. Central to this process is the idea of 'studentship' which, in its broadest sense, is used by Bloomer (1996) to refer to the 'variety of ways in which students can exert influence over the curriculum in the creation and confirmation of their own personal careers' (p.140). This important concept of studentship, which needs to be applied to guidance and counselling provision as well as learning (Bloomer, 1997; Hyland, 1998b), will be employed to combat the mechanistic and technicist determinism (Standish, 1997) which arises from the McDonaldised and overly economistic model of education and training described earlier.

3) *Vocational Studies, Work and Society*

The 'new vocationalism' of the 1970s and 1980s continues (in a modified and reconstructed form) to influence VET policy and practice in the late 1990s and, thus, much like a computer virus, threatens to thwart and frustrate New Labour's plans for education and training subsumed under the lifelong learning banner. There are three main shortcomings of this model of VET:
i) It is based on the false premise that the main problems of VET rest somehow with the skills deficiencies of school leavers and employees. Hence, the tendency of new vocationalism to 'juvenalize and personalize' (Stronach, 1990, p.157) the problems of unemployment, and to offer

simplistic solutions to the problems of post-Fordist economic trends in the form of remedying skills deficits or skills shortages.

ii) For the last few decades vocational studies has been based upon grossly distorted and simplistic conceptions of what employers want or what industry needs (Hyland, 1996d; Finn, 1990; Wellington, 1994; Rikowski, 1998a). The upshot of this has been, on the one hand, the futile pursuit of illusory or radically misguided goals and, on the other, a dangerous reductionism which results in narrowly-focused skills training typified by NVQ occupationalism. Such a combination of errors not only fails to address the serious problems of VET in post-Fordist times but also produces a one-dimensional and morally improverished conception of VET as a process through which the student/trainees's 'personal powers, capacities, capabilities, skills and talents' are shaped so as to match the capital and labour power needs of industry as these change over time (Rikowski, 1998a, p.13). It is this extremely limited and utilitarian requirement which really lies behind the calls for 'flexible' and 'multi-skilled' workers on the part of employers and industrialists (Sieminski, 1993; Hyland, 1996b,d).

iii) Stemming directly from the processes and practices endorsed under (ii), there has been a marginalisation or neutralisation of the values dimension of VET which has generated an uncritical, monolithic and ethically vacuous approach by which something called 'moral competence' (Wright, 1989; Hyland, 1992a, 1995a) is recommended largely as a means of ensuring that students develop 'employability' qualities of the sort favoured by the Confederation of British Industry (CBI, 1989) and the Industry in Education (IIE, 1996) organisation. All this is highly regrettable since, from the point of view of *all* stakeholders whether they are employers, students, trainees,employees or citizens, attention to the moral dimension of VET is essential in order to achieve the social and educational goals implicit in lifelong learning policies.

In order to remedy all these shortcomings the positive conception of VET which underpins the accounts of contemporary policy and practice in the field offered in the following chapters will build on Dewey's broad conception of vocational education (Hyland, 1993) as an activity which transcends the vocational/academic divide and 'stresses the full intellectual and social meaning of a vocation' (Dewey, 1966, p.316). I will suggest that this perspective should inform all VET schemes – even short courses and those aimed at upgrading specific occupational skills in the workplace

– though it will clearly have a particular application in the 14-19 age group where it might form an education/learning for work core component of some form of unified curriculum which integrates vocational and general educational elements and courses.

This approach to VET is designed to satisfy a number of different criteria: the normative values implicit in all educational activity (Peters, 1966), the spirit of criticism characteristic of the liberal education tradition and essential for ensuring rational progress in education and training (Bailey, 1984; Barnett, 1994; Pring, 1997) the Deweyan conception which breaks down the vocational/academic divide (Hyland, 1993, 1995a), the general educational requirements of lifelong learning for all stakeholders and citizens (Ranson, 1994, 1998) in accordance with the New Labour values of inclusiveness and social justice (Fryer, 1997; Kennedy, 1997), and the 'spiritual and moral values' which, in the Dearing review of qualifications for 16-19 year olds were proposed as an 'essential element in education' (Dearing, 1996, para.2.10). Above all, this conception of vocational studies for lifelong learning will be one which:

> acknowledges social and personal aims, values and needs, and locates education and training goals in relation to the kind of society we wish to see develop and the qualities in people that are to be fostered and nourished (Skilbeck et al., 1994, p.46).

In the chapters which follow it will be argued that only by means of such a social theory of lifelong learning can the government's avowed vision of a 'new learning culture, a culture of lifelong learning for all' (Fryer, 1997, para.1.1) be realised.

2 The Reconstruction of Education and Training

In his introduction to the blueprint document for the UfI, Hillman (1997) observes that:

> Deficiencies in British education and training have been a cause for concern for policy-makers for 150 years. Partly in response to world-wide recognition of the importance of lifelong learning, there has been a flurry of reforms in the last ten years. The result has been an array of short-term and narrowly focused initiatives which have confused rather than clarified the situation for the learner (pp.29-30).

In a similar vein, Esland (1990) noted that although VET issues have 'remained high on the political agenda' since the 1970s oil crisis and recession, the state's response has typically been one of 'crisis management...giving rise to schemes and initiatives designed to limit the social damage which followed widespread de-industrialization' (p.v). Many of these schemes and initiatives formed part of the 'new vocationalism' of the 1980s and the 'flurry of reforms' noted by Hillman would include, amongst others, the establishment of the MSC, TVEI, YTS schemes, TECs, Training Credits, and NVQs/GNVQs.

Underpinning these accounts of VET is an underlying 'history of failure' which, in Maclure's (1991) view, has persisted because of the:

> strength of the individual and institutional resistance which has thwarted one attempt after another to reform vocational education and training over many decades – a cultural phenomenon which goes back at least as far as the abortive attempts to reform technical and vocational education in the last quarter of the nineteenth century (pp.6-7).

Aspects of this historical legacy will be touched on in Chapter 4 in the discussion of employers' complaints about the failure of schooling to supply industrial requirements. At this stage it would be worth examining briefly aspects of the history and origins of vocationalism in education –

culminating in the 19th and early 20th century attempts to establish vocational and technical provision – before reviewing some key developments of the last few decades as these came to be subsumed under the 'new vocationalism' banner. Following this, the important concept of apprenticeship (in former times, indispensable from conceptions of VET) will be examined, in particular its decline and reconstruction in the British state system in recent times.

Vocational Studies – A Brief Historical Outline

Noting John Stuart Mill's remark that the Ancient Greeks were the 'beginners of nearly everything, Christianity excepted, of which the modern world makes its boast', Castle (1967) assembled a body of carefully considered evidence to show that the 'Greeks were the first real educators of our western world' (p.11). Maclure (1991) has referred to the 'historic failure of English education to integrate the academic and the practical, the general and the vocational' (p.28). Although there is a tendency to view this educational schizophrenia as a relatively recent phenemon (perhaps developing after the establishment of the tripartite system following the 1944 Education Act; Dent, 1968), its Western origins can be found in the Greek tradition researched by historians such as Castle and Curtis & Boultwood (1970).

Castle shows how the vocational/general educational divisions can be discerned in the rival education systems of Sparta and Athens. Although all of the free citizens of the Greek city-states were committed – in terms of politics, morals, and social life – to the all-embracing concept of *arete* (all-round virtue or excellence in all walks of life) the Spartans interpreted this ideal in a radically different way from the Athenians. As a 'society of professional soldiers' the Spartans 'had little time for aesthetic cultivation and, indeed, continuous war had no doubt reduced [their] capacity to appreciate any cultural values that were not associated with military efficiency' (Castle, 1967, p.17). Thus, *arete* came to be interpreted strictly in vocational/utilitarian terms in a Spartan curriculum made up of 'military drill, hunting, swimming, riding, scout-craft, spying, and strenuous work under supervision in the gymnasium' (ibid., p.21).

In Athens, on the other hand, a state which was geographically open, rich in trade with overseas countries, and characterised by emerging conceptions of political democracy and citizenship (though also, of course, heavily dependent upon a substantial underclass of slave workers!), *arete* was 'no longer valour or service to the state, but personal political leadership, the management of other men' (ibid., p.50). Thus, the Athenian curriculum was more holistic, cultural and liberal; indeed, in the writings of the two Great Athenian philosophers of the period, Plato and Aristotle, we can find the origins of that general education which provided the foundation for the 'Seven Liberal Arts of the middle ages, the *trivium*, grammar, rhetoric and logic, and the *quadrivium*, geometry, arithmetic, astronomy and the theory of music (ibid., p.59).

In addition to the differences between Spartan and Athenian education, the vocational/academic divide is clearly articulated in the perspectives on education provided by Plato and Aristotle.   However, in spite of the different approaches to education which characterise the philosophers – perhaps stemming from the fact that 'Plato was essentially a mathematician, Aristotle a physician and biologist' (Curtis & Boultwood, 1970, p.31) – the practical/general educational division in approaches to the curriculum is contained *within* each of the philosophical approaches rather than *between* them. To be sure, Plato's *a priori* rationalist approach to knowledge led to a rather different curriculum (valuing maths, logic and dialectic) from the generally *a posteriori* empirical tendencies of Aristotle (favouring biology and the sciences).   In the end, however, both philosophers – having taken note of the differences between vocational and general educational pursuits – tended to opt for those general activities which are constitutive of what later became 'liberal' education (though, as observed in the last chapter, the concept of 'liberal' education is itself a multi-faceted concept).

Schofield (1972, pp.151-2) locates the original source of liberal education as being associated with 'freeing the mind from error' in Plato's distinction between 'genuine' knowledge (acquired through rational reflection) and mere 'opinion' (knowledge acquired for specific purposes). The former concept of knowledge, disinterested knowledge, came to be thought of as superior and intrinsically valuable, whereas the latter, instrumental or practical knowledge, came to be associated with more practical and less valued vocational pursuits (Lewis, 1991). In *The Politics* Aristotle offers an account of rival educational purposes and forces which is uncannily similar to the vocational/academic discourse running through educational debates since the establishment of formal schooling in the 19th century. In Book VIII he writes:

> For in modern times there are opposing views about the practice of education. There is no general agreement about what the young should learn either in relation to virtue or in relation to the best life; nor is it clear whether their education ought to be directed more towards the intellect than towards the character of the the the soul (Sinclair trans., 1962, p.300).

Aristotle's own educational preferences are, however, advocated forcefully in his insistence that the 'citizen must take part in only those useful occupations which do not degrade the doer'. He continues:

> We therefore call degrading those occupations which have a deleterious effect on the body's condition and all work that is paid for. For these make the mind preoccupied and unable to rise above menial things...It is proper for a free man to do something for himself or for his friends or on account of its value in itself, but he that does the same action on others' account may on occasion be regarded as doing something paid for or servile (ibid., p.301).

We can see plainly in this forthright statement of educational preferences by Aristotle – not just the seeds of that differential approach to knowledge in terms of its alleged intrinsic/instrumental value (criticised in Chapter 1 and returned to again at the end of this chapter) – but also the origins of that classical humanist version of liberal education which underpinned the 'gentleman ideal' which dominated the English public school and university tradition of the 18th and 19th centuries (and, of course, has not completely disappeared to this day). Wilkinson (1970) provides a graphic description of this ideal in his observation that:

> The gentleman was taught to consider himself above specialisation, whether in the sense of regional style or that of technical know-how. Both of the latter were reserved for his social inferiors, since specialization in any form was deemed narrowing. With regard to technical specialization,therefore, such expertise was the mark of one who had to use knowledge to earn a living and not for the leisured pursuit of wisdom and beauty. In any case, thought the gentleman, effective leadership depended upon general qualities of mind, on moral stature and mannerly self-assurance; endowments like these these far outweighed any amount of specialized skill (p.133).

It is not so much any particular content that is characteristic of this classical humanist heritage, but rather its historical association with power relationships in an hierachical society (Green, 1990). In fact, as Skilbeck (1987) argues, this tradition has demonstrated a 'remarkable capacity to change and adapt, from mathematics and philosophy, to theology, to classical languages, to literature, for example, according to changing cultural circumstances' (p.15). In this way a certain differential form of education (rather than any particular content) has come to be associated – as with the rulers in Plato's *Republic* – with an aristocratic elite. As Skilbeck puts it:

> In the twentieth century, the knowledge content of classical humanism is not static, but it is still held to confer leadership rights. Invariably, in classical humanist doctrine, the potential leaders are given a different and separate education from that of the masses (ibid.).

Notwithstanding such differentiation and hierarchical conceptions, it is still possible to discern a particular form of vocational impulse in this classical humanist tradition. In Plato and Aristotle, for instance, education served the purpose of preparing citizens for various kinds of service to the state, just as the classics were thought to foster the requisite values for colonial service in 19th century England. Moreover, the evolving medieval schools and universities which laid the foundations for this liberal tradition also had explicitly vocational purposes. As Coffey (1992) argues:

> formal education in England was originally specifically vocational and continued to respond to demands for training for clerical, administrative and legal operations generally. Developing grammar, trade and craft schools all served primarily vocational purposes (p.12).

The establishment of the degree system itself – particularly the differentiation between Bachelors and Masters – was inextricably connected with vocational/professional education and structured in terms of the medieval guild system. As Carr (1997) explains:

> For a Bachelor to become a Master of Arts he had to become a member of the Masters' Guild. What has to be remembered is that, in medieval universities, the liberal arts which formed the basis of the academic curriculum were construed as crafts – the crafts of the free person – so that a Master of Arts was someone who had mastered the craft skills that membership of this particular

guild required...Like becoming a Master carpenter or Master shipbuilder, becoming a Master of Arts required serving an apprenticeship by spending anything from three to six years learning to master the skills of a craft (pp.318-19).

The origins of university teaching and learning in the guild craftsmanship tradition – historically connected with the development of skills and artisanship in vocational education (Ainley, 1993) – is well worth noting by those attached to maintaining a division between academic and vocational pursuits.

Until late medieval times most British (more properly, English) schools - including, at this time, the public schools such as Winchester and Rugby (Leach, 1904) – were essentially 'common' schools which accepted 'poor' scholars alongside the sons of the gentry and charged nugatory fees. In the theory of education developed by Erasmus in the early 16th century – though unequivocally rooted in the traditional classicist mould – there is the idea that schooling is for all young people (though mainly boys rather than girls!), and that the ultimate aim was 'world citizenship' (Curtis & Boultwood, 1970, pp.129-130). However, all this was to change; as Kenneth Richmond (1945) explains:

> The conviction that there are two distinct brands of education, one for the rulers and another for commoners, dates from the sixteenth century. The divergence was not at first clearly marked; under the Stuarts, for example, the rich were far less cut off from intermingling with other classes in the schools than they are today; but the eighteenth century confirmed it as a hard-and-fast rule. Only towards the close of this period was there any observable distinction between the old Grammar Schools and the Public Schools (p.53).

Of course, the notion of a differential education system which caters for separate schooling for rulers and ruled is as old as Plato's *Republic*; Kenneth Richmond's point applied to the practical application of this notion to actual schooling practices in Britain. For the status of vocational studies, such stratification was disastrous, since it emphasised both the divisions between vocational and liberal studies and definitively classified vocational learning as second-rate and inferior.

During the Renaissance and Reformation periods, although higher education was dominated by a self-perpetuating aristocratic elite, the grammar schools did still provide for the sons of wealthy tradesmen and, by the 18th century, many of them had a 'quite varied social composition with some broadening of the curriculum, particularly in mathematics and natural science' (Williams, 1971, p.154). However, although the:

> eighteenth century is remarkable for the growth of a number of new vocational academies serving commerce, engineering the arts and the armed services...of the new professions, particularly in science, engineering and arts, a majority of entrants were trained outside the universities, as were also most of the new merchants and manufacturers (ibid., p.155).

In fact, the university curriculum in the main was to remain ossified in the classical tradition until the reform of Oxford and Cambridge in the 19th century and the growth of provincial institutions in the early 20th century (Barnard, 1961).

Until the 19th century – in spite of massive upheaval and change generated from around 1750 by the Industrial Revolution (Plumb, 1961) – working-class education remained unplanned with a 'haphazard system of parish and private adventure schools' and, accompanying the growing urbanisation of working people, with the Charity School movement concerned mainly with the 'moral rescue as opposed to the moral instruction of the poor' (Williams, 1971, p.155). An Act of 1576 had empowered magistrates to establish workhouse schools 'to the intent that youth might be accustomed and brought up in labour and then not likely to grow to be idle rogues' (Coffey, 1992, p.26) and, in the early 18th century, the Society for Promoting Christian Knowledge recommended a half-time education system – designed to prepare boys for apprenticeship and girls for domestic service – whereby children devoted alternate days to work and school (Simon, 1974).

The Industrial Revolution was neither caused nor accompanied by the growth of formal education (Dore, 1976); countries such as France and Prussia had established compulsory state schooling long before Britain yet did not industrialise until well after the British Industrial Revolution (Green, 1990). As Ashby (1958) has suggested:

> The Industrial Revolution was accomplished by hard heads and clever fingers. Men like Bramah and Maudslay, Arkwright and Crompton, the Darbys of Coalbrookdale and Neilson of Glasgow, had no systematic education in science or technology. Britain's industrial strength lay in its amateurs and self-made men; the craftsman-inventor, the mill-owner, the iron-master...formal education

of any sort was a negligible factor in its success. The schools attended by the prosperous classes followed a curriculum which had scarcely changed since the school days of John Milton two centuries earlier' (p.50).

In fact, as Coffey (1992) argues, in spite of the massive industrial changes, education in the early 19th century bore little connection with the world of work and 'the economy did not to any noticeable extent depend upon the educational system for a supply of schooled artisans' (p.27).

At the Great Exhibition held at the Crystal Palace in 1851 Britain's position as the 'foremost industrial nation' (Musgrave, 1970, p.144) was displayed for all the world to see. However, by the time of the Paris Exhibition of 1867, a member of the Exhibition jury, Dr Lyon Playfair, was moved to write to the Taunton Commission (then considering the state of technical education) urging them to consider the state of 'scientific instruction' as part of their remit so as to help Britain keep pace with foreign competition (ibid.). Following the report of the Royal Commission on Scientific Instruction in 1884 a Technical Instruction Act was passed by Parliament in 1889 which legislated for:

> instruction in the principles of science and art applicable to industries, and in the application of specific branches of science and art to specific industries or employments. It shall not include the teaching of any trade or industry or employment (Musgrave, 1964, p.106).

The rather theoretical thrust of the Act reflected both the territorial power of craft guilds to preserve the secrets of their occupations and the also the state of the debate about the differences between technical education (principles) and technical instruction (practice). This ambiguity merely exacerbated the class divisions both between vocational and general education and *within* vocational/technical education. As Musgrave notes, 'technical education for the upper levels of the labour force might still be seen in terms of general princples, but at the lower levels to teach the practice was now becoming the custom' (ibid., p.109).

In terms of state schooling more generally, Forster's Elementary Education Act of 1870 (effectively establishing compulsory state provision for the first time had 'primarily an economic purpose' (Coffey, 1992, p.50). Introducing the Bill in the House of Commons in February 1870, Forster argued that:

Upon the speedy provision of elementary education depends our industrial prosperity. It is of no use trying to give technical teaching to our artisans without elementary education; uneducated labourers – and many of our labourers are utterly uneducated – are, for the most part, unskilled labourers, and if we leave our work-folk any longer unskilled...they will become overmatched in the competition of the world (Maclure, 1973, pp.99ff).

If we replace 'elementary education' by 'key skills' and substitute 'global competitiveness' for the 'competition of the world' it is utterly remarkable how the justification of education by Forster in 1870 matches in all important particulars the arguments put forward by Mr Blunkett in the 1998 Green Paper *The Learning Age*. Educators inclined towards pessimism might well reflect on how little progress has been made in 128 years of state education!

The Balfour Education Act of 1902 effectively established an embryonic co-ordinated national system of education – based on the foundation of 'central and local government partnership' (Kenneth Richmond, 1945, p.88) which characterised the British system until the 1988 Reform Act – and in the early years of the 20th century there was a shift of emphasis from elementary to secondary provision. In the late 19th century, so-called higher-grade departments offering 'practical and quasi-vocational curricula' (ibid., p.91) for children aged 12 to 14 had been introduced into some of the elementary schools. However, when a recognisably national secondary system did eventually appear in the inter-war years it was constrained by the hierarchical and stratified conceptions of the Victorian curriculum in which vocational studies always had an inferior and subordinate place.

Informed by a 'spiritually predestined class system' (Coffey, 1992, p.62), such a sysem of education was completely dominated by class interests and divisions, and could not escape the power relationships and educational connotations linked to such divisions (Green, 1990). The Victorian legacy has been clearly described by Kenneth Richmond (1945):

> The Victorian attitude to education was much the same as it was to all other public services: it had its First-Class compartments, the Public Schools with the doors and windows locked against riff-raff; its Second-Class, the old Grammar Schools intended for the sons of the bourgeoisie, the professions; its Third-Class, the Elementary Schools for the 'lower orders', artisans (p.90).

Such divisiveness and stratification – continuing through to the tripartite organisation of schooling following the 1944 Education Act and beyond – effectively prevented the emergence of any idea of a 'common school' (Coffey, 1992, pp.64-5), and ensured that the 'perennial liberal versus utilitarian debate continued to be fought mainly on class lines' (ibid., p.73). Moreover, the long-established British 'resistance to the provision of technical education at the secondary stage' (Lester Smith, 1966, p.209) meant that not even the Victorian conception of 'artisanship' could emerge to ensure that secondary schooling might, at the very least, come to incorporate some sort of meaningful or worthwhile form of vocational studies.

The technical schools established in the wake of the 1944 Act – like the provision for day-continuation classes for young people up to the age of 18 which followed the 1918 Act – were short-lived, partly because of the 'hostility of both parents and employers of labour' (Dent, 1968, p.36), and partly because of the continued dominance of liberal/general conceptions of education at the secondary stage. In summarising developments in schooling between 1922 and 1947, Coffey (1992) concluded that although:

> it emerged that it was regarded as an important part of the school's business to prepare pupils for the world of work...a vocational bias in the curriculum and explicit skill training for occupations appeared, however, only in less prestigious secondary schools...Vocational and practical subjects in general had not attained the importance of the more prestigious 'academic' and 'pure' subjects (p.153).

This second-class status of vocational studies – accompanied by its neglect and lack of development during the massive expansion of secondary stage academic examinations in the post-1945 settlement – effectively prevented either the bridging of the academic divide or the upgrading of the vocational aspect of education. As McCulloch (1986) noted, the 'technical and vocational end of education somehow got lost' in the relentless 'drives towards comprehensives' in the 1960s, a loss described by Halsey, et al. (1980) as 'one of the tragedies of British education after the second war' (p.214).

The history of vocational studies from the post-1945 period to the birth of the the MSC and the new vocationalism in the 1970s has been fully documented and explored by a range of commentators (Evans, 1992; Ainley, 1987, 1990; Ainley & Corney, 1990; Sheldrake &

Vickerstaff, 1987) and referred to in connection with specific topics in other chapters of this book. In offering a summary of developments during this period, it is difficult to disagree with Maclure's comments about the failure of all efforts to reform VET in the post-war years. In response to the relative economic decline as a result of the loss of empire and protected markets, the traditional *laisser-faire* approach to training in Britain was increasingly challenged in the 1960s. State intervention in VET came with the 1964 Industrial Training Act which established a Central Training Council (consisting of six employers and six trades union representatives) which adivised a regional network of Industrial Training Boards (ITBs) which, by 1966, covered 7.5 million workers (Lees & Chiplin, 1970). Training was financed through the grant/levy system imposed on firms which, though a constant cause of complaint by employers (especially small firms), did successfully expand employee training and FE day-release opportunities for workers throughout the 1960s (Evans, 1992).

In spite of its success in certain areas, the 1964 Act never amounted to a national policy for VET and, over the years, came in for increasing criticism by employers and industry representatives. Farley (1983, p.53) summarised the main problem areas in terms of the Act's lack of progress in avoiding shortages of skilled labour, criticism from employers about the ITB financial sanctions, inadequate co-ordination of skills training in different occupations and a failure to provide for the needs of young people in semi-skilled and unskilled jobs. The 1973 Employment and Training Act set out to remedy some of these problems by setting up the MSC which, formally established in 1974, was designed to bring together all the main mechanisms within the labour market. As Farley observed:

> The establishment of the MSC marked an important step in linking training with other labour market activities. At the same time it unified, administratively, training services aimed at companies and other employing bodies, with training services aimed at individuals who are unemployed or who want to improve their employment opportunities by acquiring additional skills (ibid., pp.53-4).

The story of the MSC – from its creation following the 1973 Act to its replacement by the Training Commission (later the short-lived Training Agency replaced by regional TECs in 1990) – has been described in painstaking blow-by-blow detail by Ainley & Corney (1990). The new quango – criticised by industrialists and educators alike and politicians from left and right – eventually came to be perceived as an 'increasingly sinister corporate creature that was changing the nature of British society – in particular, jobs, training and education' (Benn & Fairley, 1986, p.12) whose ultimate purpose was the 'radical restructuring of the British working class' (Finn, 1986, p.54). As Ainley & Corney (1990) noted educationalists 'conceived of the MSC as determined upon narrowing the school curriculum and thus ensuring that the middle class received a standard education whilst the working class was entertained by something called training' (p.1).

The short lived experiments which marked the MSC's period of corporate power in the 1970s and 1980s – Unified Vocational Preparation, the Youth Opportunities then Youth Training Schemes, the Certificate of Pre-Vocational Education (CPVE) and TVEI initiatives, and the New Training Initiative which eventually gave rise to the review of vocational qualifications and the establishment of the NCVQ in 1986 (Farley, 1983; Finn, 1986) – have all been fully documented and stand as a constant reminder of the difficulties of reforming VET in Britain. Clearly, injecting increased resources, finance and vastly expanded personnel into VET is just not enough (as the current New Deal planners would do well to remember).

Throughout the years of MSC power there was always a tension between training for employment and seeking to deal with the worst effects of massively increased unemployment and, in the absence of a co-ordinated national plan and VET system, the difficulties proved too great to overcome. Ainley & Corney's (1990) summary of MSC achievements represent a fitting epitaph for the quango:

> The MSC aimed to integrate mental and manual labour in a new system of vocational education. It raised the issue of training in relation to the demands of new technology for a modernized economy. The MSC sharpened the focus on a fundamental choice within British political, economic and social life – if Britain wanted to remain a prominent eceonomic power in the world economy, then it not only had to have a highly skilled workforce but also a highly motivated one. However, it has been difficult to realize this vision in practice. The New Training Initiative was never comprehensive; it never applied, as was intended, to the employed as well as the unemployed...In general, the MSC's training tended to narrow the range of skills of its trainees to the performance of itemized competencies in isolated subdivided tasks (p.140).

The decline, re-emergence and eventual reconstruction of apprenticeship in the last fifty years provides a graphic illustration of the problems and barriers to reform in the British VET system.

Apprenticeship – Alternative Perspectives

The idea of apprenticeship – viewed as some sort of teaching/learning process whereby a novice or inititiate would be able to 'come out of their time' and achieve 'mastery' in a particular sphere of activity (Parkin, 1978) – goes back to the earliest times when people first organised themselves into delimited communities. Both the formal and informal educational practices of the earliest societies – with a specifically vocational function of securing survival, nourishment and reproduction – require systems in which boys and girls could learn to hunt, fish, fight, prepare food and clothing, and care for the young (see, for instance, Benjamin's [1939] Saber-Tooth Curriculum made up of the skills of fish-grabbing, horse-clubbing and saber-tooth tiger-scaring).   Such practices were eventually formalised and systematised as tribes developed religious, puberty and organisational/leadership mores and rituals (Wilds & Lottich, 1970).

Gospel (1998a) has produced a substantial body of research and writing on the topic and offers a clear and coherent definition which captures all the key features of what might be described as the 'traditional' model. He defines apprenticeship as a:

> method of employment and on-the-job training which involves a set of reciprocal rights and duties between an employer and a trainee (usually a young person): the employer agrees to teach a range of skills, usually of a broad occupational nature; in return, the apprentice agrees to work for an extended period at a training wage which is low compared with the qualified workers' rate but which rises periodically as the apprenticeship nears completion (p.437).

Having clear links with high levels of craft, skill and mastery (Ainley, 1993; Rikowski, 1998c), apprenticeship has traditionally held a central and vital position within vocational and technical education in Britain,and changes in the institution of apprenticeship can be seen to parallel changes in the nation's social and cultural history of the sort noted in the preceding section.   Emerging from the craft and guild system of medieval times, traditional apprenticeships required young boys (and less typically, girls) to 'live-in' when they were apprenticed to a master in a particular trade or craft. Founded on long periods of time-serving, well established rituals and practices and acknowledged high status based on esoteric techniques passed on (largely by example and practice rather than formalised training) from one generation to the next, good apprenticeships allowed the talented to achieve mastery and to rise economically and socially (Liepmann, 1960; Williams, 1963).

Medieval apprenticeships reflected the fact that almost all education in this period consisted of 'on the job' training based on fixed periods of indenture which, as a general rule, was for seven years between the ages of 14 and 21 (Lawson & Silver, 1978). The institution was codified by law during the reign of Elizabeth I through the 1563 Statute of Artificers which imposed the traditional seven-year indenture on some 30 crafts and, along with the 1601 Poor Law Act, allowed pauper children to become apprentices (Coffey, 1992). By the mid-19th century this form of apprenticeship was being increasingly replaced by 'live-out' arrangements as, largely because of the changing nature of work and social life following the Industrial Revolution, the institution spread to non-artisan trades such as metalworking and electrical engineering (Adams, 1996).

The decline and dilution of apprenticed trades and occupations continued into the 20th century as a result of 'modern mass production' (Schofield, 1923, p.194) and, particularly after the First World War, the tendency of employers to split traditional jobs, particularly in the case of skilled metalworkers, into constituent parts (reminiscent of the more recent functional analysis methodology of the NCVQ) with the allocation of lower-level tasks to women and young 'trainees' who were paid far lower wages than 'time-served' workers. From the 1920s on, the apprenticeship system was subjected to fierce criticism on the grounds that it 'involved unnecessary time-serving (satirised as time-wasting), that it did not train to consistent standards, was not well suited to modern technological occupations, perpetuated outdated and irrelevant demarcations between trades and was predominantly restricted to young male workers' (Adams, 1996, p.6).

The arguments of critics such as Wilkinson (1931) and Hazell (1934) that the 'sitting next to Nellie' method of training apprentices should be replaced by systematic training linked to technical education gradually began to influence leading employers and politicians, particularly after the publication of Williams' (1963) comparative study of apprenticeship which portrayed the British system in an unfavourable light.   The organised and systematic apprenticeships of our European competitors – particularly the German dual system which ensured that around 70% of school leavers received general and vocational training (Deissinger, 1997) were contrasted with the outdated, ad hoc and inflexible nature of British practices.   Williams' criticisms (1963) concerned both the quality (no formal external monitoring of training, low day-release participation rate) and the quantity (inflexible five-year training period, rigid divisions between skill areas and between 'skilled' and 'unskilled' occupational tasks) of training, and these were taken into account by those politicians and industrialists responsible for implementing the 1964 Industrial Training Act.

As mentioned in earlier sections of this chapter, the 1964 Act introduced ITBs and imposed a levy-grant system on firms to finance vocational training. Although the ITBs were responsible for the expansion of apprenticeship for young men from 35% to 43% of the age group between 1950 and 1969 (though the figures for young women fell from 8% to 7% in this same period; Roberts, 1971, p.43) the grant-levy system was always unpopular with employers and was abolished by the 1973 Employment and Training Act which established the MSC. Rikowski (1998c) argues that, through the introduction of standards-based, modularised training, apprenticeship under the ITBs gradually moved away from the 'classical' time-serving model. The 'new' model of apprenticeships was not to reach maturity, however, until the time of the New Training Initiative in the early 1980s when the MSC effectively replaced the old system by YTS schemes which were a deliberate attempt to abolish time-serving in favour of training linked to occupational standards (Short, 1986; Gospel, 1998a).

Combined with the de-industrialisation of Britain throughout the 1980s the activities of the MSC resulted in a steep decline in apprenticeships – from 107,400 in 1978 to 34,500 in 1990 (Gospel, 1995, p.37). Along with employers' perennial complaints about the failure of schooling to match the demands of employment, the destruction of apprenticeships fuelled an increasing concern over the erosion of the country's craft and technician skills base. In response, the Conservative government – after introducing a number of reforms which de-regulated the training and youth labour market – set about re-designing apprenticeship on the basis, in Rikowski's words, of 'low youth wage expectation and the dominance of employer interests' (1998c, p.16).

The Modern Apprenticeship (MA) programme – announced in 1993 with a three-year budget of £1.25 billion – was established as a prototype in 1994 and launched nationally in 1995. Principal aims of MAs included the provision of employer-based learning for 16-24 years olds to NVQ level 3, the improvement of the supply of skills at an intermediate (craft, technician and supervisory) level to remedy identified shortages, and the incorporation of 'job-specific, key skills and broad occupational knowledge' to ensure that 'Modern Apprenticeship offers both a relevant and flexible structure to the training needs of industry' (Skills & Enterprise Network, 1997, p.1). At the end of 1995 there were an estimated 15,500 young people on MA schemes, 38% of which were in the engineering industry, and 58 in firms employing less than 25 people (ibid.). By October 1997 there were 144,576 MAs in the programme, 56% male and 44% female (Gospel, 1998b, p.22) – a significant and welcome increase in young women participants over the previous apprenticeship systems (National Traineeships numbered 83,000 and other work-based training for young people 144,700 at the time; Educa, 1998a, p.6). At the beginning of 1999 – according to DfEE figures (1999a, p.3) – almost 225,000 young people had already completed MA schemes, 126,000 were currently undertaking them in 80 industrial sectors, and the Secretary of State announced plans to increase numbers by 10,000 throughout the year.

Adams (1996, pp.40-45) has analysed the MA project in some detail and presents a useful summary of the key differences and similarities between MAs and old apprenticeships. The key differences concern the formalised training plans of MAs aimed at NVQ level 3 as against the less formal and flexible model which characterises old apprenticeships, a noticeably larger number of female MAs than the older system, and a more flexible approach to time-serving. However, although MAs are theoretically divorced from the fixed periods of indenture characteristic of the old apprenticeships, 'contracts have emerged as a significant feature of MAs, despite their redundancy in the traditional apprenticeship' and the 'minimum time period required to obtain an apprenticeship [i.e. reach NVQ level 3] in certain occupations is not significantly different from their predecessors' (ibid., p.41). As Gospel (1998a) notes, the new schemes incorporate 'both traditional; and novel features' including a 'written agreement on traditional lines between the employer and apprentice, specifying rights and obligations' (p.21). He goes on to observe that:

A crucial part of the Modern Apprenticeship is that the whole of the wage and part of the training costs are borne by the employer. But government also contributes towards the cost of off-the-job training, establishing for the first time in Britain the principle of state support for part-time education and training for employed young people (ibid.).

Rikowski (1998c) comes to similar conclusions in noting that MAs were 'viewed by the DfEE as being based on the best of traditional apprenticeships' with periods of training linked to 'dedicated employers'; indeed, in some respects, they were not 'unlike post-1964 modern or even classical apprenticeships' (pp.16-17). Rikowski goes on, however, to make the interesting observation that 'although MAs clearly have links with the past through their attachment to a lifelong learning' they can 'best be described as *Post*modern apprenticeships' since they 'imply a different approach to both apprenticeship and mastery' (p.17, original italics). Indeed, Rikowski suggests that, unlike former models of apprenticeship, the new (post-) modern versions linked to lifelong learning imply that there is 'no end point to learning' and that, since 'learning is incompatible with mastery', postmodern apprentices are 'always going to be subject to the vagaries of rapid technological and labour market changes'. In postmodernised apprenticeship the 'horizon is always just distant...it shifts with rapid technological change' (ibid., pp.17-18, 20).

   Offering a post-Marxist analysis of the current culture of lifelong learning linked with the rhetoric about multi-skilled,flexible workers, Rikowski outlines the main differences between old-classical,new-modern (post-1964) and postmodern (post-1993 MAs) apprenticeships as follows (Figs.2.1 and 2.2):

Old-Classical Apprenticeships:

- time-serving
- training by 'sitting by Nellie' (observation of the master) and learning by doing (participation in production)
- evening classes (not compulsory)
- emphasis on indentures - document signed by parents, apprentices and employers - which laid out rights and duties of the three parties
- methods of entry through trade unions or informal links (sons of employees)
- specialised training in single trade
- inculcation of 'craft pride' and 'craft mysteries'.

New-Modern Apprenticeships:

- training to standards of craftsmanship (through module system)
- supervised off-the-job training
- compulsory day release for college study
- contract of employment
- emphasis on attainment of formal qualifications (e.g. City & Guilds)
- 'scientific' entry: tests, structured interviews, application forms and stipulated qualifications
- flexibility: trade specialism, but some training in other trades
- results oriented and importance of quality.

Fig. 2.1: Classical and Modern Models of Apprenticeship
Source: Rikowski, 1998c, p.18.

Postmodern Apprenticeships:

- training to standards of NVQ Level 3
- contract of employment
- 'scientific' entry: structured interviews, application forms ... etc.
- flexibility 1 - expanded form (e.g. mixing GNVQ with NVQ, customising NVQs for firms immediate or medium-term needs)
- flexibility 2 - increasing importance of core, key or transferable skills for: internal flexibility in-company; transferability within and between companies and industrial sectors; for retraining (in case of unemployment); and for *progression* (including higher education entry)
- set within a *lifelong learning* context and trajectory

Fig. 2.2: Postmodern Apprenticeships
Source: Rikowski, 1998c, p.19.

The upshot of this comparative analysis is that:

> postmodern apprenticeship is an aspect of lifelong learning. But as lifelong learners within capitalism we only become lifelong apprentices. Postmodern apprenticeship is hence a springboard to lifelong apprenticeship and a denial of mastery (p.25)

He goes on to oberve, however, that this new strategy 'does not mean that there is no Master within postmodern apprenticeship' (ibid.); in a society dominated by capital, 'Capital is the Master of human souls' and, in the constant pursuit of employment, apprentices and all multi-skilled, flexible and lifelong learners in general may be described as 'models of capitalised trans-human existence' (pp.25-26).

This rather bleak picture of a world dominated by capital in which workers may, as it were, strive to 'become capital' (p.29) is not, however, totally pessimistic since lifelong learning can also provide the means to understand and criticise the dehumanising effects of the 'domination of capital within personhood' (ibid.). Global capitalisation has a tendency to 'reduce persons to labour power' but 'labour power is under the sway of individual and collective acts of willing and desire' (p.30) and is thus subject to criticism, change and development. In more recent work, Rikowski (1999) calls for a critical pedagogy to foster the transition to a state of affairs beyond capitalism (this notion is examined in greater depth in the last two chapters). The possibility of such development will turn on the particular philosophy of lifelong learning which underpins education and training policies. Behaviouristic and McDonaldised approaches can only perpetuate what Rikowski calls capitalised trans-human life-forms; more open and less constrained conceptions of work, education and training require the support of social theories of lifelong learning such as those outlined in the last chapter, and VET programmes will need the support of a rationally justifiable values foundation (examined in more detail in Chapters 7 and 8) if we are to achieve a learning culture which results in what Chomsky (1991) called a 'humanistic conception of education and work' which allows some role for the 'creative impulse' (p.20) which is a central aspect of unconstrained work and an essential pre-requisite of fully developed human agency.

In addition to these moral and philosophical shortcomings there is ample evidence that, in spite of the official DfEE rhetoric about the success of MAs, they have not fulfilled their potential and do not in any way add up to a coherent national policy in this sphere. As a recent Centre for Economic Performance (Hart, 1998) survey observed, although:

> take-up of modern apprenticeships trebled between 1994 and 1997...they are still the post-school choice of only 10% of young people compared to two-thirds in Germany (p.27).

The fact that they are tied rigidly to the 'pseudo-minimalist approach' of NVQs as opposed to the 'broad-based skills acquired by apprentices in traditional occupations' (Adams, 1996, p.47), is certainly not conducive to the development of lifelong learning goals. Research on Training Credits by Hodkinson & Sparkes (1995) reported a mismatch between NVQ specifications and the needs of employers and trainees, and the tendency of competence outcomes to distort and frustrate training plans (findings also noted in the SME studies by Matlay & Hyland, 1997). In addition, the major Ernst & Young (1995) evaluation of the first year of MAs noted that one of the main problems of convincing employers of the values of being involved in the MA scheme is the difficulty of having to 'convince them of the benefits of NVQs' (p.11). However, as Gospel (1998a) argues, the overall aims of these reconstructed apprenticeships are laudable, and the scheme offers valuable potential for the future development of VET in the UK. The status of MAs under New Deal arrangements and since the NCVQ remit was subsumed under the QCA will be examined in later chapters.

Vocationalism and Vocational Education

The history of vocational studies and apprenticeship has demonstrated the persistence of certain key problems standing in the way of reform. The dominance of academic or general education – linked to national examinations controlling entry to high status careers – has meant that, not only has the so-called liberal/academic divide been maintained, but also the position of vocational studies has remained subordinate and largely undeveloped. Historical, philosophical and political factors have combined to influence educational developments in this sphere and it would be worthwhile briefly reviewing some of the principal factors before offering some positive (though not necessarily original) recommendations for reconciliation and progress in this field.

Conceptual Dichotomies and Dualisms

There are a number of perennial and stubbornly persistent dichotomies in educational theory and the history of educational ideas. In the sphere of teaching, Meighan (1981, p.161) offers the following list:

- teacher-centred/child-centred,
- meaning receiving/meaning making,
- authoritarian/democratic,
- open schooling/closed schooling,
- traditional/progressive; and
- dependent/autonomous.

The distinction between liberal (academic, general) and vocational (practical, technical) education – dating as mentioned earlier in the chapter, from the time of the Ancient Greeks and influential to the present day – is just one of these entrenched dichotomies which seem to resist all attempts at reconcialiation and reform.

As noted earlier, the stratification of British schooling which occurred during the 16th century also led to a bifurcation between academic and vocational studies.   From that time on, educational theorists and philosophers have attempted to understand, explain and remedy this state of affairs.   During the 19th century, even though science and technology were beginning to enter the secondary school and university curriculum (Wardle, 1976; Musgrave, 1966), the dominance of the 'gentleman ideal' effectively ruled out the development of vocational studies. As Coffey (1992) notes, even though Thomas Arnold's conception of the 'Christian gentleman' was vocational as well as religious and social, it was founded essentially on the tradition of classical education and 'the ability to quote and to recognize classical tags were still seen as the *sine qua non* of entry to gentlemanly rank' (pp.37-8).

The advance of science, technology and industry in the second half of the 19th century, however, did eventually bring about a serious debate on the merits and legitimacy of the dominant classical tradition. Asking the crucial question concerning 'What knowledge is of most worth?', Herbert Spencer launched a fierce attack on the liberal tradition. He argued that the knowledge 'which our school-courses leave almost entirely out, we thus find to be that which most nearly concerns the business of life' (Low-

Beer, 1969, p.23).   Advocating the vital role and function of science defined as 'organized knowledge', Spencer goes on to suggest that it 'is a knowledge that has got itself taught in nooks and corners, while the ordained agencies for teaching have been mumbling little else but dead formulas' (ibid.).   In a similar vein, and also exercised   by the 'dead formulas' which stood in the way of scientific advance, T.H. Huxley, attempted to revise liberal education in the sense of giving it a practical purpose (as, indeed, it had originally) aimed at developing an intellect which was like a 'clear, cold, logical engine, with all its parts of equal strength, and in smooth working order; ready, like a steam engine, to be turned to any kind of work, and spin the gossamers as well as forge the anchors of the mind' (Curtis & Boultwood, 1970, pp.447-8).

Huxley's idea of a well-balanced and harmonious conception of liberal education was, thus, a revised version of the Ancient Greek notion of *arete*, suitably modernised by a range of new industrial metaphors.   Similar arguments were being advocated in the late 19th century by the influential philosophical 'idealists' such as T.H. Green (Gordon & White, 1979), though, for these reformers, the ethical aspects of human nature were given pride of place in theories of liberal education (just as the revised liberal educational views of J.S. Mill and the Utilitarians had primarily social and political aims; Coffey, 1992, pp.44-6).   Thus, what we have at this time is not so much an attempt to bridge the vocational/academic divide, still less to upgrade vocational education, but a project designed to present new interpretations of liberal education which incorporated the scientific and technological advances of the Industrial Revolution (Wardle, 1976).

Reconciliation Strategies

Arguably, the first genuine critic of liberal education *per se* was John Dewey, who combined trenchant attacks on the classical tradition with equally forthright diatribes against narrow vocational instruction. Attacking all 'either-or' dualisms which recognise 'no intermediate possibilities' Dewey (1963) observed that the:

> history of educational theory is marked by opposition between the idea that education is development from within and that it is formation from without; that it is based upon natural endowments and that education is a process of overcoming natural inclination and substituting in its place habits acquired under external pressure' (p.17).

This observation served as a preface to the recommendation of educational methods based on experience – described as the 'means and goal of education' (ibid., p.89) – though it was the application of this general approach to vocational education which is most relevant to the present discussion.

In *The School and Society* (originally published in 1900), Dewey (1915) had observed that:

> While training for the profession of learning is regarded as the type of culture, or a liberal education, the training of a mechanic, a musician, a lawyer, a doctor, a farmer, a merchant, or a railroad manager is regarded as purely technical or professional. The result is that which we see about us everywhere – the division into 'cultured' people and 'workers' (pp.17-18).

The key argument is that, although both 'cultural' and 'utilitarian' subjects were included in the school curriculum, the cultural was not useful and the utilitarian was not liberating of imagination or thinking power. In order to attack the false dualisms in education, Dewey's philosophy drew on the anti-Cartesian pragmatic conception of knowledge originally developed by C.S. Peirce and later refined and modified by William James (Peters, 1977; Hyland, 1993). According to Dewey, people develop knowledge, not in a passive or spectatorial manner as Cartesian philosophy would have it, but through the active pursuit and construction of knowledge. On this account, knowledge and truth are neither given nor immutable but constructed by humans out of their 'experience'. This concept of experience – which for Dewey is the 'name given to all that passes between the organism and its surroundings' (Geiger, 1958, p.17) – holds a central position in Dewey's epistemology. It is through experience that enquiry, or the pursuit of knowledge, is to be conducted and in Dewey's hands this becomes a very practical activity directed towards the solving of problems and the removal of obstacles in the way of general social progress.

In the *Aims of Education*, Whitehead (1962) argued that the 'antithesis between a technical and a liberal education is fallacious', and that there can 'be no adequate technical education which is not liberal, and no liberal education which is not technical' (p.74). In a similar way, Dewey attacked 20th century educational practice on the grounds that it had become 'highly specialized, one-sided and narrow'. It was an education:

dominated almost entirely by the medieval conception of learning... something which appeals for the most part to the intellectual aspect of our natures...not to our impulses and tendencies to make, to do, to create, to produce, whether in the form of utility or art (1915, p.26).

Dewey's philosophy stresses the value of 'education which acknowledges the full intellectual and social meaning of a vocation' (1966, p.318) and, as such, is fully in keeping with the social theory of lifelong learning sketched at the end of the last chapter. The idea of a vocation as something which 'signifies any form of continuous activity which renders service to others and engages personal powers on behalf of the accomplishment of results' (ibid., p.139) is a broad one which, instead of standing in opposition to leisure and cultural pursuits, is made to embrace them. Such a conception includes:

> the development of artistic capacity of any kind, of specific scientific ability, of effective citizenship, as well as professional and business occupations, to say nothing of mechanical labour or engagement in gainful pursuits (ibid., p.307).

Thus, in seeking to break down the 'antithesis of vocational and cultural education' based on the false oppositions of 'labour and leisure, theory and practice, body and mind' (ibid., p.301), Dewey offers us a philosophically cogent template for the reconstruction of VET as we approach the millennium.

Very few attempts to break down the liberal/vocational divide have been characterised by the philosophical scope and vocational vision which is the hallmark of Dewey's writings in this sphere. Most of the early forays – such as those by Spencer, Huxley and Mill in the 19th century – called for modifications of liberal education to incorporate the technical. An interesting version of this form of revisionism is demonstrated in Adams' (1933) *Modern Developments in Educational Practice* in which we find the insistence that 'all education must affect our future life either adversely or favourably, and to that extent all education is vocational, as preparing us for the vocation of life' (p.50). A more recent example of this sort of strategy is Silver and Brennan's (1988) advocacy of 'liberal vocationalism' in higher education, which includes both the introduction of 'hybrid' courses which combine arts and science subjects and also the incorporation of liberal/general education elements into vocational programmes in engineering and business studies (not unlike the liberal studies introduced into FE vocational courses in the 1950s and 1960s; see Macfarlane, 1993).

Although these strategies for reconciliation are useful in suggesting possible models of development, they display a tendency towards reinforcing the divisions by the very process of seeking to highlight similarities between them. Whitehead's (1962) approach to bridging the liberal/vocational divide, for example, takes its starting-point from the explicit distinctness of the 'literary curriculum, the scientific curriculum and the technical curriculum'. For Whitehead, 'each of these curricula should include the other two' (p.75); on this account, Whitehead's approach to curriculum design and qualifications might be regarded as an early version of the 'frameworking' and, perhaps, even the 'unifying' positions descibed by Hodgson & Spours, 1997, 1998; see also Chapter 3). Preferences in this area will tend to be influenced by epistemological stances, in particular whether educators adopt approaches based on Hirst's (1974) theory of distinct forms of knowledge, or favour more integrated or holistic conceptions (Pring, 1976). In any event, discussions about whether to liberalise vocationalism or to vocationalise liberalism (Pring, 1995; Lewis, 1997) have often served to reinforce rather than remove the differences.

Pring's (1995) detailed examination of these issues usefully highlights the principal problems. Commenting on the two leading approaches to reconciliation, Pring observes that the 'first is that of having two sorts of education, preserving the liberal ideal for the few, and offering a vocational alternative for the many. The second is to dilute the liberal with a vocational emphasis' (p.186). The historical survey earlier in the chapter has shown that the first approach – division and stratification – has been the hallmark of British developments from the 19th century down to and including the 'new vocationalism' of recent times. Although the introduction of GNVQs in 1992 (Higham, Sharp & Yeomans, 1996) has been claimed by some commentators to be an example of Pring's second mode, the dilution of the liberal in favour of vocational, the actual impact of recent initatives has been to reinforce divisions. Indeed, instead of the old two-track, vocational/academic divide, we now have a three-track system which separates (occupationally-specific) NVQs from (broad vocational) GNVQs and (academic) GCSEs and A-levels. (Hyland, 1994c; Hodgson & Spours, 1997).

Whilst acknowledging the difference between academic and vocational programmes at the level of content, Pring (1995) recommends bridging principles at the level of methodology and ultimate aims. As he notes:

'Liberal' is contrasted with 'vocational' as if the vocational, *properly taught*, cannot itself be liberating – a way into those forms of knowledge through which a person is freed from ignorance, and opened to new imaginings, new possibilities; the craftsman who finds aesthetic delight in the object of his craft, the technician who sees the science behind the artefact, the reflective teacher making theoretical sense of practice (p.189, original italics).

Vocational Learning

I would endorse much of Pring's argument here, particlarly the latter part concerned with the reconstruction of the nature and value of work which will be revisited in Chapter 7. My only quarrel would be with the notion that vocational studies can be liberating only if properly taught. In line with the lifelong learning criteria noted in the last chapter, I would prefer to place the emphasis on *learning* rather than teaching (whilst accepting that both are necessary), particularly the sort of learning directed towards student autonomy and empowerment which figures prominently in conceptions of 'studentship' and 'careership' (Hodkinson, 1996; Bloomer, 1997).

Moreover, it is surely worth noting that the one common unifying element in relation to the main either-or divisions in this sphere – vocational/academic, general/practical, education/training, theory/practice – is precisely and centrally the process of *learning*. All the activities, whether they are classified in terms of one side of the divide or the other, involve, in some degree, processes of learning. Of course, learning itself is not an uncontested concept, as the perusal of any text book on learning theory or educational psychology will demonstrate. However, we might take comfort here from Child's (1981) argument that:

Whilst there is no complete agreement amongst psychologists about the details of learning processes, they do accept the basic premise that learning occurs whenever one adopts new, or modifies existing, behaviour patterns in a way which has some influence on future performance or attitudes (p.81).

Although rather abstract and theoretical, this definition by itself is enough to disqualify a number of vocational strategies – in particular, McDonaldised programmes and those founded on the behaviourist functional analysis system which underpins NVQs (Hyland, 1994a; Marks, 1996; Bates, 1998) – and point towards certain others based on cognitive/experiential studies which allow at least some scope for student actvity and negotiation (Halsall & Cockett, 1996; Hodkinson, Sparkes & Hodkinson, 1996; Bloomer, 1997).

What needs to be added to this emerging conception of vocational learning is that – if it is to satisfy the criteria of a social theory of lifelong learning outlined at the end of Chapter 1 – it must also take note of the idea of both the context and the degree or quality of any learning involved. The well-known distinction between learning 'how' and learning 'that' (based on Ryle's [1973] analysis of knowledge in terms of 'knowing that' and 'knowing how') is commonly applied to VET in the form of ascribing the 'how' label to vocational studies on the grounds that they are practical and work-oriented. However, there is little philosophical justification for such a rigid division and cogent arguments for the insistence that all activity even the most basic tasks – involves both forms of learning and knowledge (Gribble, 1969; Geach, 1971; Hyland, 1994a). For all forms of human action and intelligent performance, theory and practice are inextricably linked and interdependent (Argyris & Schon, 1974).

In relation to the context of learning – especially vocational learning which, by definition, is designed to be applicable to work situations – a large body of research studies concerned with 'situated cognition' have demonstrated the importance of locating all learning within the framework of relevant social practices to ensure a deep level of understanding and meaning. Brown, Collins & Duguid (1989), for instance, argue that all learning is essentially 'situated' in the sense that what is learnt cannot be separated from the activity which generates the learning or from the context, culture or social practice within which the learning takes place. Similarly, Lave & Wenger (1991) claim that all learning is the product of 'social participation' and maintain that conceiving of:

> learning in terms of participation focuses attention on ways in which it is an evolving, continuously renewed set of relations; that is, of course, consistent with a relational view of persons, their actions, and the world, typical of a theory of social practice (pp.49-50).

Just as the behaviourist thrust of the NVQ functional analysis strategy failed to meet the basic modification criteria of learning, so the concept of situated learning grounded in social practices has provided a powerful tool in the critique (examined in more detail in the next chapter) of the atomistic and contextless nature of CBET.

Similar arguments concerning degrees and levels of learning can be made in support of a social theory of lifelong learning. For genuine learning to take place – that is learning based on full understanding and engagement – it will need to satisfy the criteria for 'deep' as opposed to 'surface' learning. This distinction has been used extensively by Gibbs (1990, 1992) and others (Biggs, 1988; Prosser & Millar, 1989) in their advocacy of an experiential approach to post-school learning by which (in a manner reminiscent of Dewey's philosophy) students become active constructors of knowledge and skills rather than passive recipients (Barnett's [1990] vision of students as critical reflective practitioners draws on similar notions). Gibbs (1992) claims that there is now a large body of research in Europe and Australia which:

> has identified students' approach to study as a key variable in predicting student performance and the quality of learning outcomes. Whether students take a surface or a deep approach (attempting to reproduce subject matter or understand it) has a profound effect on the quality, structure and permanence of students' learning (p.149).

The key differences between deep and surface learning are neatly summarised by Ramsden as follows (Fig.2.3):

Deep approach
Intention to understand. Student maintains structure of task.

Focus on 'what is signified' (e.g. the author's argument,
    or the concepts applicable to solving the problem).
Relate previous knowledge to new knowledge.
Relate knowledge from different courses.
Relate theoretical ideas to everyday experience.
Relate and distinguish evidence and argument.
Organise and structure content into a coherent whole.
Internal emphasis: 'A window through which aspects of reality
    become visible, and more intelligible'

Surface approach

Intention only to complete task requirements.
Student distorts structure of task.

Focus on 'the signs' (e.g. the words and sentences of the text, or
  unthinkingly on the formula needed to solve the problem).
Focus on unrelated parts of the task.
Memorise information for assessments.
Associate facts and concepts unreflectively.
Fail to distinguish principles from examples.
Treat the task as an external imposition.
External emphasis: demands of assessments, knowledge cut off from
  everyday reality.

Fig.2.3: Characteristics of Deep and Surface Learning
Source: Ramsden, 1992, p.52.

The advantages of fostering deep learning strategies have been clearly
identified in a wide range of empirical studies. Deep learning has been
linked with:

- more effective study habits and management (Biggs, 1987; Marton,
  Housell & Entwistle, 1984)
- superiority of understanding and grasp of underlying principles (Prosser
  & Millar, 1989; Ramsden, 1992)
- superior essay and assignment writing (Biggs, 1988; Housell, 1985)
- higher final exam grades (Watkins & Hattie, 1981; Schmeck, 1983;
  Biggs, 1987; Ramsden, Beswick & Bowden, 1986)

From the point of view of vocational learning – particularly in its
concern to upgrade the status of vocational studies in the integration of
theory and practice – the fostering of deep learning approaches in students
seems to be highly desirable. Gibbs (1992) offers some recommendations
for course tutors and lecturers who wish to encourage such learning which
include, ensuring that motivation is achieved by allowing students some
scope in negotiating content, encouraging active approaches which link
past experience with new concepts, facilitating group and collaborative
work and utilising 'interdisciplinary approaches' which contribute to a
'well-structured knowledge base' (pp.155-6). It is also crucial for tutors to
'clarify assessment criteria' so that 'students are in no doubt that mere
memorization will not be rewarded' (ibid., p.163).

The inclusion of such approaches to teaching and learning – which draw on the well-established traditions of experiential strategies described by Kolb (1993) and also the important theory of andragogy advocated by Knowles (1970) to facilitate the learning of adult students – in vocational studies brings into the picture the important values dimension referred to by Pring (1995) in his liberal/vocational reconciliation strategy. He maintains that in:

> trying to reconcile different traditions of liberal education and vocational preparation...we need to ask more fundamental moral questions about what it is to live fully human lives and what the connection is between personal development and the wider social framework in which that development might take place (pp.194-5).

Such a recommendation is on all fours with the social theory of lifelong learning referred to earlier, and provides clear links with the values dimension of VET which will be discussed in more detail on Chapter 7. The issues to be addressed at this stage concern the practical business of trying to implement such strategies against the background of the historical vocational studies legacy and the current framework of qualifications and skills training stemming from the 'new vocationalism' of the 1980s and its aftermath.   In particular, the problems of bridging the divide and unifying/integrating vocational and academic tracks needs to engage with the all-encompassing system of NVQs/GNVQs which now dominate and drive the debate about the post-school curriculum.

3 Vocational Skills, Qualifications and NVQs

Making use of Anglo-American comparative data to examine the current state of VET in industrialised nations, Lewis (1997) makes some interesting observations about different conceptions of the modern workplace as we approach the new millennium. He examines three different, if partly overlapping, versions of the contemporary discourse (though the labels assigned to them are mine) about education and work (pp.478-9):

Technological Optimism

In analyses of changing work patterns offered by commentators such as Hirschhorn (1984) and Zuboff (1988), there is the argument that in the post-industrial (or post-Fordist) society workers are more reflective, more aware of the need for constant learning in the work environment, and more in tune with the ideal socio-technical system in which work and learning are integrated. Zuboff, in particular, talks about 'informating technologies' which demystify shop-floor knowledge and skills thus 'translating the production process and making it visible' (1988, pp.9-10). There is also the suggestion that modern workplaces are learning organisations which call for 'relations of equality' which can 'encourage a synthesis of members' interests' so that the 'flow of value-adding knowledge helps legitimate the organisation as a learning community' (ibid., p.394).

De-skilling Pessimism

On this account, only an elite of core workers will require high-level knowledge and technological skills, and the majority of the workforce (trained under the narrow occupationalism of NVQs) will be effectively de-skilled and destined to 'occupy an uncertain future being assigned to the periphery of the labour market' (Sieminski, 1993, p.99). Such inter-pretations of contemporary work include Marxist-inspired critiques such as those of Braverman (1974) who views technology in the main as reinforcing worker alienation by further separating the conception of work from its alienation, and post-Marxist analyses such as Rikowski's (1998b) which, as noted in the last chapter, equate global capitalism with the creation of workers as 'capitalised trans-human life forms' (p.27) constantly seeking to acquire the skills necessary to stay abreast of the demands of post-Fordist enterprises. Rifkin's (1995) provocative thesis *The End of Work* paints a similar picture which emphasises the realities of mass, world-wide redundancies in the face of developing industrial technology.

Compatibilist Flexibility

The least provocative and most conciliatory version of modern work interprets the rise of post-Fordist firms (characterised by small-batch, short-run productions rather than Fordist mass production; see Brown & Lauder, 1992) as calling for flexible, multi-skilled workers whose skills will require constant upgrading to keep pace with technological advances. This interpretation (interspersed with elements from the more optimistic first version) is broadly the one which underpins the current lifelong learning agenda and New Deal projects (DfEE, 1998a). It acknowledges some level of redundancy and unemployment as a result of post-Fordist re-structuring/re-engineering (since why else would we require WTW and Job Start schemes?) but generally endorses the optimistic re-skilling agenda and, in the hands of commentators such as Piore & Sabel (1984), waxes lyrical about the recapturing of craft skills thereby ending the 'dominion of specialised machines over un- or semi-skilled workers' (p.261).

The powerful critique of the 'post-Fordist myth' by Avis (1996) and others (Flude & Sieminski, 1999) provides a useful counter-balance to the the more heady, 'idealist' (Rikowski, 1998a,d) versions of the contemporary debate about learning and the future of work. New working practices may indeed reinforce alienation, de-skilling and result in practices which are socially unjust and undemocractic but, as Avis acknowledges, more optimistic accounts 'celebrate the creative potential of labour' and 'veer towards a notion of a socially responsible and constrained capitalism' (p.80). Such compatibilist views also incorporate positive roles for education and training under the banner of lifelong learning. In order to connect such versions with both the 14-19 curriculum (education or learning *for* work) and post-compulsory VET (education or learning *at* work) it is necessary to address the concept of skills, particularly key or core, transferable skills, in more depth since the interpretation of vocational skills has for a long time dominated the debate about reconstructing VET and vocational qualifications.

Skill-Talk and Vocationalism

The re-interpretation of the aims and content of education in terms of skills paralleled the vocationalisation of education in the 1970s which was described in Chapter 1. Through the activities of the MSC running through the YTS schemes and the new vocationalist initiatives of this period (Wellington, 1987; Hyland & Johnson, 1998), the educational task, and the increasing merger of education and training (Holt, 1987; Dearden, 1984), was gradually re-interpreted in terms of skills and later (following the establishment of the NCVQ in 1986) competences. By the late 1970s Hart (1978) was noting that 'you cannot dip much into educational writings without realising that the ambit of so-called "skills" is growing' (p.205), and a decade later commentators were observing 'that the word "skill" is ubiquitous in contemporary educational discourse' (Barrow, 1987, p.188) to the extent that 'skills are now officially seen as an essential part of the curriculum' (Griffiths, 1987, p.203).

Although there are contexts in which the concept of 'skill' (and, indeed, that of 'competence'; see Ashworth & Saxton, 1990; Hyland, 1994a) is clearly relevant and applicable, there are three principal reasons for objecting to its wholesale and undiscriminating use to describe the outcomes of education and training.

1. It is neither a clearly articulated nor well-founded conception with no common agreement or shared understanding about whether it applies to the cognitive, affective or psycho-motor domains of human activity. The term is used 'indiscriminately of what are at best very different types of skill' (Barrow, 1987, p.188). The following are all examples of essential 'skills' recommended in the educational literature of the last two decades or so:
a) File or sort things, fill in a record book or manual, cutting with one blade (FEU, 1982); taking orders, making conversation (MSC, 1977); to write legibly (DES, 1985).

b) Communication, problem-solving, numeracy, information technology (NCC, 1990), planning, fault-finding, making comparisons (Annett & Sparrow, 1985).
c) Working with others, improving one's own learning and performance (NCVQ, 1992); considering others views (DES, 1985); human relationship skills (Nelson-Jones, 1989); 'enterprise skills' (Training Agency, 1990).

As Jonathan (1987) has argued, when faced with lists which 'include life skills, reasoning skills, survival skills, etc.' (p.93) we are bound to ask questions about whether the same concept of skill is being used in all cases and, indeed, whether the concept has not become entirely vacuous as a result of attempts to make it bear far more weight than it can possibly carry. A common error in this sphere involves making the false move from identifying features common to *different* skills and, from this, inferring the existence of a common *skill* (related fallacies are discussed in the critique of transferability in the next section). As Dearden (1984) observes in this respect:

> ...there may indeed be features common to all skilled performances in virtue of which we call them skilled, but it does not follow that it is the *same* skill which is present in each case: in the skater, the juggler, the flautist, the chess player and the linguist (p.78, original italics).

Moreover, if relatively low-level activities such as 'taking orders' are to be labelled as skills alongside 'improving one's learning performance' and 'considering others' views', it is not obvious how the conceptualisation of such varied accomplishments as skills adds anything at all to the basic description of content or processes. Clearly, items in list (a) above are simply discrete occupational tasks, list (b) items could more properly be described as common learning experiences, whereas type (c) items are, arguably, not skills at all but virtues, values and dispositions normally conveyed through the hidden curriculum.

The more recent origins of skill-talk in education can be found in the increasing use by the MSC of the notions of 'skills mismatch' and 'skill shortages' (Ainley & Corney, 1990) to account for the 'weird discontinuities of economic development' (p.94) in the 1980s with recession and massive unemployment existing alongside specialised job vacancies in selective locations. From this time on the skills mantra was used to explain such anomalies with the result that all employment and economic problems could be explained in terms of the skills deficit of individuals rather than the failure of government and industry to invest in education and training (Finn, 1990).   Reinforced by economic analyses such as that by Finegold and Soskice (1988) about the 'low skills-low quality' equilibrium which bedevilled British industry and was responsible for our poor economic performance compared with global competitors, the skills argument received its official reification and, linked to post-Fordist speculations about the need for flexible, multi-skilled workers, came to dominate all policy decisions about VET.

However, the calls for a 'skills revolution' by the CBI (1989) and the need for Britain to cope with a 'skills challenge greater than any since the Industrial Revolution by the Trades Union Congress' (NCE, 1993, p.29), need to be understood primarily in terms of rhetorical sloganising rather than systematic economic or educational analysis. The legend 'Developing Skills for a Successful Future' which introduced and overarched all the new NTETs (NACETT, 1995, p.10) can, thus, be interpreted and understood primarily in terms of its power as a marketing or political slogan. Skill-talk, very like notions of 'competence', 'quality', 'standards', 'lifelong learning' and the like, seems to have all the hallmarks of first-rate educational slogans (Hyland, 1994a; 1998c).   Firstly, talk of skills fully satisfies the 'motherhood and apple pie' test by advocating practices to which no one could possibly object, and, secondly, it is so vague and nebulous that it can be made to include just about anything that is currently fashionable or desirable.

However, although it is not difficult to account for the continued popularity and persuasiveness of 'skills for employment' and 'personal skills which employers require' (IIE, 1996, pp.8-9), it is not clear how a concept with such an unclear logical status and apparently without any precise definition or range of application can possibly carry the weight of an education and training policy or programme. Writing on the history of workmanship, Pye (1968) went so far as to refuse to use the word 'skill' on the grounds that it was a 'thought preventer' which 'does not assist useful thought because it means something different in each different kind of work' (pp.23-4).   This is similar to Dearden's argument referred to earlier about the tendency to conflate skilled performances and, in a similar vein, Barrow (1987) is highly critical of the indiscriminate use of the concept which fails to differentiate between motor skills, intellectual skills, perceptual skills and creative skills. He concludes:

> In as much as physical, intellectual, perceptual, social, creative, and interpersonal operations seem on the face of it and for the most part decidedly different kinds of activity, it is to be deemed unfortunate at the outset that the word 'skill' may serve to blur the differences (p.188).

Philosophical investigations of the concept have noted the primary emphasis on physicality and practice (Scheffler, 1965; Johnson, 1998) ; its original home seems to be in the area of psycho-motor or physical dexterity and 'expertness that comes from training or practice...especially involving the use of hand or body' (Barrow, 1997, p.190). Griffiths (1987) explains that the 'concept of skill is significant because of its associations with practice, the practical, activity, art, craft, techniques and technology' (p.204), and Ainley (1993) similarly charts the history of skill in the evolution of 'artisanship' (p.6) which combined the practical activities of artists and craftspersons. The more recent, undifferentiated use of the term in the new vocationalist schemes and in core/key skills discourse clearly wants to extend the application of skill-talk, without any discernible attempt at rational justification, to just about every possible aspect of education and training. Educational slogans thrive on ambiguity and the blurring of distinctions and definitions (Scheffler, 1960), and the failure of the skills debate to move much farther than De Bono's tautological definition, 'a skill is a skill' (1978, p.45), might be a necessary prerequisite of the gross over-extension of the concept to encompass all manner of human activity. Perhaps this is also why the FEU (1982) version of a so-called 'elaborated definition of common core skills' (pp.45ff.) consists of nothing more than list after list (covering some 130 items in all) of specific tasks and achievements.

2. A second objection to the indiscrimate use of skill-talk in education is that (like the competence movement, Hyland, 1994a, 1997; Marks, 1996) it belittles the role and status of knowledge and understanding in education and training thereby seriously impoverishing learning of all kinds. Examining the evolution of the term within lexicography, Barrow (1987) noted that the application of skill to areas of 'knowledge, understanding and judgement is specifically referred to as obsolete' (p.190) within standard dictionary definitions. Even a superficial reading of the skills literature is enough to reveal the strangeness of referring to the skills of 'filing' and 'cutting with one blade' alongside those of 'reasoning' and 'thinking' (Hyland, 1998c).   More importantly, however, such equivocation leads to a vicious reductionism which, as Johnson (1998) observes, mutates knowledge, understanding and values to produce a 'checklist of routines which are then misapplied to complex activities such as thinking or teaching itself' (p.210).

The downgrading of knowledge in the skills literature is on all fours with its cavalier treatment by competence proponents, and both have their origins and rationale in behaviourist psychology (Hyland, 1994a,b).   As Jessup (1991) claims in his justification of the NCVQ strategy, the primary concern is not with learning, knowledge or understanding but with evidence of competent performance, with identifying 'what people need in their heads to perform effectively with their hands, feet, voice, eyes, and so on' (p.121).   Furthermore, there 'is no justification for assessing knowledge for its own sake but only for its contribution to competent performance' (ibid., p.123).   Similarly, Elliott (1993) in his critique of the use of competence approaches in teacher education notes that the behaviourist foundations imply that 'the significance of theoretical knowledge in training is a purely technical or instrumental one' by which knowledge 'belongs to the realm of inputs rather than outputs' and 'can only be justified if it is a necessary condition for generating the desired behavioural outcomes of learning' (p.17).

Such belittling and downgrading of knowledge and understanding in the educational endeavour was a prominent characteristic of the skills and training lobby attack on the so-called irrelevance of liberal education (see Bailey, 1984, in this respect) which has been referred to in earlier chapters. A particularly advanced and extreme form of this critique is to be found in articles by Hills (1989) which claim that skills 'can, in stark contrast to knowledge, be the bringer of great wealth and prosperity' and that we should therefore 'reduce the pedestal on which knowledge has rested' (p.15).   Elsewhere, Hills (1990) has put forward the notion that 'for the young especially, knowledge, as such, does little for the character or personality, whereas every skill adds to person's intrinsic value' (p.19).

I am not sure what Hills means by 'knowledge as such' but I am absolutely certain that his treatment of knowledge and skill is fundamentally and comprehensively mistaken and completely erroneous. All (alleged or so-called) skills, from learning to type or ride a bicycle to making comparisons and analytic reasoning, are rooted in and totally dependent upon relevant forms of knowledge and understanding. The behaviourist thrust of both the skills lobby and the competence movement has been epistemologically naive (Hyland, 1996d, 1997a; Bates, 1998). We find no adequate distinction in the skills literature between theoretical knowledge (knowing that) and practical knowledge (knowing how) and no account of how knowledge is connected with and generative of different levels of skills and competences. The introduction of 'underpinning knowledge and understanding' to NVQs in the late 1980s demonstrated some level of acknowledgement of the problems though the attempted solutions, supplementing atomised competence statements and performance criteria with equally atomised bits of knowledge and understanding (Hyland, 1994a), demonstrated both the attachment of competence theorists to behaviourist fundamentalism and also the indequacy of such approaches to VET.

The skills literature displays the same attachment to that view of knowledge contained in Bloom's (1956) taxonomy of educational objectives which is criticised by Wilson (1972) for its obsession with the idea that 'knowledge is like a physical object which can be broken down or built up into a hierarchy of component parts' (p.106). This false picture of knowledge not only mistakenly divorces the theoretical from the practical but also implies that some basic tasks, such as filing or answering a telephone, require little knowledge whereas other activities, such as management or planning, need a foundation of high-level or advanced knowledge. Gribble (1969), in aguing against attempts by Bloom and others to develop hierarchies of knowledge which separate factual knowledge from comprehension and application, demonstrates how satisfying the full knowledge conditions (taking knowledge in the strong sense as 'justified true belief', see Scheffler, 1965) for basic propositions such as knowing that 'London is the capital of England' involves quite complex conceptual understanding. He explains that:

> knowing something involves judging that something is so, and judgement is a complex mental operation. Mental abilities and skills are not separate from knowing something for we are unable to specify mental abilities and skills independently of the various forms of knowledge (p.58).

Skills and competences require a foundation of knowledge and understanding just as education requires an infrastructure of training which can lead 'to the confident deployment of skill and technque in a wide variety of situations' (Winch, 1995, p.324). In this respect it is noticeable how the paradigm example of the driving test which used to be offered by NVQ proponents to illustrate the importance in VET of 'what people can do rather than what they know' (UDACE, 1989, p.6) has been conveniently dropped since the driving test was supplemented by a written test of knowledge of the highway code!   In a similar vein, Holland (1980) advances the idea that:

> In wrestling with the problems that are important in a field of study, ideas not skills are what count; and the problems get solved, or transformed, or by-passed, by the man with the profounder conception (p.23).

Thus, an over-emphasis on skills might easily lead to a descent into the impracticable since those who possess only techniques or knacks do not fully understand the basis of practice. Such an epistemologically vacuous conception of skills training flies in the face of current conceptions of lifelong learning and the knowledge requirements of post-Fordist industry (Zuboff, 1988; Handy, 1989).

3. There is a more sinister aspect of skill-talk which separates theoretical from practical knowledge and performance which, according to Johnson (1998) 'places under threat rich and deep conceptions of teaching, knowledge and the person' (p.211).   Such a view relates to Hart's (1978) argument that 'certain activities stand in a peculiarly intimate relation to the kind of people we are' whereas 'there is something peripheral in the exercise of a skill...skills are mere appendices to our humanity and not continuous with and constitutive of it' (p.215).   What is being criticised here is, not just the tendency to reduce complex human characteristics and achievements to interpersonal skills or moral competences, but also the idea that the complete educational endeavour can be reduced to skills training of various kinds.

 The point can be illustrated by considering the senses in which both knowledge and morality (or ethical dispositions) are connected to ideas of personhood in ways in which skills are not. In terms of the conditions of knowledge, belief and understanding as oppposed to skill, Mike Smith (1984) points out that, although we can choose whether or not to exercise a skill:

one cannot decide to know or understand something in the way that one can consciously decide to read a passage, make and execute a pass in football, or carve a piece of stone (p.228).

The connections between the subjective conditions of knowledge (personal belief, understanding and commitment) are integrally linked to the objective conditions (justification by reference to agreed public criteria) demonstrate how knowledge is constitutionally linked to personhood in ways that skill, which does not seem to require the same form of level of commitment or relationship, is not. A similar point can be made in terms of the contrast between skills and moral virtues or qualities of character. As Richard Smith (1987) argues:

> I choose whether to exercise a skill or not from moment to moment. My skill and I are separate: it is not an essential part of me. You learn nothing about what sort of individual I am if you discover that I have or lack some skill or another: to practise something as a skill is to do so in such a manner that it gives nothing away about the person beneath the persona (p.198).

Personal qualities, qualities of character such as temperance, industry, patience, and so on, are fundamentally constitutive of persons, definitive of what people are, in the sense in which skills are not. The notion of a good surgeon, or good chef, plumber, nurse, teacher, electrician, airline pilot, etc., is not synonymous with the idea of a person who possesses a range of skills. Such conceptions need to incorporate the vital ethical dimension of working life in which virtues, attitudes and values shape social practices by determining how people actually use the skills they have acquired in pursuing aims and goals.

Although Johnson (1998) is surely correct in warning us of the threat to 'rich and deep conceptions of teaching, knowledge and the person' of reducing educational values to 'moral skills' or 'human relationship skills' (p.211), it is worth also noting Richard Smith's (1987) account of how certain foundational conceptions of moral and educational commitment may, in fact, be generated through certain 'craft skills' developed in fields such 'carpentry, leather-working and gardening' (p.198). This interesting speculation is illustrated with the observation that in:

> watching a skilled carpenter, for example, I am struck by his patience and persistence, his sympathy with his material and his passion for a kind of

accuracy, for doing the job really well without falling into the trap of fussy perfectionism. His carpentry does tell me a ceratin amount about him as a person...In particular, I learn about the degree to which he possesses the procedural virtues, patience, capacity for enduring disappointment and so on, and, though caution is necessary here because procedural virtues are not readily generalisable and the patient carpenter may be short-tempered with his children, it is equally true that some of these virtues may go beyond matters of procedure and begin to look more like ends in themselves, as for example concern for precision shades into devotion to truth and knowledge (p.198).

This makes an extremely important point, broadly similar to the observation by Peters (1996) noted in Chapter 1 about the potentially intrinsic value of activities such as cooking which seem to have an exclusively *prima facie* extrinsic or instrumental value, which relates directly to my own conception of the values dimension of vocational studies described in Chapter 7. Although it may still be the case that skills, unlike moral qualities and knowledge, are only contingently related to persons and realised primarily in activities which have a predominantly extrinsic/instrumental focus, vocational studies, pursued in ways inspired by the *ideals of craftsmanship* noted by Smith and others (Ainley, 1993; Corson, 1991; Hyland, 1995, 1998b), can transform VET and dissolve the gap between liberal and academic pursuits.

Key Skills, Core Skills and Transferability

The idea of underpinning the secondary school and post-school curriculum with some form of 'core skills' element goes back at least as far as the 1959 Crowther Report (and, arguably, even further back to the medieval grammar schools which prepared scholars for the 'bachelor' requirements of medieval universities; Cobban, 1988) which recommended supplementary broad-based general studies in the late secondary stages, following which a 'liberal studies movement' was taken up in the FE sector in order to ground vocational courses with some sort of general educational foundation (Macfarlane, 1993). Green (1997a) explains that core skills emerged out of an 'historical absence in the UK' by which 'alone among the major European nations in the 19th century, England developed a technical and vocational education that had no inherent connection between general education and schooling' (p.90). With the curriculum and qualifications developments of the 1970s and 1980s, especially the growth of Business and Technology Education Council (BTEC now Edexcel) cross-modular assignment work (Hyland, 1980; Gardner, 1979), the general studies movement was transformed into a common skills or core knowledge programme. Lawson (1992) has suggested that the contemporary emphasis on core skills can be interpreted as a logical development of the National Curriculum and a 'vindication of the idea that there ought to be a core of educational experience...and the extension of the idea to the 16-19 phase' (p.85).

These conceptions of common learning and core experiences, though far from being the equivalent of the common learning systems which support VET programmes in Europe (Skilbeck et al., 1994; Green, 1997a), play an important role in attempts to unify the 14-19 curriculum. However, in their earlier existence as 'core skills' which grew out of the 1970s YTS schemes, their function was rather less ambitious since they tended to be justified by the new vocationalist 'deficit' model (Esland, 1990) which held that school leavers did not possess the requisite skills demanded by employers. A number of studies by the Adult Literacy and Basic Skills Unit (ALBSU, 1987, 1989) had provided detailed evidence of the reading, writing and numeracy difficulties experienced by around one-quarter of school leavers, and this was reinforced by the 1993 Audit Commission report which indicated that around 150,000 young people aged 16-19 were leaving schools and colleges without achieving the intended qualifications (Audit Commission/HMI, 1993).

All such evidence, combined with the massive increase in participation in FE by 16 to 19 year olds, led to the embedding of core skills and learner support services in FE colleges (Harris & Hyland, 1995). The FEU document *A Basis for Choice* (FEU, 1979) had advocated a core entitlement of knowledge and skills for all students and various core skill projects were funded by the MSC as part of the New Training Inititative (Lawson, 1992). By the late 1980s a number of bodies, including the CBI, NCVQ, HMI, FEU and BTEC, began to move in a similar direction and a 'core of related knowledge,skills,qualities and attitudes has featured in the requirements of BTEC, the TVEI and the CPVE' (Maclure, 1991, p.38). The 1989 HMI document on post-16 core skills included ten elements, knowledge about information technology, using information technology, knowledge about industry and commerce, knowledge about society and the environment, communication, literacy, problem-solving, practical skills, working co-operatively and adaptability (HMI, 1989), and the CBI added 'values and integrity' and 'positive attitudes to change'. Building on these initiatives, the NCC, working closely with the FEU and NCVQ, agreed a joint strategy in support of the idea of 'a common set of core skills which would be incorporated in both A/AS-levels and the post-16 curriculum in school on the one hand, and in NVQs or as units within the NVQ framework, on the other' (Maclure, 1991, p.39).

Such developments culminated eventually in perhaps their most formalised and prescriptive interpretation in the core skill units of GNVQs (Fig.3.1).

Communication Level 2
Element 2:1: Take part in discussions with a range of people on routine matters
Performance Criteria:
1. own contributions are clear and appropriate on the subject matter
2. own contributions are made in a tone and manner suited to the audience
3. contributions from others are listened to attentively
4. own understanding of points made by others is actively checked and confirmed

Range: Subject matters: routine matters (e.g. responding to day-to-day enquiries; discussing routine tasks)
Mode: face to face; using the telephone
Audience: people familiar with the subject matter and in frequent contact with the individual (e.g. supervisors, colleagues, peers, tutors); people familiar with the subject matter but not in frequent contact with the individual (e.g. some customers/clients)

ASSESSMENT

Core skills units levels	National Curriculum Levels
1	4 and below
2	5 and 6
3	7
4	8 and 9
5	10 and above

Fig. 3.1: Example of a GNVQ Core Skill Unit
Source:NCVQ, 1993a ,p.4.

In the original documentation, GNVQs were designed to have six core units, problem-solving, communication, personal skills, numeracy, information technology and an optional foreign language unit (NCVQ, 1992, p.78), and this specification was based, exactly and in all particulars, on the jointly agreed framework for post-16 education orginally published by the NCC. Two groups of core skills, Group 1: communication, problem-solving, personal skills, and Group 2: numeracy, information technology, and a modern foreign language (Macfarlane, 1993, p.56), were outlined in the NCC scheme but, for reasons not altogether made clear, only three core skills came to be incorporated into GNVQs. Selecting 'communication' from Group 1 of the NCC list and 'application of number' (rather than numeracy) and 'information technology' from group 2, these three became 'mandatory core skills units' which would 'form part of the requirement for the GNVQs which will be offered by BTEC, City & Guilds and the RSA Examinations Board' (NCVQ, 1993b, p.2).

The most recent phase in these developments came with Sir Ron Dearing's review of 16-19 qualifications in which, without any noticeable preamble or explanation, the core skill units were summarily re-christened as 'key skills'. After first mentioning certain 'general skills', skills in 'effectively working with others, presentational skills, problem-solving and the ability to manage one's own learning' (Dearing, 1996, p.17), said to be favoured by employers and which GNVQs and also A-levels could be expected to foster, the 'three key skills in communication, the application of number and information technology' (i.e. the three GNVQ mandatory core units) were prescribed both for schools and post-compulsory education. In addition, a separate, though obviously related, new 'AS in key skills' (ibid., p.18) was proposed along with a strong recommendation that the key skills be used to underpin and support all post-16 work up to and including university programmes.

Although there appear to be sound and cogent educational arguments for ensuring that all post-16 learning (including, at the appropriate level, work-based and learning at work programmes) is underpinned by certain common elements such as numeracy, literacy, IT and, in relevant contexts, a modern foreign language and the like, I would contend that the idea of context-independent, free-standing and generalised core/key skills is educationally untenable. There are two main reasons for this:

1) Since there are no common or agreed definitions of such skills, with proponents differing about whether core/key skills apply to specific tasks, specialised areas of knowledge, outcomes of behaviour, ways of thinking or the attitudes, values and personality traits of students, such generalised skill-talk is fatuous and redundant, and should be replaced by descriptions of common curriculum experiences.

2) If key skills are meant to pick out general, transferable skills which are context- and domain-independent (and clearly such wide-ranging applicability, in the pursuit of flexibility and multi-skilling, is precisely what much skill-talk *is* wanting to recommend) then such skills can be shown, on both logical and empirical grounds, to be entirely illusory.

As was observed earlier, skill-talk in education is not just an alternative way of approaching curriculum design or emphasising the vocational and economic functions of schools and colleges but also, through assertions about the transferability of skills 'from one job to another with little or no modification' (Annet & Sparrow, 1985, p.12), a means of implying or suggesting a broad range of applicability for any skills prescribed.   It is, therefore, a short step from referring to the 'extent to which skills learned in a particular context can be used in other contexts' (FEU, 1982, p.8) to identifying 'core skills' which are 'generic, transferable skills which underpin a whole range of activities in daily life' (FEU, 1994, p.82). As an Employment Department (ED, 1993) report in this field noted:

> The core skills movement is based on beliefs about transfer. It assumes that it is possible to identify generic skills that are transferable across education and work contexts and that the acquisition of such skills will enhance learner flexibility, adaptability and autonomy (p.9).

This concept of core skills has proved to be universally appealing and, perhaps even more than skill-talk itself, possesses all the hallmarks of a powerfully persuasive educational slogan. Once enshrined in the new vocationalist literature, particularly after the publication of the influential New Training Initiative (DOE, 1981), some notion of transferable skills became the easy answer to the very difficult problem of upgrading VET and providing employers with a flexible and adaptable workforce. Core skills have lost none of their popularity in recent years, figuring prominently in the White Papers on Competitiveness (DTI, 1994, 1995) and also in New Labour documents on education and the economy (DfEE, 1998a,b).

Searle (1987) has argued that the whole rationale of the MSC and new vocationalist initiatives, including all the various training schemes from the 1970s YTS programmes through to NVQs and GNVQs in the 1980s and 1990s, can be seen as 'pivoting on the concept of transferable skills' (p.128). Even grander claims were made by Jonathan (1987) in her suggestion that 'transferable skills are seen as the key to three separate sorts of problems: economic, social and educational' (p.100). Similarly, transferable core or key skills are currently much in vogue in higher education circles thanks to the public relations efforts of the NCVQ and its supporters (Hyland, 1996), the pressures to identify the 'outcomes' of undergraduate studies to enhance employability skills (Otter, 1995; Hyland & Johnson, 1998), and the marketing and conference activities of the Higher Education for Capability organisation (HEC, 1997).

As in the sphere of skill-talk generally, the claims made about core skills tend to be based upon rather vague and nebulous descriptions of the nature and scope of what is actually being recommended. Indeed, the cavalier treatment of central, pivotal concepts is an especially worrying feature of all the arguments concerned with skills, core skills and competences. In the YTS projects, for instance, core skills were seen as being equivalent to 'basic/generic skills' (Evans, Brown & Oates, 1987, p.43) and 'basic skills' were also referred to as generic and transferable in documents produced by the Institute of Manpower Studies (IMS, 1982) to refer to skills which appear in at least 50% of employers' job description (see also IIE, 1996). Confusingly, as Halsall (1996) observes, the terms 'core, transferable and generic are used interchangeably' and there is no indication as to whether they are to 'be applied across different subjects or across different educational, occupational and social contexts, or both' (p.77). In recent literature on employability skills the idea of 'soft skills' such as 'oral and written communication, team working, listening and problem solving' (Skills & Enterprise Network, 1998a, p.1) has appeared and, just to complete the picture, the notion of 'broad skills...higher order skills which people can conceptualise as applying to a whole variety of contexts' (Wolf & Silver, 1995, p.1) has emerged to compound further the definitional problems in this highly troubled sphere of educational discourse.

The fact that there are serious 'disagreements about the content of core skills' (Hodgson & Spours, 1997, p.15) is probably responsible for the confusion over the criteria for the application of the label, and the introduction of new terms such as 'key skills' simply exacerbates such problems. Just to make matters worse, there are different views about whether core skills should be integrated or taught separately from mainstream NVQ, GNVQ or A-level programmes. Oates & Harkin (1995) insist that 'core skills teachers...should plan learning programmes that integrate the core skills' (p.196) with the implication that core skills mean very little outside the contexts of specific NVQ or GNVQ programmes within which they are designed essentially as support mechanisms. As Oates & Harkin argue:

> The implementation of core skills is better perceived not as an *addition* to tasks but as a challenge to deliver the whole curriculum in ways that enable students to be more active in learning and gathering evidence of attainment (ibid., p.196, original italics).

Not only does this integration model fly in the face of Dearing's recommendation of a separate AS in key skills, and also the actual practices of schools and colleges, some 'favouring embedding, others stand-alone strategies' (Spours, 1997, p.62), but also requires levels of resourcing, time and student support which, in practice, have not been found in evaluation reports of GNVQs in which core skills units are meant to be mandatory. The 1992 Ofsted report on GNVQs had noted that in many institutions 'core skills requirements were considered late in the course and in several cases were not covered effectively' (Ofsted, 1992, para.50), and a later survey found that:

> standards of work in lessons designed to cover the core skills in isolation from the vocational units...at all levels were barely satisfactory. There were few examples of good work stemming from the range requirements of the core skills unit (Ofsted, 1994, para.32).

Similarly the 1994 FEFC survey reported the failure of some teachers to 'recognise the importance of developing and assessing core skills through vocational work' (FEFC, 1994, p.5), criticisms also noted in the FEU survey conducted by Wolf (FEU/Nuffield, 1994; other core skills limitations are referred to below in the context of the 14-19 curriculum debate).

The precise nature of core skills teaching, including practical matters concerned with context, implementation, tutor support, and classroom hours timetabled, has significant implications in terms of potential transferability for, as Coates (1991) reminds us, the 'requirement that core skills should not be detached from their context...decides the question of whether core skills would provide credit transfer between different qualifications' (p.51). In fact, whether core/key skills are embedded in programmes or taught separately, there is still very little hard evidence to support the idea of transfer, if transfer is taken to mean the existence of 'generally applicable skills' (FEU, 1982, p.xi) which 'are used in carrying out all tasks or activities whether in education or training, at work or in life in general' (BTEC, 1993, p.57).

Halsall's (1996) conclusion that 'there is little empirical or philosophical evidence to suggest that core skills are transferable to all contexts and learning activities' (p.78) seems to be well supported by the relevant research. An early survey of the field commissioned by the MSC reported that 'there is, as yet, no common understanding of what they [transferable skills] are or how they can be learnt' (IMS, 1982, p.2), and this was confirmed in Fay's (1988) conclusion that there is 'no real agreement about the nature and mechanisms of transfer' (p.31). In a review of the MSC's transferable skills as seen through the eyes of 26 occupational bodies there was, according to Evans & Malcolm (1985), 'no hard evidence of transfer' (p.15). Similarly, in the University of Surrey's review of the YTS core skills project it was noted that it is in the 'area of transfer that the project has most frequently been criticised as resting on untested assumptions' (Evans, Brown & Oates, 1987, p.58), findings confirmed by Larkin (1989) and also by Singley & Anderson's (1989) study which concluded that 'unfortunately the evidence for the existence of general transfer is not good' (p.25).

Indeed, the weight and direction of evidence in this sphere is such that, notwithstanding the obvious commitment to notions of transferability, even the Employment Department survey had to acknowledge the fact that:

> numerous studies that have looked for evidence of transfer of various skills and knowledge across domains reveal a preponderance of negative findings, leading many researchers to conclude that learning is inherently context specific (ED, 1993, p.10).

Furthermore, all the research on the ways in which professionals develop expertise (Chi, Glaser & Farr, 1988; Tennant, 1991; Wolf & Silver, 1995) indicates that high-level occupational skills, in addition to many of the so-called 'basic' skills, are highly domain-dependent and not generalisable. Thus, problem-solving, fault-finding, making comparisons, team working, or any other alleged core, key or generic activity will be fairly meaningless until it is located within a particular framework of knowledge, beliefs and organisational values.

In terms of the philosophical evidence, there is a long-established school of thought which fiercely opposes the idea of general powers of the mind. Ryle's (1972) well-known account of the nature of rational thinking, for example, is unequivocally context-specific and insistent that there are vast differences between different disciplines and domains of knowledge and understanding. He observes that a:

> first-rate mathematician and a first-rate literary critic might share the one intellectual virtue of arguing impeccably while their other intellectual virtues

could be so disparate that neither could cope even puerilely with the problems of the other (p.191).

After acknowledging that 'certainly there is something common to all instances of what we call good judgement', Dearden (1984) goes on to explain that:

> This may arguably be said to be getting something right in difficult circumstances, but it is very different and specific accomplishments which are necessary to get things right in different circumstances. The judgment of the politician, the cricket player, the car driver, the investor and the pilot are very different things, and we should be very unwise to assume that an excellent wicket keeper would therefore be just the man to exercise political judgment in a damaging strike (p.78).

Dearden goes on to refer to the central ethical concept of goodness, and reminds us that:

> As Aristotle argued against Plato, there is no single good present in all cases, but many different goods resting on different bodies of knowledge: the good general is not possessed of the same abilities as the good doctor, and he is different again from the good gymnast (ibid.).

In a similar way, Powell (1968) argues that epithets such as 'careful', 'vigilant' and 'thorough' are without meaning until the details of their context and application have been filled in and, thus, 'it follows from this that they will be field-dependent and of low generality'. He goes on to argue that:

> there is no such animal as 'Careful Man'; there are simply men who do particular things in particular ways and it is always necessary to specify these in some detail before we can understand what is meant by careful surgery or careful driving (p.45).

The context-bound character of high-level skills and abilities is also endorsed by Phillips Griffiths (1965) who argues forcefully against the widely held held belief that higher education can be regarded as some form of general preparation for working life (cf. Barnett, 1994; Hyland, 1997b). As he observes, although the use of 'imagination, wisdom and intelligence' is undoubtedly required for higher level study, this does not entail or imply any general fostering of such qualities. In pursuing 'history or physics or philosophy...one becomes better at history, physics or philosophy' but this does not mean becoming 'a wiser father or trade union leader; or a wiser, more imaginative, more logical and intelligent man' (p.205). Such accounts highlight fully the shallowness and folly of defining the outcomes of higher education in terms of 'employability', 'analytical reasoning', 'problem solving' or 'critical thinking' skills (Hyland, 1998c). Indeed (contra de Bono and others), such arguments should be sufficient to caution us against applying the concept of skill to any multi-faceted and complex human capabilty like 'thinking'. As Gardner & Johnson (1996) rightly insist, the thinking involved in 'determining truth is a domain-specific activity' (p.453) and, since thinking is always by definition about 'something', the context-dependency of this 'something' must decisively count against the notion of generalised thinking skills of any kind at all.

Of course, such arguments are not and could never be sufficient to prevent people from using generalised skill-talk in the attempt to harness the persuasive force of the powerful slogan (and related notions of transferability, flexibility, multi-skilling, and the like) in making recommendations for practice. Thus, we are always likely to come across assertions such as the one headlined in a recent British Chambers of Commerce survey of employers' skill needs claiming that 'employability is the most vital skill needed by the nation's workforce' (BCC, 1998, p.1). The argument that 'employability' is not and could never be described as a skill would probably not be well received by those members of the professional training lobby steeped in skill-talk, though this should not prevent such arguments being advanced. Referring to the nature of arguments in another context, Warnock (1967) observed:

> That moral argument is not more effective than we find it to be is probably attributable to the cross that all arguments have to bear; an argument offers reasons to people, and people are not always reasonable (p.72).

In many cases it is tempting to conclude that the application of the label of transferability to alleged core skills such as 'cutting with one blade', 'sorting/grading objects' and 'making comparisons' (FEU, 1982) is simply a mistake or the use of the wrong descriptive term. Clearly chefs as well as surgeons and fishmongers can be experts in 'cutting with one blade', and 'making comparisons' is done by economists, historians, poets, interior designers and meteorologists without the implication that there is much in common between all these diverse activities. There seem to be two main fallacies which are responsible for the tendency to claim more in the way of skill transfer in such cases than the evidence justifies. First, there is what might be called the fallacy of misplaced concreteness which consists in attempts to reify aspects of human behaviour. Thus, there is a jump from performing an action or task (say, summarising a series of points or solving a maths problem) *skilfully* to the mistaken identification of a discrete *skill* possessed by the performer (when, clearly, no such skill exists). Secondly, there is the generalising fallacy which consists in implying that because some putative skill, for example, problem-solving or report-writing, can be performed in a *range of similar* contexts, then it is transferable to *all* contexts without the need for modification.

The dangers of such fallacious reasoning have already been fully illustrated but, just in case the myths still retain some of their attraction, we might usefully consider the following questions. Is it reasonable to expect someone who has learnt to solve problems in, say, business studies, to be able to transfer this learning to other spheres such as counselling, town planning, engineering or catering without acquiring a large additional body of domain-specific knowledge, techniques and practices? Indeed, even with the benefit of this additional body of expertise, the idea of *generally* transferable problem-solving (critical thinking, fault-finding, or any other alleged generic) skills is still highly dubious and suspect. There is no general routine, no single set of procedures, no algorithm that *will at one and the same time* facilitate the solving of a chess problem, diagnose an electrical fault, sort out an error in calculating money, show people the way out of difficulties in personal relationships and help to clarify a difficult passage in a science or philosophy course book.

Belief in the existence of such generally transferable core skills is simply wishful thinking, without philosophical or empirical support, and can be explained in terms of the vast educational advantages which would be gained if such skills were real rather than fictitious and illusory. Such skills, insofar as they hold out the promise of providing the much-vaunted flexibility and adaptability required of employees in post-Fordist industry, are, as Hyland & Johnson (1998) observe, 'simply too good *not* to be true!' (p.170). However, if some people are still bewitched by the reification and generalisation fallacies which support the illusions, we might ask them to consider why, in spite of the fact that we often make wise decisions, accurate assessments, or have a knack for making firiends, we do not naturally speak of 'wisdom', 'accuracy' or 'friendship' skills!

The idea of core/key skills has important implications for the debate surrounding the 14-19 curriculum, and inconsistencies and weaknesses in core skill prescriptions will naturally have far-reaching implications for any proposals advanced in this sphere concerning qualifications frameworks and the links between general and vocational education. However, before examining these issues, we need to examine changes which, arguably, have had the greatest impact on VET over the last few decades and these are the consequences flowing from the introduction of CBET into the field through the NVQs and GNVQs developed under the aegis of the NCVQ.

NVQs and the Rise and Fall of the NCVQ

The story of the establishment of the NCVQ in 1986, and its revolutionary implications for VET in this country, has been told by many commentators in the field (Burke, 1989, 1995; Bees & Swords, 1990; Fletcher, 1991; Jessup, 1991; Hodkinson & Issitt, 1995; Bates, 1998), including myself (1994a). Rather than going over old ground it would, perhaps, be best to offer a brief summary of the basic accounts before moving on to the critical analysis of NVQ developments to the present time which, along with the issues examined in other chapters, will help to construct a framework for later chapters which examine more recent New Deal and lifelong learning contributions to the VET debate.

The foundations for a major overhaul of VET programmes, methodology and qualifications were laid with the publication of *A New Training Initiative* (DOE, 1981), though this itself can be seen as a continuation of MSC skills strategies and assessements for YTS referred to earlier. Even in the early stages, accountability in terms of 'outputs...the standards that need to be achieved at the end of a learning programme' (Jessup, 1990, p.18) was predominant. There was an insistence that 'at the heart of the initiative lie standards if a new kind' (DOE, 1991, p.6), and it was the pursuit of such standards, based on competence outputs constructed through the functional analysis methodology of CBET designed eventually to cover all occupational sectors, which was to provide the driving force for the development of NVQs.

The project was continued and reinforced in subsequent government White Papers, *Training for Jobs* (DOE, DES, 1984) and *Education and Training for Young People* (DOE, DES, 1985), and was brought to full fruition in *Working Together – Education and Training* (DOE, DES, 1986). Following recommendations made in this White Paper the NCVQ was established with a remit which included the design and implementation of a new national framework of vocational qualifications with the aim of securing national standards of vocational competence throughout all occupational sectors. From the start, the key aims of the NCVQ were to 'improve vocational qualifications by basing them on the standards of competence required in employment' and to 'establish an NVQ framework which is comprehensible and comprehensive and facilitates access, progression and continued learning' (NCVQ, 1989, p.2). The NCVQ was not itself an awarding body but undertook to accredit or hallmark qualifications awarded by other bodies such as BTEC, RSA and City & Guilds, insisting that it would 'only accredit qualifications which meet employment needs' (ibid., p.3).

All NVQs had to consist of 'an agreed statement of competence, which should be determined or endorsed by a lead body with responsibility for defining, maintaining and improving national standards of performance in the sectors of employment where the competence is practised' (NCVQ, 1991, p.1). For NCVQ purposes there are 11 occupational sectors, plus lots of subsidiary sectors, and, according to Smithers (1993), the industry lead bodies numbered over 180. The agreed statement of competence in each occupational sphere 'should be derived from an analysis of the functions within the area of competence to which it relates' (NCVQ, 1991, p.2) and had to be linked to 'performance criteria' which 'identify only the essential aspects of performance necessary for competence', and also 'range statements' which 'express the various circumstances in which the competence must be applied' (ibid., p.3).

This process of 'functional analysis' used by lead bodies to determine competence involved the identification of the 'expectations in employment as a whole...breaking the work role for a particular area into purposes and functions' (Mitchell, 1989, p.58). The end result was the identification of 'key purposes' for all the various occupational sectors, accompanied by key 'units and elements' linked to relevant performance criteria and range statements (see Fig. 3.2 for a practical illustration).

UNIT: RECEPTION
ELEMENTS:
01 receive and direct visitors
Notes:
Underpinning skills and knowledge: structure, location and responsibilities of people in organisation; policy and procedures of organisation on greeting visitors, security, safety and emergency; messaging procedure; telephone system and operation; effective use of information sources; dealing with difficult/aggressive visitors (e.g. recognise and react appropriately to physical communication signals); car parking arrangements available to visitors; effective communication (oral and written)
Range:
Routine and non-routine visitors must be dealt with. Contingencies must be dealt with: callers without appointment (with both urgent and non-urgent requirements), callers who are late/early for appointments, callers who require baggage or other effects to be cared for during visit, receipt of deliveries, emergency situations
Performance Criteria:
1. All visitors are greeted promptly and courteously.
2. Visitors' names and needs are identified.
3. Visitors are only given disclosable information.
4. Visitors are directed and/or escorted in accordance with organisation policy.
5. Reasons for any delay/non-availability are explained politely.
6. All records are up to date, legible and accurate.
7. Messages are accurately recorded and passed on promptly to correct location.
8. Security and safety procedures are followed at all times.

Fig. 3.2: Example of NVQ Units and Elements
Source: COVTEC, 1992, p.1.

In addition to all this, there was a hierarchy of five levels of competence, from basic tasks to high-level management and supervisory functions (see Fig. 3.3), and these levels have since played a major role in the debate about 14-19 qualifications since they have been employed to map and demonstrate equivalence between vocational and academic qualifications from school to post-graduate level (discussed in more detail in the next section).

The following definitions of the NVQ levels provide a general guide and are not intended to be prescriptive.
Level 1: competence in the performance of a range of varied work activities, most of which may be routine and predictable.
Level 2: competence in a significant range of varied work activities, performed in a variety of contexts. Some of the activities are complex and non-routine, and there is some individual responsibility or autonomy. Collaboration with others, perhaps through membership of a work group or team, may often be a requirement.
Level 3: competence in a broad range of varied work activities performed in a wide variety of contexts and most of which are complex and non-routine. There is considerable responsibility and autonomy, and control or guidance of others is often required.
Level 4: competence in a broad range of complex, technical or professional work activities performed in a wide variety of contexts and with a substantial degree of personal responsibility and autonomy. Responsibility for the work of others and the allocation of resources is often present.
Level 5: competence which involves the application of a significant range of fundamental principles and complex techniques across a wide and often unpredictable variety of contexts. Very substantial personal autonomy and often significant responsibility for the work of others and for the allocation of substantial resources feature strongly, as do personal accountabilities for analysis and diagnosis, design, planning, execution and evaluation.

Fig. 3.3: The NVQ Framework
Source: NCVQ, 1992, p.12.

In spite of growing criticisms of NVQs and CBET (Marks, 1996; Bates, 1998), especially Smithers' (1993) much publicised report which described the whole project as a 'disaster of epic proportions' (p.1), the NCVQ framework has continued to enjoy official government endorsement since its initial approval in the 1991 White Paper *Education and Training for the 21st Century* (DES, 1991) which also heralded the birth and development of GNVQs which now hold a pivotal place in the debate about the 14-19 curriculum and the relationship between vocational and academic qualifications. More recently, following recommendations made in the 1996 Dearing survey of 16-19 provision (Dearing, 1996) the NCVQ, along with the School Curriculum and Assessment Authority (SCAA), has been abolished and replaced with the overarching QCA (DfEE, 1996), following which there was a major overhaul and review of the whole NVQ system (DfEE, 1997a). At the time of its abolition in October 1997, an editorial in *Educa* (1997a) observed that this development was thought to be 'more significant than the disappearance of SCAA, which is likely to see greater continuity of functions in the new organisation'. The editorial went on to observe:

NCVQ was set up in October 1986. The quinquennial review in 1995/96...showed that there had always been confusion over its roles and responsibilities and the division of functions between the NCVQ and the

Department. Its position as a promoter of NVQs had also become anomalous, given that the original expectation that older style qualifications would disappear had not been realised. When it was set up, NCVQ was intended to be 'an engine of change independent of existing interests'. There is plenty of indication in the comments now being made by government ministers that it embraced this role too enthusiastically (p.2).

In my original book on NVQs, I argued that the qualifications, and indeed all qualifications supported by the functional analysis methodology which underpins the CBET strategy of NVQs, were 'logically and conceptually confused, epistemologically ambiguous, and based on largely discredited behaviourist learning principles' (Hyland, 1994a, p.x). This conclusion was supported by philosophical argument, policy analysis and empirical research available at the time. In order to bring the critical evaluation up to date I intend to examine NVQs and related developments in the five years since 1994 making use of broad headings which I have utilised in other recent analyses of the field (Hyland, 1996d; 1997a, 1998d).

NVQ Weaknesses

The failings of CBET as a model for upgrading workforce skills and enhancing the development and status of VET have been apparent since the late 1980s (Hyland, 1992, 1993b, 1994a,c; Marks, 1996; Bates, 1998) though, thanks largely to a generous NCVQ marketing budget (Targett, 1993, 1995; Robinson, 1996), official endorsement by government and the CBI, a captive market guaranteed by tax concessions and state-controlled funding mechanisms (Field, 1995), and a public relations machine supported by carefully vetted research consultants (Smithers, 1993, 1996), it is only in the last five or six years that the full extent of NVQ shortcomings has been revealed by independent researchers.

Not only have NVQs failed to achieve the key objectives originally set for them in terms of the needs of employers, students, trainees, VET qualifications, programmes and staff, and vocational learning and teaching generally, they have also managed to devalue and emasculate vocational studies by seeking to popularise an approach to learning outcomes which is 'normally inappropriate to the description of human action or to the facilitation of the training of human beings' (Ashworth, 1992, p.16). The replacement of traditional VET courses with NVQs has led to widespread de-skilling, a loss of significant theoretical content and a systematic narrowing and delimitation of vocational scope and focus in fields such as construction (Callender, 1992), plumbing and electrical installation (Smithers, 1993), and in catering, business studies and hairdressing (Hyland & Weller, 1994). Raggatt's (1994) survey of a wide range of NVQs offered in FE institutions concluded that the staff considered the approach to be far too 'minimalist' with a content which was 'too narrow, concerned only with the performance of simple tasks' (p.66).

Concerns over standards in this sector have been prominent since the introduction of regular monitoring and inspection by the FEFC (FEFC, 1994b). A 1997 FEFC survey of vocational qualifications standards, in addition to observing that vocational students in England spend an average of 19 hours per week on programmes as opposed to the 30-40 hours of their Continental counterparts, reported continuing concerns 'over the effectiveness of quality assurance procedures, with particular concerns about the clarity of the standards on which NVQs are based' (Educa, 1997b, p.2). The participants in the 1998 TES/Lancaster University (TES, 1998) survey of FE provision reported widespread dissatisfaction amongst staff and students about the 'highly questionable' nature of NVQ procedures and standards; many respondents felt that NVQ certificates were 'not worth the paper they were written on' and had 'served to debase qualifications' (p.33).

The major Beaumont (1996) review of NVQs, notwithstanding the fact that it was accused by one of its more critical members, Professor Smithers, of 'spin-doctoring' and soft-pedalling in order to hide fundamental inconsistencies, shortcomings and problems (Smithers, 1996), still could not disguise the fact that 'there was a lack of clarity about who [NVQs] are aimed at or what they relate to', and that the 'existence of concerns about consistency is enough in itself to threaten the credibility of NVQs' (Beaumont, 1996, pp.36, 38). More importantly, the many problems and anomalies subsumed under the innocuous and superficial label of 'language' problems in Beaumont were, for the most part, not superficial but quite serious defects and difficulties inherent in the CBET model of functional analysis and its behaviourist learning foundation (Hyland, 1996d; 1998d).

All the problems of VET in terms of supplying employers' skill needs and remedying problems are still with us and, indeed, are more pronounced than ever according to a recent DfEE document which noted that 'UK skills shortages are worsening generally' (1998d, p.1). Studies indicating employers rejection of the NVQ system as a training strategy (IES, 1995; Matlay & Hyland, 1997; see also Chapter 4) have been reinforced by the growing number of companies initiatially tempted by the superficial attractions of NVQs, British Home Stores, Burtons and the Conran Catering group (Merrick, 1994; Ward, 1995a,b), but which have now abandoned this approach and returned to their own in-house schemes. The recent resurgence of vocational qualifications 'other' than NVQs (Ward, 1998) is also significant in this respect (this issue is taken up again later).

Moreover, as will be noted later, all the New Deal policies and schemes are premissed on the (implicit) failure of the current system at all levels. The NCVQ simply failed to achieve its targets for covering all occupational sectors and encouraging employers and workers to adopt NVQs, and managed to hide this failure for years through exaggerated and massaged figures. Robinson's (1996) survey based on the government's own figures on NVQ take-up indicated that the qualifications cover no more than 3 or 4% of the total workforce. A 1997 DfEE study reported that the 'take-up of NVQs/SVQs is still low nationally compared with other vocational qualifications' (DfEE, 1997c, p.4). Instead of the 3 to 4 million awards at one time claimed for NVQs (Robinson, 1996), the offical figure by the end of 1997 was 1.9 million (DfEE, 1998d, p.9). There were 459,000 awards for 1996/1997 which, on a Labour Force Survey figure for total employment of 27,044,000 in May 1998, is somewhat less than 2% of the workforce (ibid.).

In addition, the trend noted in previous surveys (Field, 1995; Hyland, 1996d) for most awards (over three-quarters) to be awarded at the lowest levels and in business and service occupations where there have been few labour and skill shortages for many years seems to be continuing. At the same time, there is a low level of NVQ take-up in engineering and manufacturing sectors (DfEE, 1997c; 1998e), particularly at intermediate craft and technician level, in which there have been acute shortages in recent times. Similar flaws and shortcomings have also been identified in the Scottish equivalents of these qualifications, the SVQs (Canning, 1998).

Industry/Employer Involvement

As mentioned in other sections, a large number of surveys have indicated that employers, who are supposed to be the key players in the NCVQ system, are either largely indifferent to or ignorant about the nature and purpose of NVQs. The national survey of NVQs by the FEFC in 1994 revealed a 'widespread lack of knowledge about NVQs, particularly in small firms, and an unwillingness on the part of many of them to become involved in workplace training and assessment' (FEFC, 1994, p.22). More damning still was the study by the Institute of Employment Services (IES, 1995) which indicated that, even though awareness of NVQs had increased over the years, employers were still not convinced about their value to the workforce. As Smithers (1996) commented, the 'more employers know about NVQs the less they like them' (p.2). Key factors in the low take-up of NVQs by leading firms were reported in a more recent survey by the National Foundation for Educational Research in which 'the time and cost involved' and 'their perceived lack of credibility or commercial advantage' (Nichols, 1998, p.36) were highlighted.

There is, in fact, little evidence to support the NCVQ/DfEE rhetoric about the 'employer-led' nature of NVQs. The occupational standards tend to be devised by carefully selected private consultancies (Stewart & Sambrook, 1995), and the so-called employer representatives on industry lead bodies tend to be made up of training and personnel managers and a 'wide sprinkling of consultants, some of whom have a long history of involvement in the Employment Dept and its quangos' (Field, 1995, p.37). Real employers, particularly those in small firms, tend to view NVQs as bureaucratic, cumbersome, costly and not worth investing in (Hodkinson, Sparkes & Hodkinsin, 1996; Marks, 1996). Rather than streamlining vocational qualifications, NVQs encouraged a massive increase in different qualifications and occupational lead bodies which, according to Callender's large-scale study of the construction industry, resulted in a 'confusing duplication and proliferation...especially in occupational areas that cut across different industrial sectors' (1992, p.26). With the demise of the NCVQ this state of affairs is at last being remedied with the plan to replace the 180 or so lead bodies with 60-70 National Training Organisations (Twining, 1998).

As mentioned in other sections, comparisons between different occupational sectors in terms of skill requirements and supply in Britain,

France and Germany (Prais, 1995; Green, 1995) have shown that NVQs are too narrow in scope and too concerned with low-level, task- based activities to raise the general standard of workforce skills. The comparative study of OECD systems by Skilbeck et al. (1994) explained the inadequacy of the British NCVQ model in terms of, on the one hand, its 'emphasis on employment-related competences' which failed to address issues of technological and industrial change and, on the other, the fact that the system 'over-emphasises outcomes at the expense of the processes and the settings through which these outcomes have been expressed and developed' (p.238).

In the small and medium-sized enterprises (SME) sector, the failure of national training strategies has been well documented (Storey, 1994; Matlay, 1996; Pettigrew, Arthur & Hendry, 1990). As will be discussed in more detail in Chapters 5 and 6, many of Labour's New Deal and lifelong learning schemes and policies, especially the UfI and WTW projects, are targeted specifically at SME owner-managers. The SME sector, accounting for over 90% of all firms in Briatin and 35% of the total workforce (Dyson, 1990), is vital to the country's industrial and economic well-being, and it is the traditionally low education and training participation in this sector which makes small firms such a crucially significant target for government policies on VET.

Our own research at Warwick on SMEs in the West Midlands Region between 1995 and 1997 (Hyland & Matlay, 1997; Matlay & Hyland, 1997) provided some interesting backgound data on VET policy and practice in this important sector. The study, involving a telephone survey of 2000 SME owner-managers followed by 74 in-depth interviews, revealed the 'paradox of training', the gap between expressed interest and documented volume of investment and participation which is examined in more detail in the context of the debate on employer involvement in Chapter 4. There was an appallingly low take-up of NVQs in the firms surveyed (see Fig. 3.4) and this seemed to correlate with other key factors influencing participation in training such as the cost of training, owner-managers' own 'incubator' experience of training, and the perceived quality of training programmes available (overwhelmingly based on the NCVQ system) and their links with specific SME skill requirements.

Band code	No. of employees	No. of firms $n = 1986$	NVQs Awareness	Understanding	Interested in adopting	Actually adopted scheme
A	1–5	1242	72	38	13	7
B	6–10	314	19	10	4	3
C	11–19	252	64	33	11	5
D	20–49	134	35	18	7	5
E	50–99	44	15	9	9	6

Fig. 3.4: Employers' Use of NVQs
Source: Hyland,1998d, p.376.

A 1996 survey by the Association of Colleges (TES, 1996) indicated that the cost of work-based NVQs is already far higher than college-based routes (a finding confirmed by other studies; Revell, 1997), and it is highly unlikely that SMEs could bear any increased costs arising from strategies designed to address the anomolies and shortcomings revealed in the critical surveys of the NVQ system. Moreover, whereas the Beaumont (1996, p.37) survey reported that 90% of firms whould give credence only to NVQs awarded by other employers (rather than by colleges or private trainers) only around 25% of NVQs are awarded via this route. In terms of owner-managers' perceptions of current VET and the dominant NCVQ model, the negative combination of high cost and failure to supply specific skills needs may explain the very low take-up of NVQ-related programmes (including MAs and Training Credit placements) amongst SMEs. Especially worrying for those concerned with implementing New Deal policies in the DfEE and QCA are the figures for the NVQ take-up in the very large group of micro-firms (Band code A and B in Fig. 3.4 above; firms employing less than 10 people) in which only 0.56% and 0.96% of owner-managers had seen any merit in participating in such programmes.

Anomalies in NVQ Assessment

Tuxworth (1989) has observed that there 'is a lack of research evidence that CBET is superior to other forms of education/training in output terms' (p.17) and, since the whole *raison d'etre* of the NCVQ approach is founded on outcomes and outputs, this is indeed a damning critique of the system. In fact the obsession with validity which characterises CBET highlights a particular weakness of all systems which are dominated by criterion-referencing and validity. Jessup's call for NVQ assessments to 'just forget reliability altogether and concentrate on validity' (1991, p.191) flies in the face of all that is recommended as best practice for educational assessment, research and measurement. Burroughs (1971), for example, recommends that 'some index of reliability ought to appear on the label sewn into every data-gathering device ever produced' (p.68) and Gay (1987) is even more forthright in asserting that an 'unreliable test is essentially useless' (p.135). With the NCVQ strategy specifically in mind Prais (1991) argues forcefully that:

> any argument that bases itself on the notion that validity (i.e. lack of bias) is all that matters is essentially wrong. We need to be concerned with the total expected error associated with a qualification-procedure (i.e.validity plus reliability); we are likely to be misled if we focus on only one component (p.87).

In a 1993 Employment Department report on NVQ implementation a number of 'assessment anomalies' were noted including 'the cost, the amount of paperwork involved, practical difficulties of assessment in the workplace and concerns about the reliability of assessments' (ED, 1993b, p.35). Similar problems concerning consistency were noted by Hyland & Weller (1994) and Beaumont (1996) and are reflected in the increased emphasis placed on requirements for 'sufficiency of evidence' (Bates & Dutson, 1995) in workplace assessment and accreditation. Failure to ensure adequate reliability is a particular problem for systems like the NCVQ model of CBET which are based unequivocally on criterion-referencing and the pursuit of content validity at all costs. Such approaches are characterised by ever-increasing demands for specification of content and prescriptive rules. As Wolf (1995) has observed the:

> more systems are based on extremely demanding and rigid requirements, as has happened with NVQs, the more likely it becomes that factors which are technically extraneous to assessment will in fact preclude effective and high-quality assessment from taking place (p.125).

Wolf (1997b) and Smithers (1999) have also noted broadly similar weaknesses in GNVQs, as did the major survey of the qualifications by

Capey (1996). The cost of adopting such strategies has been high indeed and paid for by the anomalies and inconsistencies of assessment noted in major critical studies and the correspondingly low status of the awards.

In addition to these technical problems, it has to be said that the conjunction of an NVQ outcomes system with a post-school funding regime which rewards successful outputs, described by Hodkinson (1997) as a 'lethal cocktail' (p.7), has resulted in assessment abuses on an unprecedented scale. The University of Sussex (1996) study of NVQ assessment practices reported that almost 40% of assessors admitted to passing sub-standard students on NVQ programmes, and, in a notorious case at Derby College, NVQ certificates were ordered for students as soon as they enrolled on the course (Ward, 1996).

The 1997 report of the Public Accounts Committee (Baty, 1997a) noted that 'incorrect payments' from the DfEE to NVQ providers had totalled £8.6 million in 1995/96, a figure which the human rights charity Article 26 has described as merely the tip of a multi-million pound corruption scandal (Bell, 1996). In late 1997 the minister for lifelong learning was forced to cancel some 1600 NVQs awarded by TECs and demand that the 25 TECs in question repay £5 million of public money spent on the schemes (Russell, 1997). Furthermore, the arrival of a new government and the replacement of the NCVQ with the QCA seems, according to the 1998 report of the new government-appointed inspectorate, the Training Standards Council (McGavin, 1998), to have had little impact on the 'mounting list of irregularities mainly concerning deficiencies in national vocational qualification assessments' (p.27). The report went on to detail the 'wide variations in the quality of work-based training schemes' and noted that 39 cases of fraudulent practice involving £6.7 million in payments were currently being investigated.

Taking a more optimistic perspective, it has to be said that abolition of the NCVQ in 1997 has resulted in far greater attention being paid to the structure and function of work-based assessment of NVQs and, under the new policies for VET introduced by the QCA, this has been accompanied by an avowed determination to eradicate fraud and corruption in the system. This and much more will be required if the status of NVQs is to be raised along with general standards of VET in this country. A start has been made in the form of the DfEE blueprint (1997a) for the reform and upgrading of NVQs which seeks to assure us that:

NVQs are moving away from rigid prescription and bureaucratic procedures, and giving industry the flexibility to set occupational standards in language that people understand (p.1).

It is not, however, just the 'language' of NVQs which is problematic (as the civil servants probably know only too well; see Smithers, 1996, 1999; Nash, 1997a) but the fundamental basis of functional analysis and CBET as a strategy for education and training. The really important reforms are those which involve the separation of the promotion, design and quality assurance functions of NVQ provision and, most fundamental of all, the intention to provide the 'additional rigour required of external verification' through the introduction of 'an element of independent assessment on the basis of needs determined by National Training Organisations' (DfEE, 1997a, p.4). Moreover, as Ecclestone (1998) has argued in relation to the problems of CBET which had been transferred from NVQs to GNVQs and noted in the 1996 Capey Report:

> after the Capey Report, quite fundamental epistemological concessions were made. The approach to mastery, so prominent in the NVQ assessment model and transferred to GNVQs, was acknowledged, tacitly, to be epistemologically flawed as well as impractical. So too was the idea that ever more refined assessment specifications would guarantee both the validity and reliability of standards. Of particular interest to researchers is that these concessions are made without any public engagement with detracting research evidence (p.688).

Such reforms are more radical than the DfEE 'newspeak' implies and, on the face of it, herald a major overhaul of NVQs which involves changing just about everything save the NVQ label. The introduction of external testing measures, for instance, is a highly significant concession which, although called for by all the critics of NVQs (Smithers, 1996; Marks, 1996), would have been anathema to the fundamentalists who dictated the NCVQ agenda just a few years ago (Jessup, 1991;Burke, 1995). Nor would the former NCVQ old guard look favourably on what is clearly the abandonment of the original (now regarded as utterly unrealistic) aim of covering the whole of the workforce with NVQs. The new QCA Chief Executive, Dr Tate, has offered employers, trainers and educational institutions the guarantee that 'traditional' vocational qualifications will be retained in the drive for a reliable and high quality VET system in Britain (Russell, 1997). Indeed, in recent years there has been an increase in the award of vocational qualifications other than NVQs partly as a result of the recognition that 'other qualifications meet a need which is not met by NVQs and GNVQs' (Ward, 1998b, p.8). The failure of NVQs in this respect has recently been described in evidence presented to the House of Commons Education and Employment Committee as a 'triumph by the market over the planners' (THES, 1998c, p.2). Such a triumph is all the more remarkable when viewed against the fact that the 'market' has been, from the outset, rigged and manipulated by special concessions and funding mechanisms to favour NVQs.

Vocational Studies and the 14-19 Curriculum

As in the debate about the problems of VET and the recommended solutions, the discourse on the structure and organisation of the 14-19 (though some commentators still prefer to discuss the 16-19 group) curriculum and qualifications system was crystallised around a powerful 'alliance of interests' (Whiteside, 1992, p.9) in the early 1990s. There emerged a common consensus about the 'definition of the problem' and broad agreement on an 'agenda for action' which included (ibid., pp.5-7):

- the need to increase participation and attainment rates post-16
- the need to devise a coherent curriculum and qualification system in which 'academic' and 'vocational' elements are equally valued and carry credit transfer
- the need to improve the quality of teaching and learning
- the need to develop co-ordinated approaches at all levels to the delivery of 14/16 to 19 education and training

The chief vehicle for such a programme of reform emerged in the White Paper *Education and Training for the 21st Century* (DES, 1991) which first introduced the idea of general NVQs which would 'offer a broad preparation for employment as well as an accepted route to higher level qualifications, including higher education' (Vol.1, p.19). Before looking at the development of GNVQs it might be worth examining the stages which led up to this particular policy turn.

Young & Spours (1998) provide an excellent summary of the 'stages of development of a national 14-19 system' in terms of distinct, but overlapping and, at times, interrelated phases or periods (pp.87-91):

1979-1986 (or 1979-1991 to incorporate overlaps): this phase involved the ad hoc expansion and pre-vocational developments (e.g. CPVE, TVEI, YTS) which characterised the period of the 'new vocationalism'. This period included a 'variety of forms of local innovation based on different, sometimes competing, conceptions of vocationalism' but ended (with the 1991 White Paper) with a curb being placed on the innovations 'by restricting internal assessment in A-levels, controlling modularisation and by developing a competence-based GNVQ to challenge and replace traditional vocational qualifications such as the BTEC National Diploma (pp.88-9).

1987-1991 (1986 onwards in terms overlap): this period began with the review of vocational qualifications which saw the establishment of the NCVQ in 1986, developed through to the establishment of NVQs and a national vocational framework and continues with the aftermath of the introduction of GNVQs and the triple-track system defined in terms of the NVQ framework.

1991-1995 (1990 onwards in terms of overlap): during this phase, although the triple-track system was firmly embedded and developed within the national 16-19 qualification framework, there still remained possibilities for creating a more unified approach (outlined in the *British Baccalaureate* proposals by Finegold et al., 1990, and the General Educational Diploma of the National Commission on Education, NCE, 1993) which were enhanced in the Dearing Review of 16-19 qualifications.

1996-onwards: the most recent phase, post-Dearing, is seen as reviewing the national framework and developing linkages between the tracks.

Educational policy and practice on the 14-19 curriculum has been almost exclusively 'qualification led' (ibid., p.87) and has, therefore, neglected other important issues concerned with processes, methodology and funding. Hodgson & Spours (1997) serve to crystallise the key issues in the 14-19 debate in their observation that:

Fundamentally, the debate about the English 14-19 qualifications system is a debate about whether it evolves in a more unified direction or whether it remains a distinctive track-based system, emphasizing the division between academic and vocational learning and certification (p.18).

The 1996 Dearing review of qualifications can be regarded as a watershed in developments in this sphere in that it, not only served to consolidate the three-track system of academic, general vocational and work-based vocational awards (see Fig. 3.5), but also (and, perhaps, paradoxically), by creating connections between the three tracks in terms of the possibility of 'allowing students to change pathways' (Dearing, 1996, p.10) and the creation of National Awards at each level plus a National Diploma at the Advanced level to 'encourage studies in depth, with complementary studies to give breadth' (ibid., p.21), pointed towards a degree of commonality and unification. As Young (1997) puts it, the 'Dearing Report's recommendations are best seen as a weak variant of a framework approach which also establishes some of the conditions for moving towards a more unified system in the future' (p.38).

Higher Degree	(GNVQ5)	NVQ5
Degrees	(GNVQ4)	NVQ4
A/AS	Advanced GNVQ	NVQ3
GCSE	Intermediate GNVQ	NVQ2
	Foundation GNVQ	NVQ1

Fig. 3.5: The Triple-Track Qualifications Framework
Source: Based on Burke, 1995, p.50.

Hodgson & Spours (1997) provide a lucid account of the nature of the current situation in terms of the crystallisation of the 14-19 qualifications debate into three basic positions identified as (pp.11-13):

Trackers: those who believe in three distinctive qualification tracks (e.g. Raffe, 1993; Smithers, 1993; Prais, 1995) based on different abilities of students and different goals and purposes between vocational and academic learning. Hodgson & Spours note that this position tends to be based on systems (such as those in Germany and Switzerland) which have separate vocational and academic pathways but in which the vocational route is 'high status due to the fact that it contains substantial elements of general education' (Hodgson & Spours, 1997, pp.11-12) and separate institutions for the different routes which are valued highly by higher education and employers

Frameworkers: those who support the retention of three tracks or pathways FEU, 1994; HMC, 1995: Dearing, 1996) but allow for overarching frameworks (such as Dearing's idea of national awards) to create greater flexibility and improve:

> access to the curriculum for adults as well as for 16-19 year olds, to improve indivividual student choice, to promote personal pacing of learning, to stimulate curriculum reform by making new combinations of study possible and thus to provide a mechanism for the gradual reform of the qualifications tracks (Hodgson & Spours, 1997, p.12).

Supporters of GNVQs see the new broad-based vocational qualifications as a means of enhancing these goals (Halsall & Cockett, 1996; Higgins & Merson, 1995).

Unifiers: those who argue for a completely unified system (Finegold et al., 1990; NCE, 1993; Hyland, 1994a; Hodgson & Spours, 1997) which would involve a core curriculum post-16 and the replacement of existing qualifications by one single qualifications structure.

Although there are points of convergence between these three basic positions, all agree on the need for 14-19 reform to raise levels of achievement, trackers and unifiers both admire the general education foundation of Contintenal VET schemes,and frameworkers and unifiers both favour the unitisation and modularisation of 14-19 education and training, the 'arguments for a unified qualifications system have become stronger' in the last few years, and there has emerged a large:

> degree of consensus between the frameworkers and the unifiers because there is a mutual acceptance that the unified system is the long-term aim (Hodgson & Spours, 1997, p.13).

Enhancing Vocational Studies and Upgrading VET

To conclude this chapter it is worth summarising all the main themes and issues discussed in terms of the central question, raised in the first chapter and alluded to in many different sections throughout the book, of how developments in educational theory and practice can be seen as contributing to enhancing the status of vocational studies at all levels of the system. The vocational/academic divide grew out of the historical legacy discussed in the last chapter which, emerging out of the social stratification of schooling from the 16th century which generated what Lewis (1991) called the 'historical problem of vocational education' (p.96) rooted in class divisions, eventually led to the yawning gulf between general/academic and practical/vocational education (incorporating the inferior status of the vocational) that still bedevils the system at all levels.

In the last chapter, in the context of discussions about education and the future of work, I expressed a preference for what was described as 'compatibilist flexibility' which, though not swallowing the 'high skills-high technology' scenario fully, acknowledged the potential in the new post-Fordist paradigms for the reconstruction and upgrading of VET. Within the framework of of my earlier writings on NVQs, GNVQs and the future of VET I have been happy to nail my colours firmly to the mast of a unified system of the kind initially outlined by Finegold et al. (1990) and modified and updated by Hodgson & Spours (1997). Indeed, in endorsing the general position of the National Commission report of 1993 calling for the replacement of all existing qualifications with a General Education Diploma, I suggested that a logical corollary of such a development might be the 'abolition of the NCVQ' (Hyland, 1994a, p.114) and the merger of the departments of education and employment. With the establishment of the QCA and the DfEE both these conditions are now satisfied. Given these trends, and the possibilities outlined above for post-Dearing progress, what are the main arguments for a unified system as far as the future of an enhanced vocational studies is concerned?

I would suggest the following as key considerations for all those committed to such ideals and objectives for VET:

1. The arguments of those identified above as 'trackers' are essentially concerned with a stratified education system, within which A-levels were a means of controlling entry to higher education, based on the tripartite divisions stemming from the 1944 Education Act. In a recent review of forty years of debate about post-16 qualifications, Pound (1998) concluded that 'A-levels provide an insurmountable barrier to the quest for breadth in the post-compulsory curriculum as a whole' (p.167). He maintains that 'while the retention of the A-level system has enabled the universities to continue to recruit well-qualified applicants...the cost of preserving such academically rigorous standards has been high'. Pound goes on to argue that:

> First, those who succeed not only sacrifice breadth in their education for narrow specialisation, but they do so at the expense of a significant proportion of candidates whose failure means they have nothing to show after a full two years of study in the sixth-form. Moreover, the very existence of the A-level route post-16 effectively ensures that an even greater proportion of the age-group embarks upon vocational courses which are still perceived as having a lower currency value (p.179).

With the transition from an elite to a mass system of higher education, especially in the light of current policies stressing social inclusion and widening participation in post-school education, there is now even less justification for the maintenance of a system whose whole *raison d'etre* is the identification of an elite group of students suitable for entry to university studies. Moreover, the growth of access and non-traditional, second-chance routes to HE has demonstrated that mature students do as well as and, in many cases, better than traditional candidates (Davies & Parry, 1993; Richardson, 1994; Hartley, Trueman & Lapping, 1997).

Gleeson (1996) has called for a 'new educational settlement' underpinned by principles of democracy and social justice and argues that a prerequiste for such a settlement is the establishment of a 'unified national qualification system, challenging traditional notions of equivalence and parity of esteem' (p.15). In addition to such moral justifications for the abolition of A-levels there are important pragmatic and pedagogic considerations which relate to the ideas of studentship and deep learning referred to in the last chapter and also to emerging conceptions of the sort of knowledge and skills required for life and work in the 21st century.

In line with a whole host of policy recommendations over the last decade, it is now time to replace the narrow specialisation of A-levels by, what Young & Leney (1997) call an 'advanced level curriculum'. Such an advanced level would be characterised by a balance between specialist studies, both discipline- or subject-based, and applied and core studies which would help lead students from 'their particular interests and specialization to the wider concerns expressed in the curriculum as a whole' (ibid., p.53). Such principles are at the heart of studentship and learning progression and, as such, should be applied, not just to advanced level study, but to the post-school curriculum in general.

2. References were made in earlier chapters to the differences identified by Skilbeck et al. (1994) between the 'schooling' and 'working life' models of vocational preparation. Alongside these Green (1997a) outlines two major strategies for ensuring that vocational studies are underpinned by the general educational foundation necessary for adult and working life. The 'general technical and vocational education' paradigm, which characterises VET in France, Germany, Japan and Sweden, is 'based on the precept that vocational learning rests on a common foundation of general education, or *culture generale* as it is termed in France' (p.92). Linked to ideas of citizenship and a minimum cultural entitlement, this approach assumes that all forms of vocational study require a general education grounding to develop the knowledge and skills required for working life. The 'core skills paradigm', operating in the United States and the UK, assumes no general educational or cultural entitlement, nor any universal minimum based on citizenship rights but, instead, bases VET on utitiltarian considerations about what is suitable, relevant and useful for vocational studies. Reflecting on the sort of developments in British VET referred to in earlier chapters, Green observes that:

> With the decline of time-served apprenticeship, and the advent of competence-based learning, this already 'lean' notion of skill has become more minimalist, both culture- and theory-free. Competence-based learning, derived from behaviourist principles, defines skill as the ability to perform pre-given tasks

with predictable accuracy...General education is only necessary to the extent that it underpins competent performance in expected work tasks (ibid., p.93).

The shortcomings of NVQs and the extent to which CBET has led to impoverished conceptions of vocational studies was described earlier. NCVQ developments have, not only served to de-skill VET in Britain but, with the introduction of GNVQs and the resultant triple-track divisions (Halsall & Cockett, 1996), have effectively prevented the fostering of parity of esteem between academic and vocational studies. If we add to this the dubious and nebulous status of core/key skills illustrated in earlier sections, there seems to be more than enough justification for Green's (1997a) conclusion that:

> the core skills paradigm represents an impoverished form of general education, which is neither adequately delivering the minimum basic skills normally associated with an effective general education, such as verbal articulacy, logical skills or mathematical literacy, nor even attempting to impart a foundation of scientific and humanistic culture adequate to the demands of active citizenship in modern societies....However, the critique must go wider than this, since core skills fall short on another count central to the reform of post-16 education, which is that they fail to provide the basis for a workable unified curriculum (p.100).

3. Only a unified curriculum can achieve the objectives of lifelong learning by helping to create a 'framework of opportunities for people to learn and to lift barriers that prevent them from taking up those opportunities' (DfEE, 1998a, p.13). A learning culture requires curricula and qualifications which acknowledge the value of *all* learning achievements and, perhaps most important of all, which allows and positively encourages the progression and continuity of learning required for raising standards and participation at all levels of post-school education and training.

As Cockett (1996) observes, progression 'can be seen both in terms of qualifications for all abilities and in terms of increasing command of the processes of learning' (p.141). In terms of the former, a unified curriculum is required to ensure that the barriers to learning based on a stratified and hierarchical division of knowledge and skills are removed so as to achieve the key objective of harmonising 'systems for measuring participation and achievement in post-16 learning' (DfEE, 1998f, p.17). In terms of the latter criterion of progression linked to learning processes, the concepts of learning careers and studentship, supported by the some form of 'entitlement to information, advice and guidance' of the sort recommended in the Kennedy report (1997, p.89), will need to be embedded in post-school learning programmes along with the other curriculum and qualification reforms (including new models of guidance and counselling discussed at greater length in Chapter 7).

The criteria for progression and continuity which need to be satisfied to achieve the learning culture which underpins current VET policy proposals are neatly summarised by Young & Spours (1998) when they identify the 'underlying principles of a 14-19 system of the future' as 'flexible in how it encourages participation, attainment and breadth of study' and 'connective between all learners and types of learning' (p.92). Reforming the post-school system along these lines is bound to be gradualist and piecemeal, though the supporters of a unified curriculum are probably right in suggesting that the foundations for reform are already in place. The contribution of New Deal and related lifelong learning initiatives to this reform process will be examined in Chapters 5 and 6 but, as a preliminary, one element of the discourse on vocational studies needs to be looked at in more detail, namely, the role and contribution of employers to the national VET system.

4 Employers and Vocational Education and Training

The idea of constructing VET programmes around the 'needs of employers' or 'what industry wants' has been so attractive to people on all sides of education and industry over the last two decades that no part of the education system has been able to withstand the relentlessness of such vocationalising influences. As was noted in Chapter 1, higher education, through pressures from government and employers codified in the Dearing prescriptions, is currently grappling with the problems arising from this onslaught. Attacks on the 'ivory tower' and unworldly status are not new and can be traced back to the foundation of Oxford and Cambridge in the 11th and 12th centuries (Cobban, 1988), but in recent times, under the banner of the globalisation and economic competitiveness rhetoric of current lifelong learning policy (Barnett, 1998), some quite extreme forms of HE vocationalism have been proposed.

A particularly vivid example is provided in the report produced for the government by Mary Lord, the director of education and training for the TEC national council, which outlines the employers' 'vision' for university education (Baty, 1997b). According to this 'vision', HE needs a 'national qualification system' which would include a 'common core of employability skills and generic competences'. Moreover, undergraduates and their lecturers should be subject to compulsory work experience, according to the TEC director, and 'work-related learning should be built into every undergraduate curriculum' so that 'when one qualifies for a degree it will show that one has the NVQ competences as well as the subject knowledge' (p.10).

It would be difficult to find a more extreme case of anti-educational (and, indeed, anti-intellectual) bigotry than this! Indeed, it is probably the best example of its kind since Arnold Weinstock (then head of GEC) charged the educational establishment of 'anti-industry bias' and a preference for 'the life of the mind over the practical life' (Weinstock,

1976, p.2) in a *Times Educational Supplement* piece in 1976. There is so much wrong with this sort of attack, apart from its irrationality, dogmatism and outright prejudice, in terms of its misunderstanding and mutation of education and training processes, that it is difficult to know where to begin in framing a response. In the first place, the TEC director's case rests on very unsteady foundations in the sense that the preferred strategy for a 'work-related' HE curriculum involves the use of 'key skills' and 'NVQ competences' both of which (as suggested in Chapter 3) or either illusory or highly suspect. Moreover, apart from the false dichotomy between the worlds of education and work (with only the latter qualifying as 'real'), Ms Lord's arguments betray an attachment to an idea of the university curriculum which probably has not existed since Cardinal Newman published his classic *Idea of a University* in 1853. Some acquaintance with developments in the HE curriculum since the 1960s, particularly with reference to the reconstruction of Newman's original conception of liberal education (Bailey, 1984; Barnett, 1990, 1994), would be sufficient to reveal a rather different picture from the anachronistic one displayed in the TEC director's critique.

Notwithstanding the vocational developments since the establishment of TVEI in the 1970s bringing schools and industry together (Bell, 1981) and, in recent years, various schemes involving collaboration between industry and higher education (Philippson, 1983), there is still a persistent and sometimes wilful misunderstanding of the nature and function of university education on the part of some sections of industry. Except for certain circumscribed areas of specialist technical or professional studies, general HE cannot simply be a servant of industry or a supplier of manpower needs as the rather extreme correspondence theories of Bowles and Gintis (1976) would have it (nor, as will be noted later, does research within human capital theory provide much evidence of a direct link between investment and *social*, as opposed to *individual*, economic benefits). Furthermore, the demands made upon knowledge and creativity by post-Fordist organisations could never be met by a mechanistic linkage between university and industry but, instead, require the fostering of those critical faculties in students which are implicit in reconstructed versions of liberal education at this level (Wyatt, 1990; Lawson, 1998).

Thus, as Bailey (1984) demonstrates, it is 'precisely the general and fundamental utility that provides part of the justification of a liberal general education' and this consists in 'its capacity to liberate a person from the restrictions of the present and the particular' (pp.28-9). Similarly, Barnett's (1994) dismissal of both 'academic competence' (the old discipline-based concept of liberal education) and 'operational competence' (the narrowly-focussed NCVQ interpretation) concludes with a vision of students as 'critical thinkers' who are capable of 'systematic reflection', 'genuinely open dialogue' and a 'continuous re-appraisal' (pp.184-5) of their own learning. Vocationalism, on the other hand, is an 'ideology representing the interests of corporatism, of economy and of profit' which means that the:

> spirit of vocationalism stands for temporariness, and a shallowness of commitment. Permanent allegiance to a set of values, or even to an organization, is too costly. What is required is adaptability, a willingness to embrace new values...(ibid., p.68).

Such creativity and adaptabily cannot be fostered by trying to develop something called 'generic competence' or by providing yet more work experience for students.

Perhaps the most serious shortcoming of Ms Lord's perspective on education and industry, however, is the simplistic assumption that it is possible to determine what employers want or what industry needs and then ensure that educational institutions supply these needs. Research and development in VET over the last twenty years has demonstrated that such superficially simple questions are in fact deeply problematic and entangled in a 'complex technicism' (Rikowski, 1998a).

Employers and the Needs of Industry

Employers have been complaining about our education and training system (and also failing to provide investment or positive contributions to it) since at least the time of the Paris exhibition in 1867 when, even then, we seemed to be falling behind our industrial competitors (Musgrave, 1966). Following a Royal Commission, the *Technical Instruction Act* designed to improve the situation was passed in 1889, though in 1901 a committee led by Lord Haldane still felt the need to remind politicians that the country had 'to train the minds of our people so they may be able to hold their own against the competition which is coming forward at such an alarming rate' (ibid., p.145). Rikowski (1998a) has illustrated, through examination of the journals of the *Industrial Society* and the *Institute of Personnel Management*, employer dissatisfaction with school leavers dating from the First World War and throughout the inter-war years, and Schofield (1923) and Wilkinson (1931) have made similar observations. The criticisms persisted after the end of the Second World War (especially in relation to the standard of technical education in the newly established FE sector, Dawn, 1995) and, notwithstanding the monumental changes to schooling in the wake of the 1944 Act and the drive for modernisation and industrial relevance through the technical schools movement (Wardle, 1976), were still present in the report of the Carr Committe, *Training for Skill* published in 1958, which recommended the improvement of training to 'enable us to maintain our place as one of the great manufacturing and trading nations of the world' (Musgrave, 1966, p.146).

Foreign competition in conjunction with the alleged decline in educational standards can thus be seen as a perennial problem yet, in spite of over a century of similar warnings about the lack of attention and investment in VET (not to mention two world wars and the more recent rapid globalisation of industrial and commercial activity), British industry has continued to lag behind that of Europe in stimulating and investing in vocational and technical education and training (Evans, 1992; OECD, 1998). It is important to note these problematic links between employers, industry and VET in Britain in order to make sense of developments in this sphere since the oil crisis and recession of the early 1970s led to the collapse of the traditional youth labour market.   Since then, vocational developments have been informed and framed by employers' complaints that schools and colleges were not meeting the needs of industry and that young people did not have the qualities that employers required. In particular, employers have been highly critical of school-leavers' technical skills, their basic literacy and numeracy, their work attitudes, social skills and general appearance (Clarke & Willis, 1984).   Reid (1980) and Roderick & Stephens (1982) provided similar reports of employers' complaints but with a greater emphasis on personal qualities and work attitudes.

Employers' complaints persisted through the development of TVEI and YTS schemes in the 1980s and, broadly speaking, maintained their general character, being partly concerned with an alleged lack of basic skills and partly bemoaning the poor work attitudes of young people in areas such as loyalty, punctuality and discipline (Brown, 1987; Wellington, 1987). In spite of the radical educational reforms resulting in the establishment of a National Curriculum following the 1988 Education Reform Act, the TVEI experiment, the spread of NVQs and the introduction of GNVQs in the 1990s, the same criticisms by employers can be seen, for instance, in the 1996 Industry in Education publication *Towards Employability*. In particular, employers were widely critical of the 'everyday life literacy and numeracy' skills of young people, in addition to their lack of qualities such as 'reliability, self-discipline, confidence' and 'work ethic' in general (IIE, 1996, p.4).

There is, thus, a timeless quality to employer complaints about the education system; the Industry in Education 'wish list' of employer requirements would not have been out of place in 1946 or, indeed, in the 19th century when the famous technical education committees were convened to deal with the emerging problems of technical education and foreign competition. As well as this timeless character, it is also worth noting the international and global nature of such employer criticism. Oxenham (1984) provides evidence from India, Zambia, Tanzania, Kenya and Sri Lanka that employers perceived educational standards to be falling, and more recent studies have produced similar findings concerning school leavers in Canada (Leroux & Lafleur, 1995), Australia (Forster, 1996) and the United States (Rosenbaum & Binder, 1997). The more recent pan-European studies of industrial needs and employer requirements (Skilbeck et al., 1994; Merson, 1996; OECD, 1998) tend to stress the need for 'flexibility' and 'multi-skilled' workers to cope with the demands of post-Fordist economies.

All of this research on employers' requirements needs to be located against the background of policy studies of VET trends and developments over the last few decades. As noted in previous chapters, taken at face value there is something grossly disingenuous about the attempt to trace causal links between the skills and qualities of school leavers and the requirements of industry. What needs to be stressed at the outset is the overtly political nature of the discourse which displaces responsibility for the 1970s recession and collapse of the employment market away from politicians and industrialists and towards teachers, schools and young people. Stronach's cogent analysis of the 1980s initiatives involving the new vocationalism illustrates clearly how the causes of economic recession and the country's poor performance against its competitors were deflected away from the lack of investment, massive reductions in manufacturing bases and declining resources and towards the 'individual attributes that young people lack' (1990, p.157). The discourse of the new vocationalism was based on a tissue of misinformation which attempted to 'juvenalise and personalise the problem...understate more parsimonious causes...equate simplistically education and economic success and deflect attention from youth unemployment' (ibid., p.173).

Such developments were characterised by Stronach in terms of the new 'vocationalist ritual' (ibid., pp.181ff) and effectively shown to be irrational and counter-productive. Thus, as the 'political crisis of youth unemployment was transformed into an educational crisis' (Finn, 1990, p.47, original italics), the mistaken assumptions and radically unstable foundations of the debate effectively prevented the emergence of genuine solutions to either the economic roots of unemployment and recession or to the reconstruction of vocational studies in the interests of students, empoyers and other stakeholders. The irrationality of all this 'had the effect of distorting public policy debate about the relationship between economic change, education and employment' (Esland, 1990, p.v). As Ainley (1988) observed in his evaluation of the 1980s YTS experiments, the new vocationalism was:

> based on the false premise of the problem of transition from school to work...The problem is not one of transition but of work itself. Vocationalism has no solution for this crisis. Training, even if it were all training in real skills, cannot of itself produce jobs, as the failure of human capital theory in the developed and underdeveloped world clearly shows (pp.116-17).

Ainley's reference to the 'failure of human capital theory' serves to highlight another problematic aspect of determining the needs of employment and industry which is concerned with the difficulty of establishing positive, evidence-based links between economic productivity or industrial success and investment in education and training.

Human Capital, Investment and VET

Although, as will be noted in later discussions of the values dimension of vocational studies, there are serious moral objections to the reduction of people to human capital (and especially to VET processes through which trainees may actually be said to *become* capital, see Rikowski, 1998a,b), it is necessary to accept the descriptive term (denotation rather than connotation) in order to examine the impact of 'human capital theory'. Woodhall (1990) suggests that the:

> concept of human capital refers to the fact that human beings invest in themselves, by means of education, training, or other activities, which raises their future income by increasing their lifetime earnings (p.27).

What needs to added to this, of course, is that such investment is not always, or even typically, at the level of individual choice but often investment by the state (through compulsory schooling and subsidy of post-school programmes), by industry (through formal human resource development and management [HRD/HRM] programmes [Truelove, 1991], education-business links, or special non-formal provisions such as the much-emulated Ford Employee Development and Assistance Programme, EDAP, 1992) and, increasingly common these days, by parents on behalf of their children.

The pioneering political economist, Adam Smith, is probably the first person to identify a relationship between education and the productive capacity of workers, though human capital theory (HCT) was not established as a distinct discipline or field of knowledge until the 1960s when the American academics Schulz (1961) and Becker (1964) published early studies. Notwithstanding the fact that HCT has dominated the economics of education since then (not to mention its ever increasing use in HRD/M, vocational studies and policy documents on education and training in general) its central claim about the efficacy and benefits of investment in human capital 'remains a controversial issue' (Woodhall, 1990, p.28) as will be noted later in the discussion of employers' use of educational qualifications as a 'screening' or 'filtering' device.

One of the most persistent critics of the claims of HCT has been Dore (1976) whose book *The Diploma Disease* represented one of the first attempts to subject the main arguments to critical academic scrutiny. Dore's main critique is not directed at schooling and education *per se* but at 'schooling which is only qualification, a mere process of certificating or credentialling'. The distinction between processes which aim only at certificating and those which result in education is explicated in terms of education as a 'process of learning...which has mastery as its object' with a view to 'knowledge for its own sake...or for self respect...for profitable use...or for some conception of a professional calling'. In the process of qualification, by contrast, the student is:

> concerned not with mastery, but with being certified as having mastered. The knowledge that he [sic] gains, he gains not for its own sake and not for constant later use in a real life situation, but for the once-and-for-all purpose of reproducing it in an examination...If education is learning to do a job, qualification is a matter of learning in order to get a job (ibid., p.8).

Dore's real objective, achieved through a painstaking comparative analysis of educational developments in England, Japan, Sri Lanka, Kenya, Cuba, and Tanzania, is to illustrate the human, financial and educational waste of resources generated through 'qualification inflation'. The *'maladie du diplome'* which flows from this involves the exponential expansion of activities aimed solely at feeding the demands for ever more certificates with, most significant and dangerous of all, an ever diminishing relationship between certificates awarded and the needs of individuals, industry or society.

In order to make sense of the debate on investment in education and training, commentators have made use of the crucial distinction between *social* (the gains accruing to employers or society in general) and *private* (how much individuals benefit through better jobs or higher salaries) rates of return. In reviewing all the international evidence drawn from studies in the 1960s and 1970s, Psacharopoulos, 1981, p.326) was able to identify four basic underlying assumptions:

1. the returns on investment to primary education (whether social or private) are the highest among all educational levels;
2. private returns are in excess of social returns, especially at the university level;
3. all rates of return to investment in education are well above the 10% common yardstick of the opportunity cost of capital;
4. the returns to education in less developed countries are higher relative to the corresponding returns in more advanced countries.

The argument of point 1) about the highest returns on investment being linked with basic primary education (particularly in the developing countries surveyed by Dore) is important since it raises questions about the precise purpose and value of post-school education and training. In terms of the relationship between economic ouput and productivity and educational investment, the evidence on social rates of return is equivocal and problematic. Although what Anderson called the '40% literacy threshold' (1965, p.361), the thesis that a 40% school enrolment appears to be a precondition of economic take-off and growth, seems to hold good for most historical and contemporary examples of development, the evidence is less good for educational investment at the secondary and tertiary stages.

The weak evidence on social rates of return runs counter to the general tendency prevalent in this country since the time of the Great Debate and the new vocationalism in the 1970s to correlate investment in VET and economic/industrial performance in a direct and often overtly causal way. As Whiteside (1992) notes, this sort of interpretation was encouraged by analyses of the British economy and society such as Barnett's *Audit of War* (1986) and Wiener's *English Culture and the Decline of the Industrial Spirit* (1981) which 'contributed to the development of a set of beliefs among politicians and industrialists that one of the central causes of Britain's prolonged economic decline lay in its education and training system' (p.4).

As Dore (1976) has argued, it 'would be hard to make out a case for believing that the economic growth of Britain was a consequence of improved or expanded education' (p.14). Although Britain was the first industrial country, Green (1990) observes that it 'was not the pioneer of educational change, whereas many of the less industrialized nations in Europe reacted much more speedily to bring education in line with the needs of developing economies' (p.309). Similarly, McMaster (1991) has argued that the 'economic miracle' in Japan actually preceded the establishment of its distinctive educational system rather than the other way around, and Wadd (1988) finds little connection between educational activity and periods of economic boom and recession. It is at least plausible, he suggests, that 'instead of higher standards [of education] securing prosperity, it is the rich countries that can afford the higher standards' (p.28). Dore makes a similar case through the vivid and forceful notion that 'rich men have Cadillacs; therefore we should get some Cadillacs in order to be rich' (1976, p.88). All this serves to confirm the claim that educational expansion, as Foster (1977) surmised, is merely the 'cart not the horse of economic growth' (p.364).

Of course there must be *some* connection between educational investment and industrial and economic development, it is just that, beyond the basic levels of the compulsory stages, the relationships between higher level investment and any form of social output or pay-off are complex and problematic. The evidence for private rates of return, the benefits to individuals of investing in education, seems far easier to obtain. In both developing and developed nations there appear to be clear positive correlations between levels of educational qualification and salary levels and status (Dore, 1976; Woodhall, 1990; OECD, 1998). However, the point noted earlier in examining the basic HCT assumptions adduced by Psacharopoulos that private returns far exceed social ones for university level qualifications is worth emphasising. Just recently there have been a number of studies reporting data which purport to show how a 'degree boosts earning power' (Patel, 1998, p.4). The Institute for Fiscal Studies (IFS, 1998), for instance, used samples from the National Child Development Survey which is following individuals born in March 1958 to show that male graduates in their thirties earned 15-20% more than their counterparts who did A-levels without going on to HE. The equivalent figure for female graduates was an average gain of 35% in earnings over non-graduates. Similar comparisons using OECD statistics have been used to demonstrate that:

> on average, men aged 30-44 who left school at 16 earn less than half the salary of their graduate counterparts...A UK woman graduate earns nearly three times as much as someone who has had only a basic education (Budge, 1998, p.23).

The sting in the tail of the recent use of such statistics (which really simply confirm what has been noted for decades about private rates of return for graduates) is that the data are being used for the overtly political purpose of justifying the aboliton of maintenance grants and the introduction of tuition fees for UK university students. If the 'payoff for today's graduates is comparable to the payoff for graduates of the early 1980s studies, it may be feasible to expect graduates to pay more of their own higher education costs' (Patel, 1998, p.4). Similar sentiments are expressed in the IFS survey in which the authors comment that:

> In areas such as tertiary education for young people, where investments are primarily public but large private gains accrue, it is legitimate to ask whether cost-sharing should be adjusted...In doing so, however, due account should be taken of existing private costs such as forgone earnings and public benefits (spin-off social gains) that are not always fully reported (Budge, 1998, p.23).

The caveat about 'public benefits' and 'spin-off social gains' is clearly to be welcomed, though the reason why these are 'not always fully reported' is that, consisting as they do in areas such as public health improvements and savings, lower crime statistics, political and community cohesion and active citizenship, they are exceedingly difficult to quantify in either financial or general utility terms. These difficulties of quantifying the social benefits of education serve to highlight another problematic feature of concentrating on private returns and that is that the higher earnings associated with higher individual investment may not in fact have anything to do with the enhancement of knowledge and skills. Critical commentators in this sphere point to the 'screening' or 'filtering' hypothesis, concisely summarised by Woodhall (1990) in the notion that:

> education does not improve productivity by imparting necessary knowledge and skills, but simply acts as a screening device which enables employers to identify individuals who possess either superior innate ability or personal characteristics, such as attitudes towards authority, punctuality, or motivation, which employers value and which are therefore rewarded by means of higher earnings (p.32).

The screening function of education is now accepted as a basic premise in the economics of education (Blaug, 1976; Dore, 1997), and it has served to focus attention within HCT on the precise ways in which the education and training system, employers' requirements and economic productivity are linked together. Where the value of such a filtering mechanism becomes dubious is when, as in Dore's account of the diploma disease, educational aims are subservient to gaining qualifications or mere certification. An extreme example of the folly of using qualifications in this way is the wastage involved in Japanese university education in which students, having gained access through the fiercely competitive schooling system to one of the top state institutions, are 'not expected to do very much at university except recover from the rigours of school and prepare for the rigours of corporate life' (Sullivan, 1990, p.27). In recent years, as the bubble of the post-war economic miracle has been pierced by recession and unemployment, calls are now being made for higher education reform, ironically by the very corporations who supported the business-university compacts which fuelled the educationally wasteful screening system for so many years. Japanese business leaders are now complaining about the country's 'outdated style of education which does not prepare students for

work in an increasingly competitive, globalised and computerised world';
apparently, Japan now needs 'more creative, individualistic and
imaginative employees' (Fitzpatrick, 1998, p.27).

In a recent re-appraisal of the diploma disease twenty years on, Dore
(1997), though noting that a number of countries, notably Cuba, Sri Lanka,
Tanzania and, in recent years, China and Japan are slowing down the
inflation and 'qualification spiral', argues that there is plenty evidence that
'the fastest example of the inflation process in recent years, of course, is
that in Britain' (p.190). This escalation of credentialling or certification
within the British system with, in particular, the expansion of university
education and the retention of more post-16 students was:

> not so much in response to popular clamour as partly to reduce the
> unemployment figures...and partly from the genuine 'human capital' belief that
> Britain's 'competitiveness' would be improved if we kept as large a proportion
> of 18-21 year olds in full-time education as the USA and Japan (ibid.).

Although Dore is sympathetic to the general and perhaps more intangible
cultural and civilising influences of expanding education as a 'route to a
decent society' (ibid., p.201), we are reminded that there is still very little
research evidence which demonstrates 'the links between learning
motivations and work motivations' (ibid., p.204).

The sceptical challenge to even the more established doctrines based on
the putatively solid ground of private rates of return is taken a stage
further by Murphy's (1993) devastating critique of arguments for the
recent expansion of HE numbers in Britain. Through a painstaking
analysis of international and national data on the alleged links between
economic productivity and the supply of graduates, Murphy raises serious
doubts about explaining the relative economic positions of countries such
as Britain, West Germany, the USA and Japan in terms of graduate
numbers. There is little correlation between economic/industrial league
tables of success and HE outputs and even less of a link between 'degrees
read and jobs done' (p.19). Moreoever, since 'graduate unemployment'
tends to 'wax and wane as the economy booms and slumps' (ibid.), this
provides little support for the argument that economic prosperity is
dependent upon the expansion of HE. Murphy concludes that, not only
are the alleged links between education and jobs 'arbitrary', but also there
is little evidence to support claims about the 'internal returns of higher
education' resting on 'value-added views' (ibid., pp.22-3) about the role of

HE in fostering desirable traits of the kind needed for employment and technological advance. He argues that:

> there is no indication at all that higher education can, as the value-added view so confidently assumes, massage and manipulate labour into the form now seemingly required by industry. Certainly to judge from the past, shaping attitudes is not a task which education appears all that well equipped to effect. For those who care to look, both educational history and educational research is well littered with the debris of schemes and dreams which, like the valued-added-view, looked to education to equip youngsters with the aptitudes and attitudes deemed by reformers to be desirable or useful (p.26).

There has never been a less opportune time to rely on such superficially attractive but fundamentally imprecise and unsupported assertions as 'learning pays' (Ball, 1991) or that learning is 'the key to successful economic development' (DfEE, 1995, p.1). The upshot of all the HCT critiques is that, particularly in times of tight money or recession, it is simply financial madness to recommend an undiscriminating and largely unfocused expansion of education and training. Not only does this lead to a pointless inflation of qualifications (with the consequent diminishing returns on investment) of the sort which has characterised British educational trends over the last few decades (Avis et al., 1996; Wolf, 1997a), but also results in a mistaken emphasis on certification rather than what Dore (1976, 1997) describes as 'genuine' education. What Dore (surely uncontroversially and unexceptionably) means by 'genuine' education and training is that form of activity which is either instrinsically justified in terms of individual and/or socio-cultural development or extrinsically connected with specific occupational/professional requirements. The undiscriminating expansion of post-school education and training *per se*, runs the risk of satisfying neither of these requirements, just as the unsystematic scramble for upgrading workforce skills, described as the 'skills mirage' (EPI, 1995) by some critical commentators, has had virtually no impact on the UK economic growth or employment rates.

On the other hand, it would be difficult and imprudent to gainsay programmes which seek to target precisely identified 'skills shortages' or 'skills gaps' (DfEE, 1998b,e), and we must acknowledge the extent to which many businesses, both small firms and large corporations, continue to invest profits in education schemes for their own workers (ED, 1994;

Hillman, 1997).   Perhaps the answer, then, lies in task-specific targeting and in the precise determination of what industrial and employment requirements are indicated at particular stages of economic development so that VET comes to have 'clear links to the labour market' (Unwin, 1997, p.72).

What Employers Want

It is worth noting at the outset the existence of a number of fairly uncontroversial case studies of employers investing in general education programmes for their employees.   The Ford EDAP scheme (EDAP, 1992) established initially in 1987 with a budget of £1.8 million has become a model for non-job-related (or non-occupationally-specific) educational development programmes involving vouchers awarded to workers to buy educational courses (originally £40 per employee, now worth around £200).   Its original objectives, agreed after consultation between trades unions, staff and management, were to:

> offer employees a wide range of personal and career development education
> and training, retraining and development activities and to make available a
> variety of employee assistance services to encourage healthier lifestyles (p.2).

Not only has EDAP been described by one union offical as the 'finest industrial relations exercise that Ford has ever undertaken' (Prestage, 1992, p.11),   the scheme has grown from strength to strength over the past decade, receiving the official endorsement of the National Institute of Adult Continuing Education (NIACE, 1998). It is true that the scheme's continued maintenance and support is no doubt partly due to its influence in reducing absenteeism and improving relations between management and unions and also between hourly paid and salaried staff.   However, alongside such obvious pragmatic and utilitarian benefits, the high take-up of courses on offer (40-45% of staff) and the predominance of *general* educational courses taken (over 65% if health and leisure courses are included, EDAP, 1992, p.4), reflect features that are fully in keeping with current lifelong learning objectives.

   No doubt a combination of utilitarian, HRD and general learning promotion objectives has led to the widesdpread use of EDAP as a model for other employer-sponsored schemes such as those developed by Rover,

Unipart, Scottish Power and Abbey National given prominence in Ufl documents (Hillman, 1997, p.15). The central idea of firms and corporations as 'learning organisations' which 'explicitly recognise work as a constant learning opportunity and improve the way it is organised and managed' (ibid., p.14) is used extensively in Ufl materials, particularly in relation to the SME sector which is vastly under-represented in terms of national training efforts. As a brokering service, the Ufl will be designed to respond to this challenge by 'making high quality education and training accessible to owner-managers and employees, in the time and place they need them' (DfEE, 1998c, p.18). Such short-course, on-site or off-the-job training, described aptly as 'just-in-time learning in the right place and in an appropriate, affordable style' (Lucas, 1998, p.36), is going to be a principal feature of Ufl provision and provides a vivid and paradigm illustration of a direct input/output pay-off for investment in VET. However, the fact that many of the current lifelong learning initiatives such as the Ufl are targeted specifically at SMEs serves to illustrate the special problems of persuading firms in this vital area of economic activity of the benefits of becoming learning organisations and investing in education and training.

The Problems of SMEs

The vital strategic importance of SMEs was noted in the last chapter in the context of the failure of a VET system dominated by NVQs to either cater for the requirements of small firms or attract them to invest in training. The White Papers on Competitiveness issued by the former Conservative government (DTI, 1994, 1995) had stressed the centrality of SMEs to the task of increasing national productivity and revitalizing the British economy. The 1995 revised NTETs included ambitious lifetime learning targets for this sector such as, for instance, that by the year 2000, '70% of all organisations employing 200 or more employees, and 35% of those employing 50 or more, to be recognised as Investors in People' (NACETT, 1995, p.15). The modest figure for small firms reflects the failure of government policy to interest SMEs in the flagship IiP scheme (Storey, 1994; EPI, 1995; DfEE, 1998b) and, more significantly, to persuade owner-managers of the value of employee training. Of SMEs employing under 50 people, over 6 million enterprises, just 12% operate employee development schemes or supported non-work-related training (BCC, 1998).

As will be noted in later chapters, many of Labour's lifelong learning schemes, including the Ufl and WTW projects, are specifically targeted at SME owner-managers (Corney, 1997). There is now open acknowledgement that the:

> failure of successive governments to convince small employers of the need to ensure continuing education and training for their workforce has been the biggest obstacle to efforts to keep Britain internationally competitive (Nash, 1997a, p.29).

In spite of all the efforts of the last few decades, notes Hillman (1997) in the Ufl policy document, it remains the case that 'in general, small firms are much less likely to either provide training or to have a training plan' (p.10). This is particularly worrying in view of the importance of the SME sector to the government's WTW and Ufl initiatives (Hyland & Matlay, 1998).

The picture in relation to the attitudes to training of SME owner-managers and the actual provision of training is far more complex than the official government statistics suggest. The Warwick research in this area (introduced in the context of the discussion of NVQs in the last chapter) which surveyed over 2000 SMEs concentrated on the pivotal role played by owner-managers (see Fig. 4.1) in the light of recent research data emphasising the crucial importance of this role in the day-to day running of small firms (Goss, 1991; Storey, 1994), in addition to European research which links company performance directly with owner-managers' capabilities (OECD, 1996).

Band code	Number of employees	All firms $n = 1986$	Who makes training decisions?			
			Owner/ manager	Personnel manager	Key personnel	Other employees
A	1–5	1242	1242	0	0	0
B	6–10	314	314	0	0	0
C	11–19	252	239	13	0	0
D	20–49	134	112	22	0	0
E	50–99	44	36	1	7	0

Fig. 4.1: SMEs and the Locus of Training Decisions
Source: Hyland, 1998d, p.274.

In addition to the failure of government policies, including NVQs, Training Credits, and more general 'back to work' schemes, to stimulate the interest of SMEs, we noted in particular a 'paradox of training' (Matlay & Hyland, 1997; Hyland, 1998d) in the form of a persistent inverse correlation between (mainly positive) attitudes to training and the actual (largely insignificant) take-up and involvement of such firms in training (see Figs. 4.2, 4.3).

Economic sectors	Very negative (%)	Negative (%)	Indifferent (%)	Positive (%)	Very positive (%)
Manufacturing	1.36	1.27	2.53	92.70	2.14
Services	1.37	2.74	2.99	91.15	1.75
Construction	1.91	1.91	3.81	89.52	2.85
Agriculture	0.00	0.00	3.22	87.10	9.68
Forestry/fisheries	0.00	0.00	4.76	85.72	9.52

Fig. 4.2: SME Owner-Managers' Attitudes to Training
Source: Hyland, 1998d, p.374.

Economic sectors	No training provided (%)	Up to 1 day training (%)	2–3 days training (%)	4–5 days training (%)	6–10 days training (%)	Over 11 days training (%)
Manufacturing	86.37	6.72	1.75	1.56	0.29	3.31
Services	85.16	5.11	2.87	3.37	0.87	2.62
Construction	91.43	4.76	0.00	0.00	0.00	3.81
Agriculture	90.32	9.68	0.00	0.00	0.00	0.00
Forestry/fisheries	66.67	14.29	19.04	0.00	0.00	0.00

Fig. 4.3: SME Provision of Training in the Previous 12 Months
Source: Hyland, 1998d, p.375.

The paradoxical nature of training provision in the SME sector is graphically illustrated if we look at the manufacturing sector in which 92.7% of respondents held a positive attitude to training whereas 86.73% had failed to provide any training at all for employees in the previous twelve months. Similarly, in the important service sector, although 91.15% of owner-managers claimed to have positive attitudes to training, 81.16% had provided no training in the preceding twelve months.

On the basis of such findings a number of recommendations are offered:

1) A System of Incentives to Encourage SMEs to Participate in VET Schemes and the National Training Effort

The Warwick research demonstrated clearly that the cost of training was a key determinant of its take-up by SMEs. Since the cost of the current work-based VET system dominated by NVQ outcomes is already much higher than college-based routes (TES, 1996; Hyland & Matlay, 1997), strategies to address such anomalies need to be implemented urgently. Employers, particularly those in the SME sector, cannot be expected to pay for the design faults of an NVQ system, often far from their specific business interests, which are not of their own making and bear no relation to their particular skill requirements (IES, 1995; Hodkinson, Sparkes & Hodkinson, 1996; BCC, 1998; DfEE, 1998e). Funding should be highly targeted and, in the light of the failure of the training market and training credits in this respect (Evans, 1992; Hodkinson & Sparkes, 1995), should make use of strategies such as those recommended by Booth & Snower

(1996) involving the linking of training subsidies with the whole spectrum of state benefits. Moreover, SME owner-managers are clearly less interested in whether their workers have NVQ 'qualifications' to satisfy national training targets than in ensuring that the skills of their employees are sufficient to secure and maintain a competitive advantage in terms of their firm's position in the market (Matlay & Hyland, 1997; DfEE, 1998e). For this reason, it is important, both for SMEs and for employers in general referred to in the next section, to distinguish between skills shortages, training needs and national policies concerned with NVQs and other vocational qualifications.

2) A System of High Quality Education and Training Which Can Raise the General Status of Vocational Studies and Qualifications

Although this cannot but seem like a 'motherhood and apple pie' recommendation which no one would want to gainsay, it is important to stress both the damage done to VET over the last decade or so by the NCVQ and related experiments and the need for urgent remedies based on a fundamentally different agenda (Gokulsing, Ainley & Tysome, 1996; Hyland & Matlay, 1998). One of the key findings of our SME survey was the importance of the past experiences and current perceptions of VET on the part of owner-managers. Negative expereiences of training and perceptions of low quality schemes reported in a large number of surveys (IES, 1995; Marks, 1996; DfEE, 1997; DfEE, 1998e) are bound to discourage owner-managers from viewing employee training as a sound investment. The crucial importance of such 'incubator' experiences (Hyland & Matlay, 1997) of training amongst SME owner-managers, on both a personal level and in terms of the general health of our national VET system, must, therefeore, assume a central place in general policy in this sphere. With this in mind, it is to be hoped that the current QCA exercise involving the review and revision of NVQ criteria and related matters will be enough to remedy the many serious problems of the system. However, as I recommend in the concluding chapter, the best long-term solution is to replace NVQs, GNVQs and academic certificates with a general diploma based on a unified learning and assessment system.

In conjunction with the general criteria and recommendations outlined at the end of this chapter, these specific SME requirements will provide a useful methodological device for interrogating the emerging New Deal,

Ufl and related policies and schemes subsumed under the lifelong learning banner examined in more detail in Chapters 5 and 6.

Employers in General

Although larger employers have a better investment record than SMEs, there still remains the more general question of trying to, in some sense, quantify the needs and requirements of employers, a task which is notoriously vexed, complex and shrouded in confusion and nebulosity. Finn's (1990) extensive research in this area reported that 'employers' educational needs were extremely ambiguous' and 'could in fact be contradictory, confused or simply unknown' (p.48).   These findings confirmed many earlier studies such as the 1980 Think Tank (CPRS, 1980) report on the 'needs of the world of work' which concluded that there:

> are serious difficulties about interpreting what the needs of industry are...These [needs] are far from uniform; there are inconsistencies between what employers say they want and the values implicit in their selection process; their conception of their needs, present and future, is frequently not explicit or clearly formulated (p.7).

Similar points were made in Wellington's (1994) research which found that schools receive inconsistent messages from employers regarding what skills and personal qualities they ought to be developing in young people as future workers.

If we add to this the vagueness and ambiguity of employers' complaints and demands referred to earlier in the chapter, the confusion is compounded. The general/specific and skills/personal qualities dichotomies which appeared in employers' complaints about the deficiencies of school leavers are paralleled in the studies of employers' needs and requirements. Thus, we have a major MSC survey reporting that employers were looking for a 'greater willingness and a better attitude to work from young people' (MSC, 1977, p.17), employers' preferences for 'learned skills [of] day to day literacy and numeracy' noted in the Industry in Education survey (IiE, 1996, p.9), SME skill shortages in 'basic, technical,computer and communication' in a recent labour market survey (Skills & Enterprise Network, 1998a, p.1), and the call for a 'workforce with imagination and confidence' (DfEE, 1998a, p.15) made in the recent DfEE Green Paper.

Given this confusing and fluid state of affairs, there is much to be said for Wellington's (1994) conclusion that the 'lack of clarity in determining employers' needs is not due to a lack of empirical research', and the 'needs of industry' is a simplistic and naive conception which does not provide 'a solid base on which a coherent plan for education and training can be built' (p.320). Although critical of Wellington's conslusions, Rikowki's (1998b) analysis of these issues does agree about the incoherence of VET programmes based on employers needs; since capital is essentially chaotic and anarchic, we should not expect the summation of its needs to make rational sense. For Rikowksi, a 'post-16 curriculum based on employers' needs would encapsulate the tensions, the oppositions and antipathetic drives of various categories and functions of capital' (p.14).

The key implication of this incoherent situation is, having accepted the 'complex technicism' and the 'enormity of the task of schooling and training for the needs of capital' (ibid., p.15) in fluid post-Fordist economies, we need to develop mechanisms designed as a 'filter for labour-power needs [which] points towards possible relationships between types of labour-power called forth by, and defined by, categories and functions of capital' (ibid., p.25). The main categories of capital (and links with knowledge and skill requirements) are identified by Rikowski as follows (ibid., pp.25-27):

- *Capital-in-general /national capital*: referring to needs which 'exist in relation to all extant capitals over the lifetime of individual workers'; the labour-power requirements are correspondingly general with an emphasis on developing transferable skills, requisite attitudes and personal qualities and 'foresight' or reasonable approximation of developing capital needs based upon 'high-quality forecasting'.
- *Fractions of capital/sectors of capital*: incorporating a wide range of public and private 'congealments of capital' covering manufacturing, finance and service industries and requiring 'general' vocational preparation of the sort which GNVQs (according to the official line) are aiming at.
- *Individual capitals*: at the level of units of capital (firms, enterprises) more occupationally-specific training and skills will be indicated.

Such a filtering mechanism can, according to Rikowski, not only be viewed 'as a framework for subsuming education and training and curriculum forms under the domination of capital', but also 'offers a device for aiding [employers] to think more precisely about their labour-power needs' (ibid., p.30).

Making allowances for the nebulosity of much skill-talk noted in the last chapter and the limitations of human capital theory and incoherent employer requirements noted above, it is still possible to offer some tentative and provisional recommendations for VET policy and practice which might help us both to inform and evaluate ongoing developments in the post-compulsory sphere as we approach the millennium.

1) An Emphasis on Training and Skills, Rather than Certification or Accreditation

Although there is much generalised talk of upgrading workforce knowledge and skills on the part of both employers and educators, when it comes to designing actual VET programmes, knowledge and skills tend to be reduced and transformed into certificates and/or NVQ levels of achievement. Thus, Modern Apprenticeships (MAs) come to be defined in terms of the achievement of NVQ level 3 (Ernst & Young, 1995; Hyland, 1996d), Training Credits are tied rigidly to NVQ criteria (Hodkinson, Sparkes & Hodkinson, 1996), the New Deal WTW programme (though promising to to provide value-added training in terms of basic skills, key skills and jobsearch skills in the full-time mode) will make extensive use of 'NVQ outcomes' as 'quantitative indicators' (DfEE, 1997b, p.21)of achievement, and the NTETs are dominated by NVQ outcomes at both foundation and lifetime learning levels (NACETT, 1995, p.10). If we add to this the privileged position of NVQ achievment in Schedule 2 funding mechanisms, it is little wonder that all of the so-called 'Target 2000' training schemes, national traineeships, New Start and Right to Study (Training & Employment Network, 1997), are also dominated by reference to NVQ levels of achievement (as indeed are the Dearing recommendations for a HE credit system covering everything from certificate to doctoral level, Dearing, 1997, para.43). There are, however, optimistic signs in this respect since (as noted in the last chapter) the resurgence of qualifications 'other' than NVQs/GNVQs is causing policy-makers to allow their inclusion, crucially so in Schedule 2, NTETS and

New Deal arrangements (Ward, 1998, p.9), in the National Framework alongside those prescribed in the former NCVQ structure.

Taking note of Dore's warnings about qualification inflation and his crucial distinction between education and training aimed at learning to *do* a job and processes aimed at qualifying people to *get* a job (1976, p.8), it is not difficult to see the dangers of this emphasis on outcomes and achievement circumscribed tightly by an NVQ agenda. As Ainley (1996) noted in his critique of the Dearing review of 16-19 qualifications, this confused agenda, unduly limited by the dominance of levels of equivalence between academic and vocational qualifications is leading us towards a 'certified not a learning society' characterised by 'chronic qualification inflation/diploma devaluation' (p.91). Of course, the unified curriculum recommended in Chapter 3 will still incorporate the idea of *broad* accredited 'qualifications'. Its ongoing development through the stages outlined by Spours & Hodgson (1997) and Tomlinson (1997) will, however, necessarily involve the emergence of a more holistic vision in which the current three tracks wither away as the present vocational and academic elements are integrated and fused together.

Thus, although we still have to identify and codify knowledge and skills against the background of the differing needs of all the stakeholders (and different forms of employment and capitals), we can make a useful start by emphasising the process (especially the 'deep' learning recommended in Chapter 2) aspects of VET and the limitations of the CBET outcomes approach typified in NVQs. As was noted in the last chapter, the cause of upskilling the workforce and upgrading VET to equivalent academic standards has been severely damaged over the last decade by the many limitations and shortcomings of NVQs. It is to be hoped that the current QCA review (DfEE, 1997a) will result in improved criteria and more rigorous assessment techniques. In addition, since the National Framework (in spite of the resurgence of 'other' qualifications) is still constructed on the basis of the old NCVQ hierarchical model of levels, policy-makers need to consider seriously the recommendation that the NVQ dominance be removed from this architectonic structure and replaced by the framework (outlined in the last chapter) based on the foundation of a genuinely unified 14-19 curriculum and general educational criteria.

2) Learning for Work and Learning at Work

The arguments for a unified system for 14 to 19 year olds were examined at length in Chapter 3 along with more general considerations relating to the upgrading of VET and the bridging of the vocational/academic divide. If the criteria of lifelong learning are to be taken seriously, a 14-19 curriculum along the lines suggested by Spours & Young (1998) will be required in order to ensure the necessary progression through to the post-compulsory stage. As indicated in the earlier outline, NVQs, perhaps, re-labelled and re-packaged, would be removed from this stage (and also from apprenticeships and traineeships) and returned to the workplace where, with the new criteria and flexibility promised by the QCA revision, they would supply the skills needed by changing employment conditions . In addition, the overarching certificate/diploma design of a unified system would obviate the need for any *named* qualifications (whether they be NVQs, GNVQs or A-levels) at this stage.

In the light of the analysis pursued in this chapter, what needs to be added to that general picture is the requirement for a general educational foundation to meet Rikowski's 'capital in general' requirements and to compensate for the vicissitudes of human capital theory and labour-power planning. VET programmes for 14-19, *Learning for Work* curricula, will need to acknowledge the failure of schemes founded on behavioural functional analysis and outdated Taylorist management techniques and, instead, look to what Skilbeck et al.(1994) refer to as the 'common learning' systems of European and OECD countries which seek to provide the 'common, fundamental learnings for working life' (p.60).   Such a foundation will be essential to the emergence of what was recommended in the last chapter in terms of a genuinely unified 14-19 curriculum which 'breaks down the physical barriers between institutions thus allowing 'young people post-14 more choice from a modularised curriculum incorporating vocational, academic and work experience for all' (Tomlinson, 1997, p.16).   Moreoever, the *educational* value of workplace learning, especially its potential to foster the 'holistic and empowering vision' (Unwin, 1997, p.84) which some VET researchers have perceived in the newly-emerging models of traineeship and apprenticeship, will be central to any 'newly forged unified system' ideally incorporating a 'strong strand of vocational education' and 'new forms and combinations of vocationalist specialist study' (Spours, 1997, p.72).

Thus, for apprentices and trainees pursuing MAs, WTW options or similar routes an element of general education will still be required, though obviously both the mode and duration of study will need to be different for those people not in full-time education and training. However, even at the level of the workplace the differing demands of capital, and the differing labour-power requirements of large companies and SMEs indicated in Rikowski's 'filter', will still necessitate some general VET requirements, especially in terms of communication and ICT skills. Thus, the 'breadth and depth of study' (Spours & Young, 1997, p.9) will still have relevance in the various *Learning at Work* programmes as a way of compensating for and ultimately replacing the narrow occupationalism of CBET strategies which 'overemphasise outcomes at the expense of the processes and the settings through which these outcomes have been expressed and developed' (Skilbeck et al., 1994, p.238). Again, the unified curriculum which tends to 'focus on the link between the economic needs of the future' and current VET provision will be needed to supply 'workers who can think creatively, understand how organisations work and can link theory and practice' (Hodgson & Spours, 1997, p.18).

3) Moral Vocationalism and Social Learning

Those charged with designing VET programmes for the 21st century would do well to take note of Green's (1995) explanation of why European systems have rejected the functional analysis model of CBET represented by occupationally-specific NVQs; he observes that there is a tendency in many Continental countries:

> to resist any approach which reduces the theoretical and general educational components of VET since these are considered essential not only for skills transfer but also for the potential of individuals both as citizens and as learners and employees seeking to progress to higher levels (p.25).

Green's comment reminds us of the importance of both a social theory of learning of the sort outlined in earlier chapters and of the need to incorporate a values dimension in all VET programmes if the wider goals of lifelong learning and citizenship are to be achieved. A morally justifiable 'philosophy of VET' (Hyland, 1995a, 1996d) will need to articulate such social and moral values (discussed in more detail in Chapter 7) if the new 'culture of lifelong learning' is to be generated through a 'partnership between individual responsibility and the wider community' (DfEE, 1998a, p.17).

Before applying these principles and criteria to current trends in the post-compulsory sector, we need to examine the elements of change and continuity in the system, taking particular note of the blueprint for VET developments provided by the New Deal, the UfI and related schemes which form an integral part of New Labour's lifelong learning policies for the new learning age.

5 New Labour Policy and the Post-Compulsory Sector

In commenting on the broad outline of New Labour policies for post-compulsory education and training, Coffield (1998), adopts a slightly ironic tone of measured caution and modest optimism in observing that:

> Much of the immediate commentary on *The Learning Age* concentrated on how wonderfully different New Labour's plans for lifelong learning are from those of previous Conservative administrations (p.27).

Unsurprisingly, the new policies are introduced and justified in terms of the failure of previous reforms to tackle the main problems of VET. As noted in the last chapter, Hillman was concerned to explain the need for a body such as the UfI in the context of over a century of inadequate, short-termist, ad hoc VET policies. In a similar vein, *The Learning Age* introduces the section on the principles of public funding and investment in learning with the observation that:

> After nearly two decades of inadequate investment in learning, we face a major challenge. The Government has already shown its commitment to education as a priority by announcing an additional £165 million for higher education and £100 million for further education in 1998-99, and by its pledge to support an extra 500,000 people in further and higher education by 2002. We are seeking views on a new partnership between Government, individuals and employers for further investment in the future (p.25).

The document goes on to describe in detail, and in an admirably frank fashion, the 'serious weaknesses' in the 'country's learning scoreboard'. These are (ibid., p.12):

- almost 30% of young people fail to reach NVQ Level 2 by the age of 19
- seven million adults have no formal qualifications at all
- 21 million adults have not reached level 3

- more than one in five of all adults have poor literacy and numeracy skills

In addition, Britain lags behind a number of competitor countries, including France, Germany and Singapore, in the proportion of the workforce qualified to level 3. Meeting this challenge and remedying the serious weaknesses in the education and training system will require 'a quiet and sustained revolution in aspiration and achievement' which will be built on the following principles (ibid., p.13):

- investing in learning to benefit everyone;
- lifting barriers to learning;
- putting people first;
- sharing responsibility with employers, employees and the community;
- achieving world class standards and value for money; and
- working together as the key to success.

Principles and priorities for public funding in order to achieve the key objectives are outlined in the following proposals (ibid., p.25):

- we will guarantee help with basic skills, with courses provided free at whatever age;
- we will guarantee free full-time education for young people up to the age of 18;
- we will share with employers the cost of learning for young people in work (for example, Modern Apprenticeships);
- we will share the cost of higher education with students through our new student support system;
- we will make provision for the highest level of postgraduate education; and
- we will target financial help for adults on those who need it most (e.g. through ILAs)

Practical and detailed strategies for achieving the key goals in the light of these principles are contained in other *Learning Age* documents such as the responses to the Dearing Report on higher education and the Kennedy report on further education. However, in the drive to develop a 'culture of learning' (ibid., p.10) emphasis is given to a number of flagship initiatives such as the UfI, WTW and individual learning accounts and it is worth looking at these in more detail before examining their progress and development in the early stages.

The University for Industry

Although the Ufl Pathfinder Prospectus (DfEE, 1998c) was published in mid-1998 as a prelude to the official launch in 2000, and accompanied later in 1998 by the appointment of a permanent Chief Executive after months of inertia (DfEE, 1998g), the original Ufl blueprint dates back to joint research and development by the Institute for Public Policy Research (IPPR) and the University of Sunderland in 1995/96 (Milner, 1998). The model envisages the Ufl in terms of performing the functions of an 'impartial broker' (ibid., p.5) seeking to connect individuals and companies to learning programmes rather than being a principal provider of learning, although the organisation 'will commission initally a limited number of flagship packages in areas of strategic importance' (DfEE, 1998c, p.27). A central guiding principle is that of making learning more accessible to people who have had least contact with formal systems. The Ufl is to be user- not supplier-led and will make extensive use of open, distance and flexible learning modes, allow for study 'outside conventional institutions' and exploit 'multiple sources of material, information and expertise' (Hillman, 1997, p.16).

Fundamental to Ufl operations is the use of information and communications technology (ICT) to access learning networks and, in the pilot project which has been operating in the north-east of England since September 1997 co-ordinated by the University of Sunderland, imaginative use of ICT systems and the Internet figures prominently. By making use of 'cyberspace' linked to a Ufl free phone helpline, *Learning Direct* (DfEE, 1998h), the plan is to enable users to gain access to a wide range of resources and programmes in a cost-efficient way. The Internet can be used to access information on the content, times and locations of relevant programmes, and includes an online database of training materials. Marketing techniques, including poster campaigns on buses and local community centres, telemarketing, and door-to-door leafleting, are then connected with the Ufl helpline and Internet facilities to complete the brokerage role which 'begins with marketing and ends when the learner is booked on to a full course with a provider' (Milner, 1998, p.15).

In keeping with the general philosophy of taking learning to the community, the Ufl will rely heavily on a network of 'learner centres' which will eventually be co-ordinated to create a national learning network combining with the evolving National Grid for Learning (Twining, 1997).

In the Sunderland pilot, agencies involved include local TECs, libraries, companies,community schools, further education colleges and a local football club, and the innovative nature of the project is well illustrated in the prominence given to the *Learning World* centre based in Gateshead Metro Centre. Said to be the largest shopping centre in Europe with 6000 employees and 26 million visitors per year, the University of Sunderland and Gateshead College have utilised the Metro Centre as a site for the learning complex. Incorporating classrooms, computer laboratories and advice and guidance resources, *Learning World*, 'only doors from IKEA is open seven days a week and has a turnover in the order of £1 million', offers courses from basic literacy and numeracy to MBAs and 'has had about 4,000 students between the ages of 7 and 70 since it opened' (Hackett, 1998, p.6).

Similar innovative projects located squarely within 'lifestyle sites' and supplying 'learning on demand' include Cyberskills workshops in South Bristol and CD-ROM learning packages of skills for employment based in Croydon Central Library (Hillman, 1997, p.19). There will also be special links with company-based schemes, particularly with the the UK automotive sector which 'involves 7,000 companies, over 90% of which are SMEs, and has an annual turnover of £12 billion' (DfEE, 1998c, p.20). All of this is designed to contribute to the 'catalyst function' of the UfI in its role of 'risk-taker, innovator and motivator' (Milner, 1998, p.17).

The UfI will be an independent agency which 'facilitates access for its customers to the education and training provision that best meets their needs' (DfEE, 1998c, p.25). This will entail a 'new kind of public-private partnership' designed specifically to achieve the two main strategic objectives which are:

1. to stimulate demand for lifelong learning amongst businesses and inividuals;
2. to promote the availability of, and improve access to, relevant, high quality and innovative learning opportunities, in particular through the use of information and communications technologies.

To meet those objectives:

the UfI will provide ways of overcoming the barriers of time, cost, fear, inadequate information, complexity and inconvenience which deter individuals and businesses, in particular smaller firms, from learning (ibid., p.9).

Initial priorities will involve a focus on four client groups and skill areas (ibid., p.15):

1. basic skills;
2. information and communications technologies for the workplace;
3. small and medium-sized businesses; and
4. specific sectors: automotive components; multimedia; environmental technology and services; and distributive and retail trades.

These priorities are intended to 'demonstrate the range of the UfI's customers and activities and its dual focus on individual employability and business competitiveness' (ibid.).

In the transitional phase, prior to the official launch in the year 2000, a team led by Dr Anne Wright who was appointed as permanent Chief Executive in August 1998 to work with the UfI Chairman, Lord Sainsbury, will 'develop legal and organisational structures and business plans for the UfI, pending the establishment of permanent UfI structures' (ibid., p.32). It is intended that the organisation be self-supporting within a few years after its national launch; it will charge a fee to providers for the use of its systems and networks and also charge for the use of the UfI kitemark. Combined with efficiency gains and, mainly through the use of new technologies, the elimination of duplication and wastage, Hillman (1997) argues that the UfI will deliver a 'more effective way of spending money' and 'will find a market and pay its way' (p.60).

The UfI Pathfinder Prospectus makes the optimistic claim that:

> As the market for lifelong learning expands and the UfI's financial performance is demonstrated, private sector financial institutions will be increasingly attracted to fund the UfI's growing capital requirements by investing directly in its activities, like commissioning new products which may require substantial resources (DfEE, 1998c, p.32).

The New Deal Initiatives

The links between the New Deal and other lifelong learning and learning age projects is clear; the scheme is specifically designed to be radically different from the past legacy of failed experiments and reforms in education and training, its moral and political justification is provided by new emphases on co-operation, mutualism and social inclusion, and, like the UfI, it is underpinned by the 'third way' (Giddens, 1998; see also Chapter 8) policy of public-private sector collaboration. In this respect, New Deal policy is epitomised in the 'Target 2000' umbrella of initiatives, including National Traineeships suggested by Dearing (1996), New Start for disaffected 14-19 year olds and Right to Study which entitles all youngsters under 18 in employment to one day a week of study at a local college (Training & Employment Network, 1997). In examining its specific remit and terms of reference, however, it is less easy to place strict limits on the applications of the New Deal concept. The following principal applications can be discerned in the policy documents and the general literature:

1) New Deal refers specifically to the WTW scheme for unemployed 18-24 year olds, launched in April 1998 and extended in June 1998 to include long-term unemployed people aged 25+ (DfEE, 1999); the original blueprint document for the scheme is actually labelled as the 'design of the New Deal' (DfEE, 1997b).

2) The New Deal is merely a part of a much 'broader welfare to work programme' (Ward, 1997, p.8) which, along with the WTW scheme for certain categories of unemployed people, includes other projects such as the scheme for encouraging lone mothers back to work (Bryson, Ford & White, 1997). The New Deal for disabled people and for unemployed people over 25 (Skills & Enterprise Network, 1998b, pp.39-40) are part of this broader framework.

3) New Deal is a more generalised term for identifying New Labour's overall policies for education and training, including links with the UfI, ILAs and the National Grid for Learning made in *The Learning Age* (DfEE, 1998a, p.11) alongside connections between the New Deal and National Traineeships (ibid., p.31) and also Modern Apprenticeships (ibid., pp.40-41).

4) In addition to the above, all of which might be described as aspects of the New Deal for *individuals*, there is also the link with the new adminstration's wider policies to attack social exclusion in the form of the 'New Deal for Communities' (Social Exlusion Unit, 1998). Launched in September 1998 with a budget of £800 million over three years, this community-oriented version of the New Deal is designed to 'give some of our worst-off local communities the resources to tackle their problems in an intensive and co-ordinated way' (p.7).

Like lifelong learning and the learning society, 'New Deal' is clearly a term which possesses too much valuable sloganising potential to be restricted to any one particular project. Its political origins are, of course, to be found in post-Depression America in the 1930s when, after his inauguration as President in March 1933, Franklin Delano Roosevelt (FDR) pledged himself to a 'new deal for the American people' (Johnson, 1966, p.570) and went on to ask Congress for the:

> one remaining instrument to meet the crisis: broad executive power to wage a war against the emergency as great as the power that would be given me if we were in fact invaded by a foreign foe (Commager, 1963, p.242).

Under the slogan 'Relief, Recovery, Reform' the next decade witnessed an unprecedented spate of legislation and reform measures, including massive public work programmes, national work-relief schemes and major reforms of banking, industry, agriculture and labour relations, which gradually brought the country out of the Depression and which made the New Deal 'different from anything that had yet happened in the United States' (Hofstadter, 1959, p.302). As Thomas Stokes, a junior member of FDR's administration, commented at the time:

> They were exciting, exhilarating days. It was one of the most joyous periods of my life. We came alive, we were eager. We were infected with a gay sprit of adventure, for something concrete and constructive finally was being done about the chaos which confronted the nation (Sauvain, 1989, pp.168-9).

Although there are some superficial similarities, no doubt of the exhilirating, joyous and adventurous as well as of the relief, recovery and reform kind (referred to again in Chapter 8), between FDR's New Deal and the New Labour version, it would be just too much of an exaggeration to describe the present state of the British economy and our VET system in terms of a crisis or an emergency. However, the persuasiveness of the slogan is clearly rooted in the idea of a sharp break with the past and can, thus, legitimately be applied to the WTW and related schemes (indeed, a previous job creation scheme launched by the MSC in 1975 was described at the time as a 'mini-New Deal', Ainley & Corney, 1990, p.33; the term was also applied to the Youth Opportunities Programme established by the last Labour government in 1978; Finn, 1997).

In terms of the current New Deal, it could be said that its *denotations* are represented by the (practical, task-related) versions (1) and (2) above, whereas the wider moral/political *connotations*, suggesting the general political campaign against social exclusion with policies in all fields designed, like lifelong learning, 'for the many, not the few' (Tuckett, 1997, p.3), are contained in versions (3) and (4). For the sake of clarity it is worth mentioning that in the present examination of VET trends I will be referring principally to version (1) outlined above in describing the WTW and related schemes. However, the other three interpretations (particularly 3 and 4) will enter into the more general discussion of the ethical and political dimensions of recent trends in education and training with which the final two chapters are especially concerned.

The New Deal is one part of the 'welfare to work' initiative announced by New Labour just before the 1997 election. Its immediate aim was to 'reduce the number of 18-24 year olds experiencing long-term unemployment...estimated to be 250,000 nationally in May 1997' (Mason, 1998, p.176). This strategy is a key aspect of the wider Labour Party promise to 'attack unemployment and break the spiral of escalating spending on social security' (Labour Party, 1997, p.7). More generally, the scheme is informed by the aim of ending the 'dependency culture' by 'improving both the employability of those out of work and by imposing an effective time limit on continuous benefit entitlement' (Finn, 1997, p.247).

The Design of the New Deal WTW

The scheme is designed to cater for:

> young people aged 18-24 who have been unemployed for six months or more and are receiving Job Seekers Allowance (JSA). It is intended to help them to find work and also to improve their prospects of remaining in employment (Ward, 1997, p.8).

The key to the whole programme is the initial 'Gateway' provision which 'aims first to get young people into work, and includes help with job search, careers advice, and preparation for and submission to a range of options' (DfEE, 1997b, p.1). Following an 'intensive period of counselling advice and guidance' during the Gateway period of from 1-4 months, the 'New Dealer' then has four main options to choose from (Ward, 1997, pp.8-10):

- *Employment option*: if a young person has not been able to find an unsubsidised job (and this is a key priority) within two months, this option offers a subsidised job with employers receiving £60 per week for 26 weeks for a job with a minimum of 30 hours per week including the equivalent of one day per week training (the training will attract a payment of £750 and be provided either by the employer or another agency).
- *Environmental task force*: this option is designed to improve the employability of young people through placements and training lasting up to 6 months (30 hours per week with one day per week training). The Environmental Task Force undertakes projects concerned with water conservation, forest and park management and the reclamation of derelict and waste land.
- *Voluntary sector*: this option has similar aims and conditions as the Task Force option but is directed towards community projects such as reducing drug abuse and improving community relations
- *Education and training*: this route involves full-time education and training for up to 52 weeks and is intended mainly for those who do not have a qualification equivalent to NVQ level 2. Employability skills are emphasised in all the programmes recommended.
  [A further option, the Self Employment route, was introduced in 1998 with the aim of encouraging up to 20,000 people to start their own businesses.]

In the subsequent development of WTW, the scheme has been opened up to people over 25 and, as an extension of subsidised employment, allows for a '6-month £75 a week tax subsidy for private sector employers who take on people who have been out of work for over 2 years' (Finn, 1997, p.248).

The government has emphasised that there will be 'no fifth option of an inactive life on benefit' (ibid., given that a fifth option is now self-employment, presumably there is no sixth option) and sanctions include withdrawal of the JSA for up to two weeks if people refuse or fail to take up one of the New Deal options.

New Deal Policy and PCET

In evaluating New Deal initiatives it is necessary to begin with general political principles (these will be examined in greater depth in Chapter 8) before examining the specific nature of the development of VET strategies in relation to recent history in this sphere. Certainly, macro-policy comes first since the overall aim of challenging the dependency culture and radically reforming the whole welfare system are foundational elements in the 'third way' conception of the new 'social investment state' (Giddens, 1998; see also Chapter 8). As the Prime Minister argued at the 1998 Labour Party conference, the present welfare and benefits system is 'chaotic, unfair and out of date'. Mr Blair went on to observe:

> I did not come into politics to dismantle the welfare state. I believe in it – so when we bring forward porposals for change in our Welfare Reform Bill...don't tell us it is a betrayal of the welfare state when in truth welfare reform is its only salvation (Schaefer, 1998, p.6).

In addition to the general political agenda, the government's inheritance from their Conservative predecessors needs to be considered. This included:

> unpopular schemes, harsh benefit regulations and an underfunded Employment Service [ES] preoccupied with benefit policing. It also inherited widespread scepticism amongst the unemployed and employers who, respectively,   see 'schemes' as something you're forced to go on with little prospect of a real outcome (Finn, 1997, p.253).

If we add to this the general under-investment in training by employers (especially SMEs) and government, the chaotic state of vocational qualifications as NVQs are radically revised under the QCA and the generally gloomy state of VET in general, we would be bound to say that *any* attempts to attack these problems are to be welcomed.

However, if New Deal projects are examined against the 'Relief, Recovery, Reform' criteria of FDR's original New Deal, it has to be said that, *from the standpoint of PCET*, there has been more emphasis on relief and recovery than on reform. The reform elements of New Deal are all concerned mainly with welfare reform and the (generally praiseworthy) aim of reducing the dependency culture by targeting society's most disadvantaged groups. This focus on those who have gained least from the system is, of course, also present in lifelong learning policies, and the policy objectives underpinning this strategy can be said to satisfy the relief and recovery criteria of the New Deal (though without the massive spending on public works which characterised FDR's New Deal). Reformist zeal is also evident in the general strategy, for WTW, the Ufl and the various community projects, which demonstrates a determination to forge local partnerships which are 'fully integrated with local regeneration strategies' (Finn, 1997, p.247).

However, there is little concrete evidence, other than the firm statements of intent, thus far of any radical programme to reform PCET in the light of its legacy of failures and shortcomings. WTW and related schemes are still connected with a three-track qualification system in which the occupationally-specific route is of poor quality and low status. Moreover, there is still an emphasis on skills and qualifications seen principally in terms of the old NCVQ agenda, whereas the progression required in order to foster a lifelong learning culture requires an emphasis on learning processes, knowledge and values.

The FE sector is being 're-formed' in the light of the Kennedy recommendations (referred to in more detail in Chapter 8) but those changes leave largely intact a system which has consistently failed those following vocational or 'second chance' routes. Indeed, many FE colleges have found themselves worse off by taking WTW recruits (McGavin, 1998b) and it remains to be seen whether the new Employment Zones linked to the integrated ES schemes designed to implement the New Deal (Finn, 1997) are sufficient to attract the vital SME sector into the national training efforts.

In the long run, perhaps it is unfair to judge the New Deal as anything more than a programme to relieve unemployment coupled with an element of employment-related training designed to help people to guard against unemployment in a shifting labour market. At this level, it might be described as a potential stepping-stone, and necessary pre-requisite, for more substantial VET improvements. Whether such potential is realised might well be determined by how many New Deal 'graduates' progress to other forms of education and training in ways which satisfy the current lifelong learning objectives. The achievement of such objectives will, in turn, depend upon whether the New Deal schemes are integrated with the evolving system of post-school education and training.

6 The Emerging National System of Education and Training

Taken alongside developments relating to the 14-19 curriculum, further and higher education and the 'Target 2000' projects, the continung growth and evolution of the UfI and New Deal initiatives within general lifelong learning policy can be seen as an attempt to shape a new post-school education and training system for the 21st century. This chapter looks at the policy analyses and empirical studies, including our own projects at Warwick concerned specifically with SMEs and the UfI, employed to evaluate these developments up to the time of writing (February 1999). In conjunction with the criteria for a social model of lifelong learning referred to in earlier chapters and the blueprint for a values dimension for VET described in the next chapter, these evaluative studies will be used to offer some provisional answers in Chapter 8 to the question of whether recent trends add up to what Gleeson called a 'new educational settlement' (1996) for the post-compulsory sector or, indeed, have been conducive to the fostering of the 'learning culture' which is the principal aim of all current policy on education and training. In the light of this evaluation, issues surrounding the status, present health and possible future of VET in Britain will also be considered.

UfI Developments

At the time of writing we are well into the second phase of transitional development planned for the UfI (see diagram below) and, just prior to the official launch, it seems timely to assess progress to date. The 'key development milestones' (DfEE, 1998c, p.38) are as follows:

1998

Spring	Pathfinder Prospectus issued Transition team established Call for applications for ADAPT *funding
Summer	Successful ADAPT products announced First Ufl learning products commissioned
Autumn	Chief Executive appointed Ufl legal entity established Development projects running
Winter	Ufl website established

1999

Spring	Franchised network of learning centres established Databases and infrastructure established National marketing campaign begins
Summer	Full Ufl staff team in post

2000	Ufl open for Business

[* ADAPT is a development project attracting European Social Funding to finance schemes for 'innovative, transnational projects which will test out aspects of the University for Industry model'; ibid., p.39; see also ADAPT, 1998].

An editorial about the Ufl published in the *Times Higher Education Supplement* in April 1998 declared, with apparent relish, that:

> The first obvious thing about it is that it is no university. It is designed to trawl the highways and byways, using all modern means of public persuasion, to draw in those who have learned little and like it less. Only very much second

and later is it to help people who are already skilled but seek retreading...Tackling educational failure and skill shortages is admirable, but calling the project a university risks debasing the currency which the government has said it wishes to defend (THES, 1998b, p.11).

Even if we allow for a certain degree of educational snobbery and elitism, the editorial still raises lots of points and questions which require attention.

It is true that, since the initial plans were officially announced in April 1997 with pre-election promises that it would be a 'virtual university' performing a role 'similar to Channel 4 TV's networking one' and expected to 'do for industry what the Open University did for higher education' (Nash, 1997a, p.29), the UfI got off to a decidedly shaky start. The last sentence in the quotation from the THES editorial above refers to the fact that, for a period in 1998 when the Teaching and Higher Education Bill was proposing plans to tighten up on the use of the university title (Baty & Tysome, 1998), there was some doubt about the legality of the UfI label. Indeed, the leader of the UfI pilot in Sunderland felt at the time that the UfI should be renamed *Learning Direct* (the free DfEE helpline launched in Spring 1998) so that it would be disassociated from 'an FE version of the Open University' (ibid., p.1). In the event, the original title has been retained though the moral and educational justification to use it has yet to be earned.

Another early problem was that the new organisation, after the original announcements and the IPPR blueprint document, appeared to be without definite stewardship and direction. Lord Sainsbury was still Chairman but, with few members of the original board remaining and more concrete proposals awaited, Hillman (1998) chose an opportune time in July 1998 to announce that the fledgling was still very much alive and about to 'emerge from its shell' (p.28) under the transitional leadership of the deputy director of Sheffield Hallam University. More recently, to move from ornithological to human metaphors, the embryo has reached the foetal stage thanks to the concrete financial pledges in the 1998 comprehensive spending review coupled with the appointment of the Vice-Chancellor of Sunderland University as the new permanent UfI Chief Executive (DfEE, 1998g). On her appointment, Dr Wright promised that the UfI would 'make a major contribution to improving the skills and competitiveness of businesses' and 'be one of the most important drivers of change in learning' (ibid., p.1). With less than a year to go before the official birth and national launch, how likely is it that the UfI will achieve these important objectives? We can offer some, necessarily tentative and provisional, answers to this question by considering the key objectives in terms of the impact on learning by individuals and by organisations.

Learning by Individuals

Expansion of and access to further and higher education has progressed apace over the last decade or so. Full-time HE numbers increased by 71% between 1989/90 and 1996/97 and FE numbers increased to 3.8 million by 1996/97 (DfEE, 1998a, p.77). In spite of all this the system was still under-performing and large numbers of students were under-achieving.

The 'serious weaknesses' of the present education and training system listed in *The Learning Age* document were referred to at the beginning of Chapter 5 and, clearly, by prioritising basic skills and targeting those people who have benefited least from formal systems, the Ufl is seeking to mount a head-on challenge to the traditional problems of non-participation in post-compulsory education. The Secretary of State's commentaries on the various *Learning Age* documents make frequent references to the fact that 'seven million adults have no formal qualifications' and 'one in five finds it difficult to read, write and deal with numbers' (Blunkett, 1998, p.18). In his justification of Ufl priorities, Hillman (1997) acknowledges that, notwithstanding the fact that:

> 83% of adults see learning as having personal significance and 92% of employers can identify the advantages of lifelong learning to their organisations...only a minority of the adult population has recently undertaken any learning at all...we have a long way to go to achieve a learning society (pp.11-12).

Hillman cites the figures taken from the 1996 NIACE/Gallup survey on lifelong learning (Fig. 6.1) to substantiate the case for prioritising learning programmes and funding in favour of certain disadvantaged or traditionally low participating groups.

FIGURE 1: PARTICIPATION IN LEARNING, 17+			
	ALL	MEN	WOMEN
Base: All respondents = 100%	4673	2270	2403
	%	%	%
Currently learning	23	25	21
Recent learning (in the last 3 years)	17	18	17
	40	43	38
Past learning (more than 3 years ago	23	25	21
None since leaving full time education	36	31	41

Fig. 6.1: Participation in Learning
Source: Tuckett & Sargent, 1996, p.219.

More recent data provided by the 1997 National Adult Learning Survey (NALS) (Beinart & Smith, 1998) are more optimistic (partly because it included non-taught and informal learning), indicating that '67% of all [5653] respondents had undertaken some vocational learning in the past three years and 30% had taken part in some non-vocational learning in this time' (p.8).

The problem of non-participation in post-school education has been well documented and researched (McGivney, 1990, 1996) and we now know quite a lot about the typical characteristics of non-participants. The 1997 NALS data, distinguishing between vocational and non-vocational learning, produced a number of key group features and differences (see Fig. 6.2).

The groups found to be more likely than others to have taken part in vocational learning included:

• males;

• those aged under 50;

• those in paid work;

• those working (or who had worked in the past 10 years) in managerial, professional or other non-manual occupations;

• those spending longer in full-time education and leaving it better qualified;

• those living in households with their parents and in households with partners and children.

Groups particularly unlikely to have undertaken vocational learning in the past three years included:

• females;

• those aged 60 or more;

• those looking after the family or home, retired or long-term sick/disabled;

• those working (or who had worked in the last 10 years) in unskilled manual occupations;

• those who left full-time continuous education aged 16 or less and with no qualifications;

• those living as a single person or living in a household with a child but no partner or living in a household with a partner and no child;

• those with a long-standing illness;

• those caring for an elderly or sick household member.

Fig. 6.2: Profile of Vocational Learners
Source: Beinart & Smith, 1998, pp.8-9.

In addition, the four most significant predictors of a person's vocational learning status were reported as (ibid., p.11) :
(i) socio-economic group
(ii) whether or not a qualification had been obtained on leaving continuous full-time education
(iii) current activity status
(iv) whether or not a respondent had started a new job recently

For non-vocational learning the first three predictors were exactly the same and (iv) was replaced by sex, with females more likely to have participated in this sphere than males.

These key features of non-participants have been replicated in many other studies (Brookfield, 1986; Munn & McDonald, 1988) and are neatly summed up by McGivney (1993, pp.14-15). Characteristics which distinguish non-participants from participants in adult learning are age (older people are less likely to be involved), educational background (the people with least initial schooling are more likely to be non-participants) and socio-economic group (the lower the social scale or class the lower the participation rate). In addition, these features are connected by McGivney (ibid., pp.17-22) with the key obstacles or barriers to learning described as:

- *Situational*: time available for attendance, costs of courses
- *Institutional*: an education system unresponsive to the needs of adult learners in terms of learning, teaching, timetabling and admissions to courses; also a lack of adequate information and publicity about learning opportunities
- *Dispositional*: problems of attitude, perceptions, expectations and motivations linked to the key features of non-participant groups

It is rather easier to describe the typical and perennial problems of non-participation in learning than it is to offer solutions. However, the whole of the current lifelong learning policy thrust concerned with widening participation and remedying basic skills deficits turns on the success of strategies designed to overcome the traditional barriers and obstacles. As Kennedy (1997) rightly observed, over the last five years the post-school system (at both FE and HE levels) has been successful in expanding access but there is now 'clear evidence that policies which are directed solely at increasing participation will not achieve the levels of learning and achievement now required' (p.20). The following shortcomings in the present system are noted (ibid.):

- in 1995 under half of 15 year olds achieved five GCSEs at grade C or above
- although four out of five 16 year olds stayed on in full- or part-time education, or were involved in work-based training, this applied to only three out of five 18 year olds
- only 2 out of 5 young people left Youth Training with a qualification in 1995/6
- less than 44% of employees receive training

She concludes by observing that:

> We are convinced by the wide-ranging and detailed evidence presented to us that there exists an immense and diverse body of people in this country which should be encouraged and welcomed into post-16 learning (ibid., p.22)

The government and the DfEE have fully accepted the Kennedy thesis and (as will be discussed in the more detailed policy analysis and evaluation in Chapter 8) the targeting of the most disadvantaged groups is a key focus and priority in all the *Learning Age* documents and features prominently in the flagship UfI and New Deal projects. The pledge is to 'implement the recommendations of the Dearing and Kennedy reports' and 'increase numbers in higher and further education by 500,000 by 2002' (DfEE, 1998a, p.56; this target figure was summarily increased to 700,000 in early 1999). All the current DfEE policies will ultimately be judged in terms of their success in achieving these targets for individual learning.

Learning by Organisations

As mentioned in Chapter 4 in the context of discussions about employer involvement in VET, although large companies and certain leading organisations have a good record on investment, smaller firms have no history of any such involvement. After decades of initiatives from the MSC schemes of the 1970s to the Competitiveness White Papers of the 1990s, it is still the case that SMEs 'lack a full appreciation of different types of learning' with 'owners and managers reluctant to invest in training because in the short-term the costs of training are more apparent than the benefits' (Hillman, 1997, p.11). Recent DfEE data confirm this general picture (Fig. 6.3) which is summed up lucidly by Hillman in the general formula that the 'larger an organisation is, the easier it is for it to train its employees' (ibid., p.10).

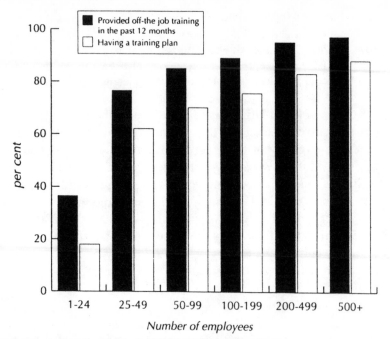

Fig. 6.3: Training Activity by Size of Organisation
Source: Hillman, 1997, p.11.

All of this serves to explain why the SME sector is a prioritised and special target for the Ufl. As the *Pathfinder Prospectus* (DfEE, 1998c) notes:

> SMEs account for a large and growing proportion of employment and are a key source of new jobs. Nearly 4 million enterprises in the UK have workforces of fewer than 250 people. They are a reservoir of the country's most highly skilled and creative individuals (p.18).

Such firms, however, face special and particular difficulties in relation to training such as the costs of training, problems concerned with allowing off-the-job training time for employees and a lack of awareness of training opportunities and benefits. In the light of this, an indicative target for the Ufl is that 'within five years, the delivery of Ufl services to 100,000 start-up businesses and 50,000 established SMEs per year' (p.18).

    In our earlier research on SMEs in the West Midlands referred to in Chapter 4, we described a 'paradox of training' in form of a mismatch between owner-managers' generally favourable attitudes to training and their very poor record in actually providing training. Factors influencing training policies of SMEs were divided between 'directly relevant' influences, the market positioning of firms, prevailing economic conditions and availability of appropriate training, and the 'indirectly relevant' which included the cost of training, time constraints and, significantly, the personal attitudes of owner-managers to training based on their own 'incubator' experiences of programmes and their general perceptions of the status, value and relevance of current VET provision (Hyland & Matlay, 1997, pp.132-3).

In our recent national survey (Matlay & Hyland, 1999, forthcoming) designed specifically to identify the views and opinions of SME owner-managers in relation to recent government policy initiatives (with a specific focus on the initial SME awareness of and attitudes to the UfI experiment) in the field, we employed a computer-generated random sampling programme in conjunction with the Yellow Pages business database to select 6,000 firms (5,951 SMEs and 49 large firms using the 250 employees limit as a cut-off point; these figures reflect the approximate 90:10% predominance of SMEs nationally, see Fig. 6.4).

Size Band	Size Definition	Number of Employees	Manufacturing (N=2,062)	Services (N=3,938)
A	Micro-Business	1-10	1,585	3,027
B	Small Business	11-49	357	768
C	Medium-Sized	50-250	92	122
D	Large Business	251+	28	21

Fig. 6.4: National Survey of SMEs (N=6000)
Source: Matlay & Hyland, 1999, forthcoming.

Interviews were conducted by telephone using a semi-structured schedule to determine the awareness of and attitudes to the UfI amongst owner-managers. Follow-up questions for those SMEs indicating an awareness of the UfI served to identify owner-managers' more specific needs and expectations.

A key element in our earlier research on SMEs was the determination of the locus of training decisions, and our finding was that such decisions resided overwhelmingly with owner-managers. These findings were confirmed and reinforced by the national sample (Fig. 6.5).

Band Code	Number of Employees	All Firms N=6,000	Who Makes Training Decisions?			
			Owner/ Manager	Personnel Manager	Other Managers	Other Employees
A	1-10	4,612	4,612	0	0	0
B	11-49	1,125	1,020	94	11	0
C	50-250	214	8	189	17	0
D	251+	49	0	49	0	0

Fig. 6.5: The Locus of Training-Related Decisions
Source: Matlay & Hyland, 1999, forthcoming.

Owner-managers, those 'highly skilled and creative individuals' praised in the DfEE prospectus on the UfI, were the sole source of executive descision-making in all the micro-firms (Band Code A) canvassed and also in over 90% of SMEs employing 50 people or fewer. Only in the larger firms with 50-250 employees do personnel managers take control of training decisions with, not unexpectedly, 100% authority and responsibility in large firms with over 250 workers.

In terms of the basic awareness of the UfI (Fig. 6.6) we noted a direct positive correlation between size of firm and level of awareness: the larger the firm the more those people responsible for training decisions knew about the recent policy developments and initiatives in the field.

Size Band	Size Definition	Number of Employees	Manufacturing (%)	Services (%)
A	Micro-Business	1-10	51.50	52.47
B	Small Business	11-49	57.61	58.36
C	Medium-Sized	50-250	86.95	88.14
D	Large Business	251+	100.00	100.00

Fig. 6.6: Owner-Managers' Awareness of the UfI
Source: Matlay & Hyland, 1999, forthcoming.

In total, of the 6,000 firms canvassed, 3,295, just over 54%, indicated their awareness of the UfI, and this group was then questioned about general attitudes to the initiative (Fig. 6.7).

Economic Sectors	Very Negative (%)	Negative (%)	Indifferent (%)	Positive (%)	Very Positive (%)
Manufacturing	0.00	1.43	1.45	94.34	2.78
Services	0.00	1.37	1.21	94.69	2.73

Fig. 6.7: Respondent Attitudes to the UfI (N=3295)
Source: Matlay & Hyland,1999, forthcoming.

Follow-up questions were then used to identify broad dispositions and intentions to support and invest (though at no specified level) in the UfI (Figs. 6.8 and 6.9).

Size Band	Size Definition	Number of Employees	Time (%)	Effort (%)	Money (%)
A	Micro-Business	1-10	77.54	73.78	68.12
B	Small Business	11-49	81.79	80.06	69.68
C	Medium-Sized	50-250	100.00	100.00	100.00
D	Large Business	251+	100.00	100.00	100.00

Fig. 6.8: Intention to Support the UfI
Source: Matlay & Hyland, 1999, forthcoming.

Size Band	Size Definition	Number of Employees	Manufacturing (%)	Services (%)
A	Micro-Business	1-10	68.32	71.27
B	Small Business	11-49	68.71	73.83
C	Medium-Sized	50-250	85.69	89.55
D	Large Business	251+	100.00	100.00

Fig. 6.9: Intention to Invest in the UfI
Source: Matlay & Hyland, 1999, forthcoming.

Finally, respondents were asked to specify their expectations of the UfI (Fig. 6.10) and responses were analysed in terms of both general and specific information and services required, and also in relation to the most frequently occurring categories.

Services Expected from University for Industry	Manufacturing Sector (N=1130) (%)	Service Sector (N=2165) (%)
1. General Information:		
Business Situation	91.86	92.10
Market Developments	88.58	83.23
Government Policies	86.11	78.57
Economic Trends	86.02	71.09
2. Specific Information on Training:		
Availability of Services	95.31	92.84
Cost of Programmes	73.84	84.62
Needs Evaluation	54.52	41.02
Sources of Finance	51.77	56.49
Skills Audit	47.61	36.81
Budgeting and Planning	31.23	33.90
Investors in People	24.78	34.59
Modern Apprenticeships	19.11	9.38
NVQs/GNVQs	3.54	3.56

Fig. 6.10: Owner-Managers' Expectations of the UfI
Source: Matlay & Hyland, 1999, forthcoming.

The relatively low level of awareness of the UfI initiatives for micro-firms, ranging from 51-58% for firms with less than 50 employees compared with 86-88% for those with up to 250 employees and 100% for large firms, corresponds exactly to what other research studies have reported about the patterns and problems of training in the SME sector. Such findings constitute a direct reinforcement of Hillman's observation about the positive correlation between the size of a firm and its interest (and, correspondingly, its capability/willingness) in investing in training. How, then can the UfI objectives and targets for SMEs be achieved in the face of these difficulties?

Research by Finegold & Irvine (1997) provided a macro-analysis of the well-established and long-standing market failure in this respect. They reported that:

one of the foremost barriers to raising investment in human capital is good information about the supply and demand for skills and the effectiveness of current employment and training programmes (p.124).

They go on to suggest the improvement of networks of information to help companies to identify 'what works at work' (ibid.). Our research tends to confirm Finegold & Irvine's perspective in this field since the most frequently cited expectations of the UfI by SME owner-managers, general information about business/market/economic trends and government policies, plus specific data about services and training programmes based on employer needs and skill audits, are concerned overwhelmingly with just this sort of information.

On the face of it, the supply of such services to SMEs is the UfI's strongest characteristic in the light of the fact that its role will predominantly be as a broker of these very services requested by owner-managers. To achieve the four prioritised objectives mentioned earlier, the UfI will plan to 'analyse the needs of the market and potential customers', 'provide and direct people to information, advice and guidance' and 'ensure the availability of, and connect customers to, high quality learning programmes' (DfEE, 1998c, pp.4-5). All this will be achieved through the learning networks and partnerships described above, and by 'harnessing the unprecedented range and power of technologies available today, from the familiar telephone and television to the newer technologies of the Internet and CD-ROMs' (ibid., p.9).

In terms of the analysis of market conditions and skills needs, there is already in place a very useful infrastructure developed for the DfEE by the Skills and Enterprise Network which provides quarterly labour market reports and regular up-to-date analyses of changing skills needs. What has been added to this under the new Labour adminstration is the establishment of a skills task force which has already published an interim report, *Towards a National Skills Agenda* (Swain, 1998). Recommending a stronger focus on priority skills in national education and training, more emphasis on workplace learning and, in line with the key UfI strategy, a stress on the use of ICT in training, the task force report was followed by a promise by the Secretary of State of a sum of £338 million to finance new projects in the field. Such a skills agenda, however, stands little chance of success unless it takes account of the issues raised in Chapter 4 about the need for workplace learning linked to the real needs of employees and employers (rather than a qualifications-driven agenda) and which also treats seriously Rikowski's 'filter' thesis which brings out the important distinctions between 'capital in general' (national) and 'individual capital' (regional or firm-linked) skill requirements.

Our earlier research confirmed other findings in this field which reported that the costs of training are, not surprisingly, key determinants of its take-up by firms. This factor is even more crucial in the case of SMEs in which, as many commentators have observed, the costs of training are often more apparent than the benefits. The central Ufl claim is that:

> by stimulating new learning markets, and by encouraging partnerships among different sectors, learners and providers, the Ufl will *help bring costs down* and make learning more accessible and affordable (DfEE, 1998c, p.9; original italics).

Whether this claim turns out to be justified is a matter for empirical investigation over the next few years. A promising start has been made, however, in the early work of the newly formed skills taskforce and the recent work of the National Advisory Council for Education and Training Targets (NACETT, 1998).

The Evolution and Development of the New Deal

The first thing to be said is that, if the evaluation of the various New Deal schemes was based on the volume of activity created and the amount of literature relating to this activity, then the scheme might already be judged to be an overwhelming success. Before the launch of the WTW scheme for 18-24 year olds, interviews and workshops were held with young unemployed people to determine their views and attitudes to the general aspects of the initiative. Respondents saw the WTW as a potential alternative to the standard Jobcentre approach which was considered 'impersonal' and treated 'unemployed people as numbers on the list rather than people to find jobs for' (Opinion Leader Research, 1997, p.5). The counselling and guidance features of the WTW Gateway stage were welcomed and viewed as a real opportunity to 'break the circle and establish stepping stones towards sustainable employment' and, of the five options available, 'private sector employment and education options were the most immediately well received' (ibid.).

These preferences seem to have been broadly matched by the actual routes taken by Gateway 'graduates'. In terms of looking at the official take-up figures for the New Deal it is useful and interesting to examine these in the initial and later phases of the first year of the initiatives. Taking the original WTW scheme for 18-24 year olds (only introduced in April 1998) the figures up to July 1998 (Educa, 1998b, pp.4-6) indicate almost 100,000 'starts', including 10,000 disabled young people, and 19,180 entrants had moved on to the following options:

- 13,700 have gone into unsubsidised jobs
- 5,500 have gone into subsidised jobs
- 3,630 have taken up the full-time education and training option
- 1,100 have started work in the voluntary sector
- 950 have joined the Environmental Task force

In addition, 25,000 employers had signed up with the New Deal by September 1998, and special projects for homeless and for unemployed people over 50 had been put in place (ibid.). The scheme has also been extended to older unemployed people and, more recently, a further £80 million has been earmarked to fund college places for any unemployed person, regardless of age and status (THES, 1999a, p.2). In December 1998 Employment Minister, Andrew Smith, declared that the early figures on the New Deal were positive; he commented that:

> It is encouraging that some of the most successful areas have already helped 40% or more young people into jobs after six months...In total, since the New Deal began 38,400 young people have gone into jobs and 22,430 have gone into education and voluntary options. The true cost of the jobs secured so far is currently around £1000 per job (DfEE, 1998k, p.1).

The most recent figures on New Deal take-up (up to the end of November 1998) are listed on page 152 (DfEE, 1999, pp.2-3):

New Deal for Young People

- over 203,000 starts on the programme, 82,600 have left, leaving 120,500 participants at the end of November 1998
- of the 82,600 leavers, 49% have entered unsubsidised jobs, 12% have transferred to other benefits (with 10% leaving for known and 29% for unknown reasons)
- Up to the end of November 1998, nearly 50,000 people have gone into jobs from the Gateway, three-quarters of which were unsubsidised jobs
- 56% of those who have left New Deal having started an option went into unsubsidised jobs. Of those leaving from the Employer Option, 76% entered unsubsidised jobs, compared with 47% of leavers from full-time education and training

New Deal for Long-Term Unemployed (aged 25+)

- 70,900 starts on New Deal by the end of November 1998, 10,700 have left, leaving 60,200 participants
- the vast majority of participants (93%) are in the Advisory Interview Process
- 28% of all leavers from the Advisory process enter jobs, 2,760 unsubsidised and 1,400 subsidised
- 83% of all leavers also leave JSA, 22% for unsubsidised jobs, 18% transfer to other benefits, 7% leave for known and 25% for unknown destinations, 11% for the Employer Subsidy, and 16% for work-based Training for Adults/Training for Work

The New Deal, the UfI and Vocational Studies

Since the New Deal projects and the UfI still have to be fully developed, the ultimate impact on VET and the PCET system will only be known after empirical investigations undertaken in the early years of the new millennium. However, even at this early stage the spate of activity in this sector since the Labour government took office in May 1997 provides fascinating material for analysis and speculation.

The impact of the WTW and related schemes, both in terms of unemployed people progressing through Gateway and at the level of employer interest generated by the sheer volume of activity, is considerable and provides grounds for a modest optimism. Similarly, the early stages of the UfI development, both in terms of learning by individuals and by organisations, indicates that the learning network approach does indeed have much potential. In this area, the *Learning Direct* helpline has been a notable success, both in terms of encouraging people to enquire about learning opportunities and also in terms of advising and directing people towards providers. In its first full year of service the helpline has received over 400,000 calls, over 135,000 of which were about FE college courses, and one in six about HE provision; 18% of callers were unemployed and 46% were in employment (THES, 1999b, p.2). A breakdown of callers interms of age and gender groupings is shown in Fig. 6.11.

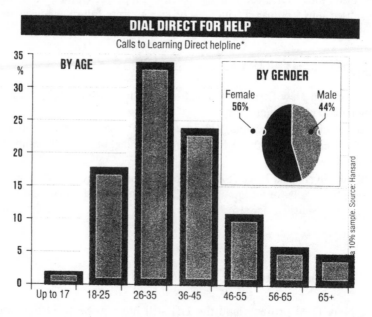

Fig. 6.11: Callers to Learning Direct Helpline
Source: THES, 1999b, p.2.

All such promising and optimistic data, however, will obviously need to be located within a framework in which longer-term plans and the impact on the future development of VET and the PCET sector still have to be determined. At this stage, investigating a system in transition, it could be said that, although New Deal activity is impressive in *quantitative* terms, the *qualitative* implications are less promising. The emphasis on moving people off JSA and into unsubsidised jobs on the WTW projects is clearly an overriding priority and this has more to do with New Labour's policy of welfare reform and short-term relief than it has with the improvement of education and training and the reconstruction of VET.

These macro-political issues will be examined in more detail in the concluding chapter. At this stage, it is necessary to offer a description of the important values dimension of VET against which all reform attempts will ultimately have to be judged and evaluated.

7 Values and Vocational Studies

At various points during the preceding chapters I have been at pains to stress the moral dimension of VET and to link this with the values connected with a social theory of lifelong learning which pays due attention to the needs of all stakeholders in the system. It is now time to spell out this values dimension in more detail in the context of the principal themes and issues already identified and in relation to the alternative models, in the main, those dominated by individualistic, technicist, marketised or overly economistic concerns, which have been criticised for their educational and ethical shortcomings. In conjunction with the recommendations for vocational studies already offered, this values dimension will both complete the critical account of VET I have been developing throughout the book and also provide a framework within which to examine developments over the last couple of years under New Labour.

I will begin by examining ethical aspects of vocational studies specifically before moving on to consider related values questions linked to aspects of VET already mentioned in other contexts such as the nature of guidance and counselling, studentship and learning careers and, on a macro level, concepts of individual autonomy, community ideals and systems for achieving social justice for all stakeholders and interested parties concerned with vocational studies.

Ethical Aspects of Vocational Studies

Alongside the historical legacy of VET characterised by social stratification and subordination to academic pursuits there has been a serious neglect of the ethical foundations of vocationalism. In view of the centrality of the broader vocational aims of much of the educational system, from schooling through to postgraduate education, this neglect of the values components of preparing people for working life is surprising though perhaps not altogether unpredictable (Wall, 1968). There is a sense, after all, in which the inferior status of VET has meant that the moral high ground would always be occupied by academic studies with its links and associations with the classical ideals of liberal education. Vocational education, on the other hand, has always been associated with lower order, working-class pursuits (Lewis, 1991; Coffey, 1992) and is very often considered, as a number of VET writers have tellingly observed (Ainley, 1990), to be typically about 'other people's children'.

It is, perhaps, this background which accounts for the current 'morally impoverished' (Fish, 1993, p.10) state of VET within which various forms of 'moral competence' (Wright, 1989) are recommended largely as a means of ensuring that young people develop the 'qualities and personal skills employers require' (IES, 1996, p.9). In the Dearing review of qualifications for 16 to 19 year olds we are informed that:

> Education means preparing young people for life in the widest sense. As adults they will assume responsibility for the quality of our society and of our civilisation. Spiritual and moral values must therefore be an essential element in education (Dearing, 1996, p.4).

It is entirely typical and symptomatic of the current technicist malaise that this telegraphic prescription is not only effectively left unelaborated but subsequently buried under a mass of recommendations concerned with credit frameworks and mechanisms for creating parity of esteem between different qualifications pathways. If, however, we choose to intrerpret Dearing in a non-rhetorical way, taking seriously the idea that the 'spiritual and moral dimensions should be taken into account and consciously included in the curriculum and programmes for young people' (ibid., p.37), then it seems clear that there are many ways in which the lack of an adequate values dimension in vocational studies can be remedied. Not only will this, I would argue, bring VET into line with a social theory of lifelong learning but should also help to upgrade vocational studies and assist in the process of bringing about that parity of esteem so highly prized and recommended by almost all commentators on the post-compulsory curriculum.

Jarrett (1991) has argued that perhaps the 'single most important goal for a teacher to work towards has to do with the basic attitude towards work' (p.206) and similar sentiments inspire Mary Warnock's philosophy of education in which 'work is, and always must be an ingredient of the good life' such that a 'life without work would always be less good than a life which contained it' (1977, p.144). What is missing from such general accounts is a more precise definition of work and, more specifically, some account of the crucial differences initially picked out by Arendt (1958) between work as creative endeavour and the more mundane sort of paid work associated with labour and toil.

Drawing on Arendt's writings, Herbst (1973) identified a number of educationally and morally significant features of the distinction between work and labour. Although the concepts have much in common, they both consume time and energy and can be done more or less efficiently, work can be identified as having an element of intrinsic value (when the work process is integrally related to its end product) whereas labour essentially has extrinsic or utilitarian value (as it is generally done for purposes beyond itself such as financial reward) and can, therefore, more properly be described as 'toil'. 'Labour is hardship…the price which we pay for whatever advantages the rewards of labour will buy' (Herbst, 1973, p.59). Another way of expressing the key difference is that 'work, unlike labour, must have a point which the workman [sic] can endorse, and a purpose with which he can associate himself' (ibid., p.61).

There are echoes here of Marx's 'philosophy of man' which 'proclaims man (sic) to be the presupposition and the end of all philosophy, all science and all human activity' (Kamenka, 1969, p.15). It is thus the 'alienation' of persons from that most basic and central of all human activities, work, which is so offensive to Marxist ethics founded on on the philosophy of man.   Kamenka (ibid., pp.19-20) outlines four main aspects of the alienation process operating under capitalism:

i) man is alienated from the things he produces and his own labour in producing them;
ii) man is alienated from other men through the competitive character of the economic system based on private property which forces everyone to live at someone else's expense;
iii) man is alienated from nature which does not confront him as a field for the creative exercise of his powers but as a source of difficulty and drudgery; and
iv) man is alienated from society as the expression of social, collective power.

Kamenka summarises the Marxist perspective in this respect:

Alienation, for Marx, then, occurs when man falls into servitude to and dependence upon his own powers or the institutions and goods he has himself created; it is overcome when man makes all his activities free expressions of his nature and full satisfactions of his needs (ibid., p.19).

Rikowski (1999) points to similar de-humanising tendencies in the idea of workers becoming 'trans-human' in the relentless pursuit, through striving to achieve the multi-skilling and flexibility required by post-Fordism, of the means of existence, of capital. As Rikowski explains:

As the capitalisation of humanity deepens and strengthens we become a life-form which increasingly incorporates the contradictions of capital. Capital assumes a number of forms: value, money, commodity, state and other forms. The capitalisation of humanity implies that, as capital, these forms take on real existence within us and within our everyday lives as human-capital (p.2).

White's (1997) philosophical analysis of these issues leads him to broadly similar (though somewhat less pessimistic) conclusions. He begins by noting the difference between 'autonomous work' whose 'end product is chosen as a major goal of an autonomous agent' and 'heteronomous work' whose 'end product is not chosen as a major goal, but is in some way unavoidable or required of one' (pp.5-6). This is illustrated in diagrammatic form in Fig. 7.1.

producing X is NOT CHOSEN as major goal	producing X IS NOT a major goal	work unwillingly engaged in
		work willingly engaged in
	producing X IS a major goal	work unwillingly engaged in
		work willingly engaged in
producing X is CHOSEN as a major goal		

Fig. 7.1: Autonomous and Heteronomous Work Patterns
Source: Based on White, 1997, p.5.

The diagram serves to illustrate that White's analysis, though clearly based upon foundations similar to those used by Arendt, Herbst and also Dahrendhorf's (1982) distinction between 'heronomous work' as human action 'imposed by external needs' and 'activity...which is freely chosen' (p.183), is both subtle and finely nuanced. Whether work is freely chosen or not, the end product may or may not have personal significance for the workers. Such an account also serves to obviate the distinction between paid and unpaid work since a voluntary worker might, conceivably, find no personal significance in a job (say, working in an Oxfam shop) whereas a nurse (who had to engage in paid work for a living) could easily invest in and derive great personal significance from her job. The recreational/vocational dichomoty is also exploded by this analysis (consider the difference between professional golfers or tennis players and golf or tennis enthusiasts) and, less obviously, the constrained/ unconstrained distinction since a voluntary worker could easily feel morally obliged to engage in such work whereas we can imagine a 'journalist with a private income for whom writing articles is a major goal' (ibid., p.49).

However, although there is 'no sharp line' (ibid., p10) between autonomous and heteronomous work in practice, we should think, rather, in terms of a continuum of activities and gradations between the two, White does end up with a reasonably tight definition of autonomous work in the form of the claim that:

> People engage in autonomous work when [a] they are self-directed in the conduct of their lives, and [b] the end-product is something of great significance in their personal vision of how they wish to live (ibid., p.10).

Significantly, however, he goes on to suggest that:

> Very few people in the history of the world, or, indeed, alive today, have been able to engage in much, if any, autonomous work. Nearly all work has been heteronomous. It is something which the worker has been constrained to do for some reason. *Some* heteronomous work, like *all* autonomous work, has been of personal significance to the agent...[but] even personally non-significant work, undertaken, perhaps, simply to earn a living, can be very enjoyable (ibid., p.10, original italics).

White's analysis has been presented in some depth since it has important implications for ethical discussions of vocational studies. It serves to remind us that a part of what Wringe (1991) calls the 'morality of work' consists in the recognition that:

> Work does not have to be sublime or spectacular...to be worthwhile. Many relatively mundane jobs can be challenging and varied, and involve standards of logic, efficiency, integrity, judgement and so on (p.38).

In a similar vein, Green (1968) argues that the 'meaningfulness of a task lies not in the work but in the worker' and that 'some people may find even cosmic significance in a task that, to others, would seem mean and inconsequential' (p.25). Craft skills and the work of artisans are highlighted in Ainley's (1993) study and, arguing along similar lines, Corson (1991) calls for a consideration of work as 'craft...pursued for its own ends...similar to recreational work in having value for its own sake' (p.171). In order to realise such (essentially Deweyan) ideals, Corson suggests a framework for learning, incorporating notions of crafstmanship, which are designed to reinforce the 'values that students see in their work and the significance of that work for themselves and for their society' (ibid., pp.171-172).

In order to ensure that this ethical dimension of VET is embedded in learning programmes, I want to suggest three main spheres in which the values associated with working life sketched above might be incorporated into a critical pedagogy designed to reinforce the principles of guidance, studentship and learning careers referred to below. The values connected with work which seem to be of particular significance for the ethical dimension can be conveniently discussed under the headings of pragmatic, aesthetic and moral.

Pragmatic

In addition to the morality of work, Wringe (1991) also writes about the 'morality of toil and the division of labour'. The first consequence of this perspective is that, since 'toil, regular, serious toil cannot itself be a necessary part of the good life', the 'facts of human existence are such that the preparedness to undertake it may be regarded as a necessary part of a life that is just' (p.40). On this account vocational studies must, therefore, be underpinned with those aspects of general education, such as art, humanities, science, sport and so on, which give meaning to those aspects of life which are not taken up with work or labour.

In addition, if vocational studies is to move beyond what Lee et al.(1990) described as the 'immorality' of the new vocationalism of the 1980s which sold 'unemployment relief as training' (p.195) under the guise of the enterprise label, it will need to incorporate that 'critical pedagogy' which Rikowski (1999) argues for in order to expose the ways in which capitalism can dehumanise working life. This will require critiques of the one-dimensional 'individualism' of the simplistic policies which claim that 'learning pays' for everybody, regardless of social conditions and economic circumstances. Alongside the interpretation of individualism within the context of communitarian and social values (discussed at greater length below) there will be a need to explode the new vocationalist myths which sought to 'juvenalise and personalise' (Stronach, 1990, p.157) the problems of unemployment. The full implications of globalisation and attendant (un)employment patterns will be required to supplement the typically bland and uncritical goals of fostering a 'positive interest in economic activity' and 'understanding the importance of competition' (NCC, 1992, p.2) amongst students.

A critical pedagogy would also need to examine the nature of post-Fordist working conditions including the critical exploration of rights, benefits and entitlements in relation to work and employment. In addition to examining the nature of work and employment on a global scale, including new definitions of work and emerging patterns of flexible employment (RSA, 1998), this pragmatic dimension should seek to provide students with the wherewithal to interrogate and, if need be, resist some of the harmful effects of commodification and globalisation. In a critical examination of the impact of McDonaldisation on youth culture, Miles (1998) makes the intriguing suggestion that:

> rationalised forms of consumption are actively used by young people as a means of adjusting to the fluidity of everyday life, of giving such fluidity a constant, though adaptable, focus…The everyday reality that stems from the consuming experience is not one of being controlled, but of being *in* control (64, original italics).

What Miles gains in optimism with this perspective is, arguably, lost in wildly utopian idealism. McDonaldisation and similar mass commod-ification processes work by subverting the rational and critical faculties of consumers. If we were all as critical as Miles assumes young people to be, the McDonald corporation and other global companies would be in serious trouble. Sadly, the standardisation of consumer fashion points to slavish obedience rather than critical subversion. In a telling comment, Miles observes:

> In one sense, Ritzer's analysis is correct in that the relationships that young people have with the goods they purchase illustrate they they are essentially modernists...who pick out what they feel is appropriate in their given circumstances. What is often appropriate is often also McDonaldised, and if as a consequence young consumers are happier and more stable, then who is Ritzer to argue otherwise? (ibid., pp.64-5).

This perspective is, not merely outstandingly naïve, but also has a pathetically hollow ring when we observe the ways in which the powerful mass advertising of everything from designer trainers to the latest blockbuster movie, described by some commentators as a general dumbing down in the hegemonic 'McMass society' (Parker, 1998, p.11), provokes a manic and hysterical following in young people. In any case, if we were concerned only with making people happy and stable (given that we could ever agree about what this means) all manner of conditioning and indoctrinatory activity might be justified. In processes of education and training, however, it is necessary to balance the values of happiness against other values such as those connected with knowledge, rationality and social justice (Dearden, 1972).

Rikowski (1999) is nearer to the critical nature of the educational task in this sphere when he describes how 'living contradictions' emerge as 'we become a life-form invaded by the alien force' (p.2) of capital and its various constraints and demands. Such contradictions, however, contain both the means and goals of a critical pedagogy aimed at providing a humanistic framwork for working life. Rikowski explains that, as trans-human, capitalised life-forms:

> our consciousness does indeed become subordinated, but always *open* and never *entirely determined*. This is because our fragmented existences and contradictory lives force us to think through, to live and work through, the contradictions, tensions, dilemmas and *conflicts* generated by capital as a conglomeration of contradictory drives and forces (ibid., p.5, original italics).

When we think these contradictions, as and through:

> ourselves as capital, it is only then that capital reflects itself as consciousness of itself in the forms that it has invaded and incorporated the human. It is through this process that capital exposes and uncovers itself within us as *it thinks itself through us*. At this moment, it reveals its weaknesses (ibid., original italics).

Expressed in more down-to-earth terms, if we are to achieve the ideals of a critical pedagogy in VET nothing has to be taken as given. Concepts of globalisation (discussed in more detail in the next chapter), post-Fordist organisation, education and skills training, and all aspects of working life have to be analysed carefully, from *more than one perspective*. Such a critical investigation will include the consideration of growing inequalities both within nations (the growing gap between 'haves and have-nots' in Britain and other industrial nations; Atkinson, 1996) and between states in the northern and southern hemispheres (Fisher & Hicks, 1985), the massive ecological consequences of global economic developments (Hutchinson, 1996) and, very important in current 'third way' politics, the ways in which the pressures of globalisation serve to 'deepen processes of social exclusion' (Giddens, 1998, p.124). In short, a critical vocational studies programme will examine *alternatives* to all aspects of current economic arrangements and working conditions, including the fundamental ideas implicit in so-called 'free market' economics. Unfettered markets contain profoundly 'irrational' (Smith, 1996) tendencies from both an ethical and a pragmatic point of view, and what Ormerod (1994) describes as a 'new economics' might usefully point out that:

> Economic success can be achieved, and achieved more successfully, within a broader and more beneficial framework than that driven by the pure individual rationality of the economics textbooks...The power of markets needs to be harnessed to the wider benefit of society (pp.204-5).

In terms of a moral and political critique of unfettered markets, 'third way' compatibilism can be bolstered by an existing and long-standing body of work in moral and political philosophy which incorporates cogent challenges to any unqualified and naïve attachment to free market capitalism. The 'prisoner's dilemma' scenario (Jonathan, 1997) used extensively in macro-policy and decision-making on the distribution of public welfare and goods, demonstrates convincingly that co-operation and collaboration between members of society produces greater and longer-lasting benefits than do the activities of rational, self-interested people acting only as self-regarding individuals.   Hence the stress on partnership and state regulation in 'third way' and social democratic politics.   In addition to all this, there is also the powerful tradition surrounding the social contract arguments advanced in Rawls' (1972) theory of justice which, in arguing what sort of society rational, self-interested people *would* choose if they were situated behind a veil of ignorance which hid from them their future relative position in society, presents a forceful, rational, logical and pragmatic (as well as an overridingly *moral)* case for communities which are characterised by high degrees of social justice, liberalism and a broadly equitable distribution of public goods and services.

Aesthetic

Norman (1983) comes close to identifying the aesthetic dimension of work when, using Marxian concepts, he writes of 'unalienated' work as 'meaningful, creative and self-expressive' which 'gives an individual a sense of his or her identity, recognised and confirmed by others' (p.175). Warnock (1977) points to cognate features of work in her idea that 'all work is effort to make or change things and reduce them to order, and all these efforts are worth making' (p.145).   Similar sentiments connected with notions of craft and artisanship were noted in Chapter 3 and connect with Jarrett's (1991) exploration of the moral character of dispositions and attitudes to work in relation to the Buddhist concept of 'mindfulness'. Defined by Snelling (1987) as a state of mind which 'sharpens and intensifies our powers of direct perception' and 'enables us to stand back from the the ongoing drama of our lives and take an objective look at the habit patterns in which we are caught' (pp.61, 67), this quality of mindfulness serves to illuminate just those feaures of work and craft connected with the aesthetic dimension.

Such features are captured in the idea of the 'gift of art' which may lead to an 'inner transformation, or deepening of the sense of life through apprehending the work's meaning' (Papanoutsos, 1988, p.93).   Nowhere is this idea more powerfully expressed than in Pirsig's (1974) *Zen and the Art of Motorcycle Maintenance* in which the writer connects notions of work and engineering craft with aesthetics and Buddhist perspectives. Describing the reflections of the motorcyclist on the beauty of the engineering which enables his machine to operate, Pirsig writes:

> Precision instruments are designed to achieve an idea; dimensional precision whose perfection is impossible. There is no perfectly shaped part of the motorcyle and never will be, but when you come as close as these instruments take you, remarkable things happen, and you go flying across the countryside under a power that would be called magic if it were not so completely rational...I look at the shapes of the steel now and I see *ideas*...I'm working on *concepts* (p.102, original italics).

It seems to be in literature and poetry where this aesthetic dimension of work and craft is provided with its fullest and most illuminating sense and meaning. Seamus Heaney's poems are instructive is this respect; in *Follower* the poet recalls his father at work ploughing fields:

> His shoulders globed like a full sail strung
> Between the shafts and the furrow.
> The horses strained at his clicking tongue.
> An expert. He would set the wing
> And fit the bright steel-pointed sock.
> The sod rolled over without breaking.

And again in *Thatcher* we read:

> Bespoke for weeks, he turned up some morning
> Unexpectedly, his bicycle slung
> With a light ladder and a bag of knives...
> He shaved and flushed the butts, stitched all together
> Into a shaped honeycomb, a stubble patch,
> And left them gaping at his Midas touch.
>
> (Heaney, 1990, pp. 6, 10).

Of course it is likely that most work, namely that which is more properly described as labour or toil, will never possess such qualities, but the possibilities inherent in this aesthetic dimension are still worth pointing out.   Speaking of the autonomous nature of work, White (1997) alludes to the Aristotelian idea of learning principles through habit and practice; for example, just as 'men become builders by building and lyre-players by playing the lyre...so we also become autonomous by doing autonomous acts' (p.114). We could add to this that we learn about the aesthetic and craftlike features of work by taking note of them and, following Dewey's recommendations, seeking to realise them in everyday occupations.

The sheer joy of useful, productive and careful work is nowhere better described than in Primo Levi's novel *The Wrench* (1988) in which the central character, Faussone, relates stories of his work as a rigger on construction sites. One of Faussone's workmates reflects:

> We agreed then on the good things we had in common. On the advantage of being able to test yourself, not depending on others in the test, reflecting yourself in your work. On the pleasure of seeing your creature grow, beam after beam, bolt after bolt, solid, necessary, symmetrical, suited to its purpose; and when it's finished you look at it and you think that perhaps it will live longer than you, and perhaps it will be of some use to someone you don't know, who doesn't know you (p.53).

Even though we must take account of the realistic view that, as Wringe (1991) observes, many kinds of work are 'not constitutive of the good life and are at best a necessary evil' (p.37) and, moreover, the research indicates that school pupils are often acutely aware of these basic facts of working life (Willis, 1977; Shilling, 1989), I would still want to argue that a VET programme which did not include the aesthetic dimension would be sadly incomplete. Along with new emphases on citizenship, the importance of this creative and imaginative dimension of learning is now being recognised in discussions about changes to the National Curriculum (Robinson, 1998) and, as Dewey argued almost a century ago, nowhere is this creative perspective needed more than in the area of vocational pursuits.

Moral

The moral dimension of VET will explore issues which follow logically from those aspects of working life identified above. Indeed, it could be said that if the pragmatic and aesthetic ideals and goals of VET are realised then the moral legitimation will naturally follow. There are certain moral principles, Trusted (1987) identifies these as 'trust and benovolence' and other moral philosophers prefer 'social justice' (Rawls, 1972) or the 'equal consideration of interests' (Singer, 1982), which become the 'working principles of a society' (Trusted, 1987, p.114) in that, without them, it is difficult to see how any society could function. Thus, a certain level of truth-telling, trust in others and concern for the interests of others is indispensable to the operation of any organisation or social grouping whether this group is assembled for economic or non-economic purposes (MacIntyre, 1981). Indeed, during the period of rampant individualism in the 1980s 'enterprise culture' (Heelas & Morris, 1992), these basic moral facts had a tendency to be overlooked, ultimately to the detriment of all members of society.

The values of the enterprise culture were naïve in supposing that the 'history of Western civilization is the history of free individuals engaged in intellectual thought' (Shirley, 1991, p.154). The idea of the 'unencumbered self' (Sandel, 1992) is largely fictitious since, as the later discussion of communitarianism will suggest, there is a sense in which all human agency has to be rooted in and realised through networks of social values and practices. Individual and personal development of all kinds, particularly the social and moral which educators are typically charged with fostering (Downey & Kelly, 1978), is inevitably and inextricably located within societal and communitarian networks.

Indeed, as Poole (1990) explains, the market itself could not function without the existence of social and moral values which are themselves non-market and certainly far from individualistic. A market consisting of purely self-interested individuals could not logically reproduce itself since, for reproduction of the system to happen:

> it would require that purely self-interested individuals enter into a relationship with each other in order to produce, nurture and care for other self-interested individuals just like themselves. To make sense of the apparent sacrifices of self-interest involved here we would at the very least have to assume the existence of goods of a quite different kind to those involved in ordinary market transactions (pp.49-50).

The operation of markets, therefore, is entirely dependent upon the inculcation of non-market values of a disinterested, other-regarding kind. In short, it requires the fostering of values which education, as Ranson (1998a) rightly argues, is typically asked to transmit, namely, such virtues as honesty, respect for persons and good citizenship. This is why Jonathan (1997), argues that markets are inappropriate in education since 'in any open society the *social practice we call education must represent the limiting case of the free market'* (p.6, original italics).

Guidance and Counselling

One of the consequences of the massive expansion of the post-school sector in recent years has been a sharp increase in the number of 16-year olds staying on in education beyond the compulsory stage, with numbers reaching an all-time high of almost 400,000 full-time students in 1994/95 (Higham, Sharp & Yeomans, 1996). Expanding the post-16 catchment in this way has meant that more and more young people who in former times would have left school at 16 or taken up youth training are now in full-time education (as noted in the last chapter the full-time education and training option has proved the most popular WTW post-Gateway route). As a direct result of this exapansion, there is now a correspondingly expanded group of students, mainly in FE colleges, who have no formal qualifications and who possess below-average literacy and numeracy skills (Harris & Hyland, 1995; DfEE, 1998a).

As a way of dealing with this new cohort of students in the post-16 sector, various forms of support and guidance services have been developed. There is a sense in which the FE sector, in its traditional role of offering 'second chance' routes to people who had been failed by the school system, already had a history of learning support and an emphasis on student tracking in the sense of providing for the monitoring, diagnosis of problems and support and counselling of students (FEU, 1993). Further impetus to such developments was provided by the post-incorporation funding formula for the sector which allocated finances to institutions on the basis of three distinct stages in students' learning programmes: entry, on programme and completion (FEFC, 1993). This 'increased emphasis on the student's initial assessment and guidance', particularly in terms of 'programme completion' and 'qualification achievement' (FEFCc, 1994, p.4), thus makes it paramount that learners enrolled on FE courses are given all the support they need in order to achieve success in terms of acknowledged qualifications.

Research evidence on student drop-out from (or non-completion of) courses, however, suggests that the post-school sector still has some way to go before it achieves the 'inclusiveness' recommended in the Kennedy report and by the Tomlinson committee (Tomlinson, 1996) which investigated the provision for students with learning disabilities in the colleges. A report by the Audit Commission in 1993 indicated that around 150,000 young people aged between 16 and 19 were leaving schools and colleges without achieving the qualifications they were registered for (Audit Commission/HMI, 1993). More recently, research on the progress of GNVQs, now a mainstream post-16 route for academically average and below-average youngsters, found that the new qualification had unacceptably high drop-out rates and failed to provide links with employment and higher education (Russell, 1997). Recent FEFC figures reveal that, although student numbers in FE grew by 16% between 1994 and 1996, drop-out rates also increased to 18% for full-time students and 16% for part-timers (Thomson, 1997).

Since further education is traditionally associated with providing second chances for people failed by the compulsory system, it is clearly ethically unacceptable to allow those opportunities to be squandered through wastage and drop-out at the post-compulsory stage. Current lifelong learning policies envisage an increase of around 500,000 new post-school learners by 2002, 420,000 of these in the FE sector (DfEE, 1998a; subsequently expanded to an extra 700,000 by 2001/2; Thomson, 1998), and the FEFC Chief Executive has indicated a full awareness of and determination to tackle the causes of student drop-out in the sector (Nash, 1997c). As the key role of the Gateway stage of the WTW scheme has demonstrated, the role of guidance and counselling is crucial to success in this sphere. Thus, the growth of student guidance and counselling services in FE in recent times (Jones, 1997) is, in quantitative terms, at least, to be welcomed. When it comes to the quality of such support services, however, there is rather more cause for concern since recent evidence suggests that the failure to provide impartial and student-centred guidance might be a principal cause of high drop-out, non-completion and failure rates in this area. Recent work by the Further Education Development Agency (Baty, 1998a) identified the failure to give impartial and realistic advice to students as a primary cause of the unacceptably high drop-out and failure rates as a consequence of piling students onto the wrong courses in FE simply to achieve enrolment quotas.

Problems and difficulties concerned with achieving impartiality and genuinely neutral, student-centred guidance were created by the new centralised control over FE following the incorporation of colleges in 1993 and, most significantly, by the overriding 'commitment to a market ideology' (Cantor, Roberts & Pratley, 1995, p.13) which has dominated and unduly manipulated post-compulsory policy and practice in recent times. In the new marketised and 'McDonaldised' FE sector learners, until relatively recently, have been encouraged, by means of glossy college brochures, smart cards and credits to purchase programmes (Avis et al., 1996), to think of themselves as self-interested consumers shopping for educational commodities (mainly NVQs and GNVQs) in the FE supermarket (Reeves, 1995; Hyland, 1998b).

Such a system, reinforced by the new funding mechanisms, resulted in the immediate post-incorporation years in a squalid scramble for students by colleges and schools which reached such levels of irrationality that the former FEFC Chief Executive felt the need to warn institutions against 'predatory trading' and 'corporate actions which may be legal but unacceptable' (Nash, 1995, p.1). Against this background of suspicion and unhealthy competition between post-16 institutions the idea of impartial guidance services was distorted in a desperate bid to boost student numbers at any cost. As Nicholls (1995) observed, whereas in former times the local education authority had a duty of service, open to public scrutiny, to ensure that each student had access to the best possible advice, post-incorporation competition had caused individual needs to be overlooked. He went on to pose the emotive question of whether 'the development of free market competition was being paid for by the life chances of young people' (p.20).

Fortunately, recent developments in the sector (following the Kennedy report and the DfEE response in the form of a new policy document for FE; DfEE, 1998f, which will be examined in greater depth in the final chapter) the folly and potential waste of unbridled competition has been acknowledged. There is now a realisation, in the words of the FEFC Chief Inspector, that 'more effective co-operation between schools and colleges over guidance is needed to ensure that 16 to 19 year olds are aware of the full range of options open to them' (Jones, 1997, p.23). The FEFC now requires college support and guidance services to satisfy certain auditable criteria which include 'the implications of choice of learning programme' and an 'assessment of the suitability of the learning programme' (Reisenberger, Hughes & Green, 1994, p.35) for each and every student admitted to a post-16 institution.

More significantly, within the framework of national efforts to achieve lifelong learning targets, student advice and counselling services are being given a much higher profile, and new concepts of guidance have emerged in recent years which emphasise that:

> Advice and guidance services are services to help people to become more aware of their education and training needs; to supply them with information about the choices open to them; to help them develop the skills to enable them to make the right decisions about their career; and to help them to decide their best course of action (Ball, 1995, p.12).

The Kennedy (1997) report went even further in its call for a 'national entitlement to information, advice and guidance' for all post-16 learners, and its stress on the need for impartial and 'specialised careers education and guidance' to 'help learners plan their long-term career pathway' (pp.89, 91). The official DfEE response to Kennedy acknowledges past weaknesses and promises to implement measures to 'ensure that all learners have easy access to information' so as to 'promote young people's entitlement to post-16 learning' (DfEE, 1998f, p.19).

Studentship and Learning Careers

Central to the emerging concept of guidance and counselling outlined above is the notion of a long-term and ongoing process through which students are enabled to gain, experientially and incrementally, greater self-awareness, self-confidence and decision-making capabilities in connection with their learning careers, personal development and working lives. In order to realise such goals against the background of the reconstructed model of VET, and particularly in the light of the moral dimension linked to a social conception of lifelong learning described earlier, models of student learning based on 'careership' (Hodkinson, 1996) and emphasising empowerment and learner autonomy will need to be implemented in the post-school sector. The concept of 'studentship' with its emphasis on the processes and features of learning characteristic of the 'deep' approaches (referred to in Chapter 3) and of the experiential tradition (Kolb, 1993) can help to facilitate good practice in this sphere.

Interpreting the idea of studentship in its most comprehensive sense, Bloomer (1996) employs the term to refer to 'the variety of ways in which students can exert influence over the curriculum in the creation and confirmation of their own learning careers' (p.140). Drawing on theories of social and humanistic learning, Bloomer (1997) goes on to elaborate, using case studies drawn from the post-school sector, this concept in terms of 'acting upon...learning opportunities in creation of their descriptive curricula and their learning' (p.137). In line with the situated cognition notions discussed in Chapter 3, Bloomer emphasises the importance of the social context of learning, incorporating also the 'strong relationship between students' views of knowledge and their preferences for particular learning activities' (ibid., p.147), in developing processes of studentship which take into account learners' dispositions to knowledge and action which are required to foster growth, personal identity and development.

Against this background the concept of a learning career is presented, not in terms of the narrow occupationalism that has been criticised in relation to CBET approaches, but as 'an intrepretive schema, linked not purely to a single domain of human activity but to *life* and to whatever impinges significantly upon that life in the experience of the interpreter' (ibid., p.149, original italics). In offering more detailed descriptions of the central careership concept, Bloomer, in an account which is remarkably similar to the rich and deep Deweyan concept of vocationalism outlined earlier in the chapter, explains that the idea of a learner career:

> allows for the incorporation of both objectively and subjectively defined experience; it has the capacity for describing,in both objective and subjective senses, continuity and transformation in learning by relating the present to both past and future; as subjectively experienced, it is about 'life as a whole' and, thus, it is not bound to include or exclude experiences from one sphere of human activity more than those from any other; and, certainly, it is not limited to the insights afforded by any single discipline perspective (ibid., p.149).

Such a conception, in addition to supporting the idea of a unified post-school curriculum and a broad educational foundation for vocational studies already recommended in earlier chapters, moves us beyond the technical rationality of the McDonaldised educational commodity market, to a more pragmatic rationality which foregrounds students own experiences of learning, work and life. As Bloomer puts it, the learning career conception:

places studentship, learning and personal development in a dynamic, mutually constitutive relationship...it also links, dynamically, the formation of personal identity and dispositions to the transformation of social, moral, economic and other conditions...It thus has the potential to yield not simply the knowledge *that* young people 'act upon' learning opportunities in the way that they do through their studentship but to generate an understanding of *why* they do (ibid., p.154, original italics).

Espousing a broadly similar approach to learning and drawing on the work of Habermas and Giddens, Hodkinson (1996) has explained the mechanisms of the present post-16 training market, based on training credits and (nominally) individualised self-interested choices of pathways for students, in terms of a system characterised by 'technical rationality' by which the 'decision-making process is seen as a production line along which the young person progresses, completing the decision stage by stage' (p.124). The technicist assumptions of the McDonaldised training supermarket are laid bare in Hodkinson's account and revealed as woefully inadequate when appled to the real-life opportunities and contexts within which youngsters have to operate in relation to education, work and training. His research on the actual operation of the training credit system demonstrated clearly that the choices and decision-making processes actually adopted by youngsters were radically at odds with the technical-rational model. In real-life contexts, as against those hypothesised by the DfEE, TECs and the Employment Service, choices and judgements were influenced by a whole range of diverse factors such as local contacts, work experience, family and peer influences and the general milieux of groups and cultures which impact upon and shape the lives of young people.

Such a combination of factors and influences leads naturally to decision-making processes which are, neither technically rational nor irrational but, in Hodkinson's terms, 'pragmatically rational' in the sense that judgements are 'embedded in the complex struggles and negotiations of the training field' (1996, p.133). Faced with a welter of competing forces and influences, the vicissitudes of government policy, the complex rules of the employment services, local industrial needs and job openings, the quality of careers and guidance services, and the pressures exerted by friends and family, it is surprising that young people are able to make any sort of rational decisions at all. Yet, as Hodkinson & Sparkes' case studies illustrate vividly, youngsters do, indeed, make pragamatic judgments about their futures based on the:

partial information which is localised...on the familiar and the known. The decision-making is context-related, and cannot be separated from family background, culture and life histories of the pupils.   The decisions are opportunistic, being based on fortuitous contacts and experiences.   The timing of the decisions is sporadic, in that decisions are made when the pupil feels able to do so and are reactions to opportunities as they are encountered (Hodkinson & Sparkes, 1993, p.250).

Such a model of real-world choice and agency in the face of complex alternatives and pressures represents a far more accurate picture and source of information than the technical-rational approach with which to inform and structure VET and careers and guidance policies and processes. Moreover, by acknowledging the legitimacy of students' developing knowledge, values, identity and pragmatic judgements, such a model is far more likely to meet the criteria of autonomy, empowerment and progression which are implicit in current conceptions of lifelong learning (Ranson, 1994, 1998).

Individual and Community in the Learning Age

The critique of individualism referred to above leads directly to a consideration and re-appraisal of the ethical foundations of vocational studies and lifelong learning.   The precise ways in which these fundamental ethical notions are reflected in and serve to inform current education and training policies under New Labour will be discussed in the final chapter.   At this stage it is worth noting that, alongside the maintenance of the essentially economistic interpretations of learning from the former Conservative to the present Labour education policies (though, importantly, the latter are supplemented by broader concepts of VET linked to expanded access and social inclusion goals),   the emphasis on individualism remains.   Thus, in justifying the new 'individual learning accounts', the Secretary of State cites their potential in 'giving the individual more say and greater responsibility over their own skills development' (Blunkett, 1998, p.18).   Of course, individual rights and entitlements to education and training must be balanced against duties, but this excessive concentration on the responsibilities of learners to manage (and in the case of many students, to finance) their own learning is, not just potentially coercive and authoritarian (Tight, 1998a; Strain, 1998), but also fails to take account of the 'social context of learning' and the 'social arrangements of resources, opportunities and culture which foster or impede learning' (Coffield, 1998, p.26).

At one level, of course, a concentration on the individual in education and training aims and goals is both appropriate and necessary. It is, after all, individuals who are the basic units of the learning society, and a morally justifiable programme will necessarily stress individual rights and the importance of individual autonomy in learning. However, without attention to the social dimension of learning, what Smail calls the 'public space' (1993) essential to the health of all democratic societies, the individualist emphasis can lead to seriously midguided and damaging conceptions of education, training, and social and working life. The extent of such damage, and the tensions and contradictions that excessive individualism can lead to, can be appreciated simply by recalling that the whole educational system can in a sense be regarded as representing the 'enduring and powerful forces of a whole society socializing its members' (Meighan, 1981, p.62). Such socialisation, by definition, involves some degree of subordination of individual interests in favour of the collective good (Jonathan, 1997).

Many years ago Hargreaves (1982) criticised the schooling system in Britain on the grounds that it was 'deeply imbued with a culture of individualism' (p.87). He went on to identify the main fault as being 'not in the humanistic sentiments and ideals which it enshrines' but in the 'repudiation of the nineteenth-century concerns with the social functions of education'. For Hargreaves the solution to the 'most pressing problems of our society' is to be found in the fostering of 'active community participation from its members' (ibid., p.135). In a similar vein, Langford (1985) has attacked the obsession 'with the difference which being educated makes to an individual' (p.3) and recommended instead a greater concern with the social dimensions of education and schooling. For Langford, to 'become educated is to become a member of society and so to have learnt what it is to be and live as a member of that society' (ibid., p.181).

The roots of individualism, along with the explanation of its persuasiveness as a general doctrine, were traced by Bertrand Russell (1946, Chap.XII) to the Greek Stoics and Cynics down through the medieval Christian tradition until the ideas found their fullest expression in the work of Descartes which itself provided a major source for the development of political and economic liberalism in the 16th and 17th centuries. Within the liberal tradition, individualistic notions went hand in hand with the growth of capitalist mercantilism and, in political theory, the basic concepts date back at least as far as Hobbes and Locke and are encapsulated in the idea of what Macpherson (1964) called 'possessive individualism' which asserts that the 'individual is the essentially the proprietor of his own person, and capacities, for which he owes nothing to society' (p.263). The obvious attractiveness, derived from the superficial self-evidential nature of their expression, of such ideas explains their enduring centrality in moral, social, economic, political and educational theories.

Within educational theory individualism finds its expression in notions of autonomous , independent and self-directed learning to which, on one level, nobody could possibly object. Once we get behind the superficial veneer of attractiveness, however, we can begin to see how such vague and nebulous concepts as autonomy and independence are meaningless until they are located within a social dimension. As Dearden (1972) has argued, by valuing freedom, autonomy and individual development in education, we do not thereby 'mark the eclipse of such other values as truth and morality' (p.461). Similarly, Lawson (1998), in qualifying the extremism of 'andragogical practices' in adult education which result in misguided attempts to abolish all teaching and guidance in favour of independent student learning, points to the weaknesses and dangers of 'deontological liberalism'. Eschewing all content in favour of process, such a philosophy is 'suited to a society which has no vision' and 'produces societies which no longer debate or seek the good' (p.41).

In his investigation of autonomy within the framework of political and citizenship education, Smith (1997) observes how, particularly in developed industrial societies, 'autonomy typically works alongside notions of choice and the market, separating individual persons from their world and from their fellows, the better to render them subject to control' (p.128). Alluding to processes paralleled by the McDonaldised world discussed earlier in the chapter which result in what Rikowski (1999) calls 'capitalised trans-human life forms', Smith argues that such facile conceptions of 'autonomy' now threaten:

> in the name of freedom, to re-shape the emotional lives and identities of young people especially, alienating them from the aesthetic and reflective modes of being in favour of slick versions of evaluation...Thus autonomy has

become a dangerous ally. Offering; like the goblin in the fairy-tale, to turn the straw of our determined, contingent world into the gold of pure freedom, it theatens in the end to come back and claim the children it promised to save (ibid., p.128).

Against such excesses, Smith, drawing on the work of MacIntyre (1981) and Marcuse (1964), points to theories of politics, morality and education which forground 'our increasing sense of the importance of involving others' in all of life's transactions. In conclusion, he recommends that:

> Autonomy, then, should not be thought of in terms of an essentially individualistic journey towards an abstract and determinate rationality, but as a process involving other people in which reasons are demanded and given in dialectic. And if autonomy means having a degree of control over our lives, then we have to help each other understand the ways in which power is taken from us and exercised over us (1997, p.134).

In similar vein, Jonathan (1997) alludes to the 'illusory freedoms' of market individualism in education, arguing that the 'distribution of education is a matter for public action' on the grounds that such distribution 'reflects and modifies public judgements of worth' (p.215). Such public/collective as opposed to the private/individualistic conceptions of the educational task, which are embedded in and realised through the social conceptions of lifelong learning discussed in earlier chapters in looking at the work of Ranson (1994, 1998) and Edwards (1997), derive much of their meaning from the revival of 'communitarian' philosophies in public discourse about education and society.

Within academic circles 'communitarianism' developed out of the debate, stimulated by the work of Rawls and Nozick, about the limits of political liberalism in modern states (Sandel, 1992; discussed extensively by Jonathan, 1997). The emphasis on liberalism, the 'deontological liberalism' and 'rights theory' criticised by Lawson (1998) which was referred to earlier, resulted in the view that individuals have the right to choose and pursue their own ends and values and that the state merely provides a neutral framework which allows members of society to make such choices. Such conceptions directly parallel the 'possessive individualism' of the economic market which is based on the belief that 'all human behaviour is conditioned by the hedonistic aspirations of each individual wanting to maximize his/her productive capacities' (Shirley, 1991, p.154).

In addition to the arguments against individualism mentioned already, not least the fact that economic individualism is parasitic upon non-individualistic social values, communitarians stress the social context of rights, duties, interests, values and all aspects of human agency. As Arthur (1998) puts it, whereas liberalism is the 'politics of rights ...communitarianism is the politics of the common good' (p.356). Arthur goes on to trace the development of 'popular communitarianism' in the writings of Etzioni (1995, 1997) which established an agenda founded on the belief that:

> Neither human existence nor individual liberty can be sustained for long outside the interdependent and overlapping communities to which we all belong. Nor can any community long survive unless its members dedicate some of their attention, energy and resources to shared projects. The exclusive pursuit of private interest erodes the network of social environments on which we all depend, and is destructive to our shared experiment in democratic self-government. For these reasons we hold that the right of individuals cannot long be preserved without a communitarian perspective [which]...recognises both individual human dignity and the social dimension of human existence (Arthur, 1998, pp.358-9).

I would argue that, not only are such communitarian ideas crucial to the 'third way' social democratic response to globalisation and new social transformations described by Giddens (1998), but they also provide an ethical foundation for the positive constructions of the learning society and lifelong learning outlined in Chapter 1 and discussed thoughout the book. In response to Rikowski's (1998a) argument that the debate on the learning society is 'idealist educational discourse' which results in the idea of lifelong learning which is an 'ungrounded abstraction' (pp.223, 227), I would suggest that a communitarian ethics, linked to the general values framework for VET described above, can, at the very least, begin the urgent and necessary process of locating vocational studies within the material and concrete realities of contemporary working life and social conditions.

8 Lifelong Learning and New Deal Values in the Learning Age

As a way of bringing together all the various arguments, developments and strands of thought discussed throughout the previous chapters, I want to try to deal with two key questions which, though fairly easy to formulate, are rather more complicated and difficult to answer.

1. How can developments in post-school VET since 1997 be characterised in terms of political, social and moral values? In other words, what particular form of learning society is current lifelong learning policy likely to achieve?
2. Is the emergent system of post-school education and training likely to enhance and foster the model of vocational studies, including the important values foundation, advanced throughout this book?

Subordinate questions related to these principal themes might seek to speculate about how any shortcomings in current policy and practice, in terms of an enhanced national VET system, might be remedied.

New Deal Education and Training in the Learning Age

In a recent collection of articles and readings on contemporary VET in the UK, Esland, Flude & Sieminski (1999) observe, in relation to the 'main parameters of policy for the Labour government after it took office in May 1997', that:

> Although there have been changes of emphasis and priority, and some alleviation of the more extreme right-wing elements of employment policy, the neo-liberal promotion of free market economic globalization has continued to

provide the overrarching framework for Britain's political economy as it enters the new millennium (pp.1-2).

I would broadly endorse this analysis, though I would perhaps want to allow for more substantive and potentially far-reaching policy shifts in terms of VET and *lifelong learning programmes*, as opposed to overall *economic policy*, than Esland and his co-writers seem to want to permit.

Although New Labour's lifelong learning policies have already been characterised in terms of maintaining a fairly high degrèe of continuity with the former Conservative adminstration's commitment to individualism and an economistic interpretation of education and training, it is also important to mark some differences in the overall values orientation which are neither superficial nor simply a result of presentational style. To begin with, it would be useful to re-examine the main developments in terms of the typologies of the learning society outlined in the first chapter.

Although Young (1998) is surely correct in characterising the learning society as a 'contested concept' (p.193), it is also true that there is now both sufficient policy development and policy analysis on lifelong learning to delimit discussions to a number of key strategies and models. It would be useful to offer brief summaries of the 'leading contestants' in the field.

1.Edwards' Typology (1997, pp.175-184):
a) An educated society
b) A learning market
c) Learning networks which allow people to pursue heterogeneous goals

2.Young's Typology (1998, pp.194-199):
a) Schooling model
b) Credentialist model
c) Access model

[+ d) An educative model, favoured by Young]

3. Ranson's Typology (1998, pp.2-10):
a) A society which learns about itself and how it is changing
b) A society which needs to change the way it learns
c) A society in which all its members are learning
d) A society which needs to democratically change the way it learns

In addition, there are, of course, the more basic liberal/economistic versions, and also the debate about the 'mythical' or 'idealist' nature of the learning society, but, arguably, the three typologies outlined above encompass and encapsulate these subsidiary debates.

At first glance, there appears to be more than enough evidence in the form of official policy and DfEE *Learning Age* documents to offer a general characterisation of New Labour's version of lifelong learning and related education and training. The economistic interpretation of learning and its individualistic emphasis runs throughout the official versions. Thus, in the Secretary of State's introduction to the *UfI Pathfinder Prospectus* (DfEE, 1998c) we are told that 'learning is the key to individual employability and business competitiveness' (p.1). This neatly encapsulates both planks of official policy as does the reference in the principal *Learning Age* document to 'learning as the key to prosperity, for each of us as individuals, as well as for the nation as a whole' (DfEE, 1998a, p.7). The document then moves on to rehearse the familiar arguments about investment in human capital, the 'knowledge-based global economy of the twenty-first century', and the need for a 'well-equipped and adaptable labour force' before instructing us that 'we must all develop and sustain a regard for learning at whatever age' (ibid.).

Thus far, and at the level of avowed policy, this fairly simplistic account can be classified in terms of Edwards' 1.b, p.180, learning for economic competitiveness, Young's 2.b, p.180, a credentialist model essentially concerned with employability qualifications and Ranson's 3.b, p.180, learning as a way of keeping pace with technological change. At this level there is little evidence of the broader concern with education implied in the educated society based on learning networks (favoured by Edwards), nor is there much reference to the access model of extending educational opportunities for all kinds of learning (not just employment-related activities) which Young's account advocates. Ranson's radical vision based on a learning democracy and the recognition that a learning society needs to re-think the fundamental social, political and moral conditions which contextualise all forms of learning is also difficult to locate within this official policy vision.

On further inspection, however, and particularly with reference to the practical implementation and *implications* of these policies, other features of the key models concerned with educational and social objectives achieve greater prominence. A key difference between the former

Conservative and the current New Labour perspectives on the ultimate purposes of the learning society is that the former saw learning for economic competitiveness as an *end in itself,* justified purely in terms of a self-sustaining and successful market, whereas the latter (though in agreement on the fundamental need for a learning society to achieve economic aims) almost always links this to the *further* (and perhaps also overriding) end of promoting wider social cohesion.

This difference is usefully illustrated in the recent NACETT report on skill needs and education and training targets which argues that:

> The primary purpose of the new targets should be to *make Britain more competitive internationally.* But they will also play a vital role in *promoting social cohesion.* Those two goals need not be in conflict with each other; sustained economic success, for example, is essential if we are to reduce dependency on the State and make work pay (NACETT, 1998, p.5, original italics).

The implied notion of 'social cohesion' here is, to be sure, rather limited and utilitarian (and absolutely faithful to the New Labour policies of welfare reform aimed at ending the dependency culture!) but a wider and more elaborate value position can be found in the general DfEE documents on lifelong learning. Alongside the (admittedly primary) emphasis on economic competitiveness and employability skills in *The Learning Age,* for example, there are unequivocal references to the development of a culture of learning which:

> Will help to build a united society, assist in the creation of personal independence, and encourage our creativity and innovation...Learning offers excitement and the opportunity for discovery. It takes us in directions never expected, sometimes changing our lives. Learning helps create and sustain our culture (DfEE, 1998a, p.10).

Elsewhere in the document there are references to the ways in which learning 'contributes to social cohesion and fosters a sense of belonging, responsibility and identity in communities affected by rapid economic change and industrial restructuring' (ibid., p.11).

All of this indicates an extension of the basic minimum individualistic and economistic functions of education and training to include broader educational and social purposes. Thus, other aspects of the learning society typologies, particularly Young's access model (2.c, p.180) aimed at ensuring a more equitable distribution of educational and life chances, and Ranson's (3.a, b, p.180) concept of a society which recognises the need to change dominant modes of learning, begin to enter the picture along with this broader vision. At this stage we are still within Edwards' learning market (1.b, p.180) approach and still primarily concerned with employability but, in the New Labour plans for funding lifelong learning, and significantly with its current targets and priorities, glimpses of the more elaborate visions of the learning society begin to reveal themselves.

The key priorities of the current lifelong learning policies, particularly in the flagship UfI and WTW schemes, are unequivocally directed towards those who have benefited least from the system. The Learning Age document again establishes the central vision in declaring that:

> We must bridge the 'learning divide', between those who have benefited from education and training and those who have not, which blights so many communities and widens income inequality (DfEE, 1998a, p.11).

To this end, the UfI, for example, will target those organisations (mainly SMEs) which have been most disadvantaged by current provision, and will focus specifically on those people 'over a fifth of the working population – around 8 million people' with 'either poor basic literacy or poor basic numeracy skills, or both' (DfEE, 1998c, p.16). Smilarly, the WTW scheme claims to be 'committed to ensuring that the New Deal will actively promote equality of opportunity and outcome for young people of all ethnic and racial groups' (DFEE, 1997a, p.37). Goals relating to the equality of outcome, as was noted in Chapter 6, have still to be achieved but, at the level of policy, the implementation of the scheme offers some justification for the vision of VET which is informed by the values of social justice.

Policy and practice in the FE sector, which has traditionally been concerned with accommodating those learners who have been most disadvantaged by schooling, also provides some evidence that current policies might be characterised in terms of the broader access model identified by Young (2.c, p.180). The agenda for this post-school sector was firmly established in the Kennedy report (1997) which was informed by the ideal of 'developing the capacity of everyone to contribute to and benefit from the economic, personal social and cultural dimensions of their lives' (p.22). In order to achieve this:

public policy for post-compulsory learning must be dramatically, systematically and consistently redirected towards widening rather than simply increasing participation and achievement. A much wider cross-section of the population needs to be involved than now (ibid.).

In the DfEE response to Kennedy (1998f) there is a clear endorsement of this key principle of widening participation in the declaration that the:

Government is committed to the establishment of a learning society in which all people have opportunities to succeed. Increasing access to learning and providing opportunities for success and progression are fundamental to the Government's strategy (p.7).

In terms of policy implementation there is also a clear intention to use 'funding as a lever of change' in order to 'widen participation in post-16 learning' (ibid., p.12). In addition to the extra 500,000 places and extra £100 million for key priorities in the sector, the Single Regeneration Budget is directed towards enhancing access through basic skills support and an extra £5 million is promised for an Adult and Community Learning fund, matched by trusts and other agencies, is to be used to finance access to basic literacy and numeracy schemes (ibid.). More recently, these targets for the FE sector have been enlarged with an additional £725 million, aimed at disadvantaged and disabled people in the main, to expand post-school schemes in these priority areas to take in 700,000 people by 2002 (Nash, Crequer & Slater, 1998). This extra funding includes £183 million specifically for student support in FE, with maintenance allowances of £40 a week being piloted for disadvantaged students, linked with a pledge to review the whole system of student support in the sector (Crequer, 1998).

These developments point towards, not just a general commitment to widening access and opportunities, but a determination to remove the traditional barriers by prioritising schemes for those who have historically been excluded. This seems to be fully in line with Young's access model (2.c, p.180) and also begins to address the features of Ranson's models of the learning society (3.c,d, p.180) in terms of mounting a campaign to include all members of society in the project of lifelong learning. Moreover, in terms of particular strategies, the range of public/private partnerships and exploitation of the National Grid for Learning and the Learning Direct helpline to tap into as broad a range of existing resources as possible, there are also characteristics in the overall policy which match aspects of Edward's 'learning networks' (1.c, p.180) conception through which 'learners adopt a learning approach to life, drawing on a wide range of resources to enable them to support their lifestyle practices' (1997, p.184).

At this stage, there is still not a full-blown commitment to other principles in Edwards' model, the 'normative goals of a liberal democratic society' leading to the 'educated society' (ibid.) which is broadly similar to Young's favoured model (2.d, p.180) and advocated also by Ranson (1998), Pring (1995) and others, though it could be argued that this goal could not be achieved until the prior foundational ones concerned with improving access and basic skills at the lower levels have been realised. Indeed, it is feasible to claim that, in addition to a broader social purpose for VET linked to wider access and social inclusion, the idea of education as a public good can begin to emerge. This may then serve to extend the more economistic versions of human capital to construct systems of what Schuller & Field (1998) call 'social capital' located in 'the kinds of context and culture which promote communication and mutual learning as part of the fabric of everyday life' (p.234) and, thus, approximate to the radical vision outlined by Ranson (1998) and others.

It is also worth noting that this emergence (revival?) of the idea of education as a public good also marks a sharp difference between New Labour policy and the former Conservative administration's commitment to the market as an end in itself. The market, as will be suggested in the discussion of 'third way' values and politics below, is still there but it is now merely a means to an end and, moreover, tempered by state regulation and social values. This is an important development since, particularly during the triumphalist period of the enterprise culture in the 1980s and early 1990s, the concept of free market forces was all powerful and, as recommended by the New Right neo-liberals (see Heelas & Morris, 1992), reigned supreme in accounts of the optimal and most efficient and socially just distribution of public goods and services, including, education.

As referred to in the last chapter, philosophers of education such as Carr & Hartnett (1996) and Jonathan (1997) have offered cogent criticisms of such neo-liberal, marketised theories of education on the grounds (surely, powerfully persuasive once recognised and acknowledged) that education is not *just one public good amongst others* but also, crucially and decisively, a *means of access* to a whole range of other goods, both public and private, such as employment, culture, values and personal autonomy. As Jonathan (mentioning that even the father of free market liberal politics, Adam Smith, saw that education, and national defence, were different from other goods) puts it:

> In education, the market model of just distribution is not just destructive of some aspects of the good itself, it also represents, not the fulfilment of priority for individual liberty as regulating principle for political association, but the frustration of that aim. Education therefore is the one good which consistent neo-liberals should themselves see as representing the limiting case for the market's claimed virtues (1997, p.238).

Winch (1998) extends this line of argument by pointing out that, against the notion espoused by neo-liberals such as Tooley (1997) that educational institutions exist to provide educational opportunities, on the contrary, 'education is a preparation for life and educational institutions exist to prepare children for life' (p.429). He asserts that:

> education, not educational opportunity, is the good that society and parents wish to have provided...one does not have to be a diehard egalitarian to see the disadvantages of very large inequalities in educational achievement in terms of future life-opportunities and in the damage to social cohesion and economic prosperity that results from the presence of significant numbers of uneducated people in the society (p.435).

Such a statement could have come from any of the recent *Learning Age* documents which promote the idea of lifelong learning on the grounds of both economic competitiveness and general social cohesion and inclusiveness. Moreover, in response to some of the criticisms (Tight, 1998; Strain, 1998) levelled at policy statements for seemingly presenting an authoritarian and coercive view of learning as something which everyone must pursue throughout life, the government might respond that their targeting of excluded and disadvantaged groups and the stress on access and foundational basic learning is the only way to promote ideals which are the opposities of coercion and exclusion: autonomy and inclusion for all citizens. Such conceptions are on all fours with White's (1973) justification of a compulsory curriculum on the grounds that the ethico-political ideal of maximising preferences can only be achieved by providing people with the wherewithal (through education) to understand and acquire preferences in the first place. In another context, it is no different from   Peters' (1966) Aristotelian view of moral development expressed in the notion of people having to 'enter the palace of reason through the courtyard of habit' (p.314).

Field's (1998) interesting and thoughtful discussion of such issues makes reference to some of these tensions in pointing out that the generalisation of lifelong learning may have 'alarming consequences' for if:

> competitiveness does depend on continuous investments in human capital... there is bound to be an element of coercion, because all our competitors need to do is to invest continuously in their human capital, and so on... Much of our rhetoric on learning, and the learning itself, is largely self-serving. Yet we also know that learning in all its various settings and modes can help solve practical problems. It can even make us happier, indirectly (by helping us get a job or repair our homes or rethink our marriage or improve our golf) and directly (mastering something new can be an effective consumer good in its own right). Anyway we are going to have to do more of it, more effectively, *whether we like it or not* (pp.7-8; italics added).

Field is absolutely right and his elegant attempt to resolve the strains and tensions of lifelong learning rhetoric could serve as a most appropriate *leitmotif* for the 'third way' politics which underpins current PCET policy and practice.

Third Way Politics and Learning Age Values

Giddens (1998) begins his discussion of the 'third way' by explaining that the term 'is of no particular significance in and of itself' and 'has been used many times before in the past history of social democracy' (p.vii). Kellner (1998) defines this particular social democractic approach in terms of 'mutualism' which he claims:

> offers a way out of the sterile argument between state ownership and private enterprise. A mutualist economy is one in which enterprises respect their staff, customers and the environment, and refuse to ride rough-shod over any of them in pursuit of profit (p.15).

In a similar vein, Leadbetter (1998) explains that the 'central ethic of the Third Way is simple and traditional: co-operative self-improvement' (p.15). He goes on to elaborate the approach in terms of a politics which:

> encourages people to recognise their shared needs and the potential for shared solutions. It promotes co-operation and collaboration, as well as ambition and striving. This is not wishy-washy political correctness. The most knowledge-intensive sectors of the economy, software and biotechnology, thrive on a mix of competition and collaboration (ibid.).

For Giddens (1998) the 'overall aim of third way politics should be to help citizens pilot their way through the major revolutions of our time: globalization, transformations in personal life and our relationship to nature'; third way politics 'looks for a new relationship between the individual and the community, a redefinition of rights and obligations' (pp.64-65). With these ultimate aims and purposes in mind, Giddens helpfully offers a list of 'third way values' aimed at achieving the 'third way programme' (Figs. 8.1 and 8.2).

Third way values

Equality
Protection of the vulnerable
Freedom as autonomy
No rights without responsibilities
No authority without democracy
Cosmopolitan pluralism
Philosophic conservatism

Fig. 8.1: Third Way Values
Source: Based on Giddens, 1998, p.66.

The third way programme

The radical centre
The new democratic state (the state without
    enemies)
Active civil society
The democratic family
The new mixed economy
Equality as inclusion
Positive welfare
The social investment state
The cosmopolitan nation
Cosmopolitan democracy

Fig. 8.2: Third Way Programme
Source: Based on Giddens, 1998, p.70.

The ultimate end of the programme is the 'social investment state' which 'defines equality as inclusion and inequality as exclusion' (ibid., p.102). The inclusive society is characterised in terms of the following features (Fig. 8.3):

The inclusive society

Equality as inclusion
Limited meritocracy
Renewal of public space (civic liberalism)
'Beyond the work society'
Positive welfare
The social investment state

Fig. 8.3: The Inclusive Society
Source: Based on Giddens, 1998, p.105.

The inclusive society designed along these lines thus becomes a society of 'positive welfare' which would replace:

> each of Beveridge's negatives with a positive: in place of Want, autonomy; not Disease but active health; instead of Ignorance, education; rather than Squalor, well-being; and in place of Idleness, initiative (ibid., p.128).

It is not difficult to penetrate the rhetorical flourishes here and discern, in terminology, philosophy, and concrete policy, the current political programme of New Labour. Many of the key concepts and principles employed by Giddens are clearly in evidence in the lifelong learning literature, and the influence of 'third way' political philosophy can be illustrated by examining two key developments in particular: the UfI scheme and the policy for further education.

The UfI scheme might have been designed by reference to Giddens' 'third way' manual of practical politics. All the key ingredients are there. The UfI, for example, is designed to be 'a new kind of public-private sector partnership' which will 'stimulate new learning markets' and 'encourage partnerships among different sectors, learners and providers' (DfEEc, p.9). Third way principles are even more influential in the original UfI blueprint devised by Hillman (1997). In oder to meet the 'four challenges for lifelong learning' (which were examined in more detail in Chapter 5) three broad strategies were considered (pp.31-2):

1. *Laisser-faire*: let the market develop at its own pace as customers (learners) compete for the goods of education and training supplied by providers.
2. *Dirigisme*: the state would assemble educational experts and industry representatives to construct a grand plan and a new educational institution to organise, deliver and assess all aspects of post-compulsory education and training.
3. *Animation*: the state co-ordinates and accelerates the nascent market through effective partnership with all relevant stakeholders and by broking supplies and demands and franchising and kitemarking suppliers of approved services.

It comes as no great surprise that those charged with drawing up the original UfI plans decided upon the 'third option'. Hillman explains the logic behind this choice:

> It is less expensive than dirigisme but entails more of a role for government than laisser-faire. It creates expectations and political liability but is much less

risky than dirigisme. At best it can realise the flexibility and responsiveness of the market while making sure that things happen faster and that commercially marginal groups are not excluded (ibid., p.33).

All the key elements of third way philosophy are cleary on display here: public-private sector partnerships, social inclusion, responsible handling of the public purse and the regulation of the market in the interests of all members of society. A broadly similar partnership strategy characterises the organisation of the New Deal WTW initiative which allows for one of three types of arrangement (DfEE, 1997b, p.3):

- a private-public agency partnership which might ask the Employment Service (ES) to undertake contracting for the Gateway and New Deal options
- a consortium, involing the Local Authority, the TEC, careers services and private and voluntary sector agencies, undertaking to deliver all or part of the New Deal under contract to the ES
- consortia with which the ES could contract to take forward the delivery of specific elements of the New Deal such as the Environmental task force

There is a clear commitment to flexibility by the DfEE in the statement that:

We would expect the arrangements for delivery to vary from area to area in accordance with the views of the local partners and the needs of the young people in the area (ibid.).

These key features also serve to characterise New Labour policy on FE since the 1997 Kennedy report (1997) established the basic agenda by pointing to the 'fair amount of chaos and confusion within further education' (p.32) since incorporation and emphasising the central role of the sector in widening participation. The unmistakable implication was that, in spite of the expansion and diversity of the five years following the 1992 Further & Higher Education Act, barriers to learning for the most disadvantaged had not been removed and the system was still denying access to those who had gained least from compulsory schooling. Admitting that competition between FE institutions had resulted in 'improved responsiveness' in some regions, there was an unequivocal assertion that 'competition has also inhibited the collaboration needed to widen participation' along with the recommendation that 'partnerships must be created to fill the strategic vacuum at local level' (p.35). The failure to address the needs of all members of the community on the part of FE colleges was also caused by the dominance of business and industrial interests on governing bodies to the exclusion of other stakeholders. No doubt influenced by the growing number of cases of fraud and corruption in the system, and by the damaging results of local competition, Kennedy observes that 'if further education is to fulfil its potential in terms of social cohesion and economic prosperity, all stakeholders need to ensure wide involvement on the part of employers and members of the community'. With changes in college governance clearly in mind, the report follows up with the radical recommendation that:

> Formal arrangements are necessary to ensure that it can respond more effectively to the needs of the wider community. This cannot be left to chance. Both governance and the [FEFC] Council have roles to play in the changes needed to promote the systematic development of community involvement in planning. The government, for example, should alter the articles of government for sector colleges to make community involvement a requirement (ibid., p.42).

Almost all of this, in both policy and practice, is now acknowledged in and realised through current policy for the FE sector. The consultation document *Accountability in Further Education* (DfEEi), after revisiting the central role of the FE sector in achieving lifelong learning objectives, observed that 'governing body arrangements are ripe for reform'. This was followed by the key prescription that:

> A central principle in determining new arrangements should be that governing bodies include members drawn from the key stakeholder groups. Those groups include the business world, as well as local government, local community interests, college staff, students and, in some cases, parents. In that way wider stakeholder involvement in college governing bodies would be secured through formal arrangements, as advocated in the Kennedy Report (p.1).

Alarmed by the large number of mismanagement cases in FE, with the Secretary of State declaring that it 'is clear that 10% of the sector is underachieving' (Baty, 1998b, p.4), the DfEE has been quick to act on the results of the consultation about accountability and college governance. Measures assuring greater accountability of instutitions plus tough rules to curb the dominance of business interests on college governing bodies' (ibid.) are to be implemented in the 1999/2000 academic session.

The other main recommendation of Kennedy concerned with widening participation and reducing exclusion by encouraging partnerships rather than competition, is also fully acknowledged in the official DfEE response to the report (DfEE, 1998f). There is a clear acknowledgement that the FE sector's record since incorporation has been poor in relation to widening participation and catering for the needs of the most disadvantaged groups in the community. If Learning Age objectives are to be achieved, all this will have to change. As the key paragraph in *Further Education for the New Millennium* (DfEE, 1998f) expresses it:

> The Government believes that the excessive emphasis in the past on market competition has inhibited collaboration, and that strong partnerships are now needed to develop efficient local strategies for learning (p.9).

Local learning networks, co-ordinated through Learning Direct, the UfI and the new Regional Development Agencies established in 1999 (Whittaker, 1998), represent the practical realisation of this principle and, at a stroke, serve to unite all aspects of lifelong learning policy into a cohesive whole.

Before leaving the topic of 'third way' politics it is worth mentioning the centrality of the concept of 'globalisation' (mentioned throughout Giddens' analysis and given a separate, concluding chapter) which features prominently in all contemporary discourse about VET and lifelong learning. In the broad Learning Age macro-policies, the concept is used in relation to the new post-Fordist, post-industrial world in which 'investment in human capital will be the foundation of success in the knowledge-based global economy of the twenty-first century' (DfEE, 1998a, p.7). On a micro-level, the perspective informs the inordinate emphasis placed on the use of IT and the Internet in, for example, the UfI pilots, and on the National Grid for learning.

This usage owes much to the sort of scenarios sketched by writers such as Kenway et al. (1993) and Edwards (1994) and who have linked new educational technologies with international markets. As Green's (1997b) detailed analysis suggests, there is a fair amount of utopian 'futurology' going on here, and it is highly unlikely that new technologies will either transform the whole workforce making us all 'multiskilled or polyvalent' (p.13) workers, or completely 'de-institutionalize education since children still have to learn how to learn' (ibid., p.171). At this level, such futuristic scenarios are as unreal and naïve as theories of andragogy which posit the notion that all adults are autonomous, self-directed learners (see the criticisms of these ideas by Collins, 1991 and Brookfield, 1986).

Globalisation theories applied to nationhood and world politics owe much to Reich's influential thesis put forward in T*he Work of Nations* (1991) in which the whole process is explained in terms of the activities of transnational corporations and global enterprise webs. In this new world order both consumerism and production are truly cosmopolitan to the extent that, in the coming century, there 'will be no more national products, no national corporations, no national industries' (p.1). Such arguments are applied to national identity, culture and politics as well as economics, and the implication is drawn that nationhood is about to become a thing of the past.

Such speculation has been subjected to trenchant criticism by Esland (1996a,b) and Green (1997b), and Giddens (1998) also offers a 'third way' interpretation in which social democrats 'seek a new role for the nation in a cosmopolitan world' (p.129). He asserts that the 'emerging global order cannot sustain itself as a pure marketplace' and that 'a reassertion of the nation is important as a stabilizing force, a counter to endless fragmentation' (ibid.). However, acutely conscious of the destructive nationalism which has blighted Eastern Europe since the end of the communist era, Giddens is concerned to recommend a positive version of cosmopolitanism of which the 'European Union is a prototype'. He explains that:

> National identity can be a benign influence only if it is tolerant of ambivalence, or multiple affiliation. Individuals who simultaneously are English, British, European, and have some overall sense of global citizenship, may regard one of these as their overriding identity, but this need not prevent them accepting the others too (ibid., p.130).

Cultural pluralism and cosmopolitan democracy are proposed as necessary features of a new global order in which national economic and territorial disputes might be settled through the mediating agency of some form of 'global governance'. The argument is that:

> The expansion of cosmopolitan democracy is a condition for effectively regulating the world economy, attacking global economic inequalities and controlling ecological risks (ibid., p.147).

Such cosmopolitanism, therefore, does not dispense with national identities and cultures but, rather, opens such cultures up to pluralistic influences; internationalism would mean nothing if nations did not exist in the first place. Green (1997b) arrives at similar conclusions when he argues that:

> rather than a full-scale globalization of education, the evidence suggests a partial internationalization of education systems which falls far short of an end to national education *per se*...The major dilemmas for governments and educationalists in the coming decade will revolve around how to reconstruct cultures of citizenship and nationhood in ways which are appropriate to modern conditions and yet conducive both to a deepening of democracy and to a strengthening social solidarity (pp.185-6).

This essentially moral response to globalisation (which, incidentally, has been flourishing at the periphery of British education since 'World Studies' was introduced into schools in the 1980s; see Heater, 1980; Fisher & Hicks, 1985; Hyland, 1986) needs to be fully integrated into the values core of VET described in the last chapter in the same way that literacy, numeracy and IT merit a place in the common knowledge core which underpins general and specific vocational preparation.

Vocational Studies and Lifelong Learning – What Future?

Before embarking upon a final evaluation of the current state and possible future of vocational studies in the light of all the issues and developments discussed in the previous chapters, it might be worth taking stock of the changes in post-compulsory policy and practice since New Labour gained power in May 1997. To this end we could usefully begin by asking whether the 'new educational settlement' in the sector called for by Gleeson (1996) has been achieved.

Although we have only two years of VET developments to analyse, it seems reasonable to suggest that the New Deal has not, and is not likely, to generate an educational settlement as radical and far-reaching as that which followed the 1944 Education Act. Perhaps, such a comparison is unfair since, whereas the 1944 Act occurred at a moment in history when social class stratification linked to educational inequality and disadvantage provided a decisive moment and pivotal turning point for policy, the 1997 position was less momentous. The 1988 Reform Act had left us with a national curriculum and standardised assessment regime at the school level, and the post-school sector has been reconstructed as a result of the consequences of the 1991 White Paper which introduced GNVQs and the three-track curriculum into an FE sector of incorporated colleges following the 1992 Further & Higher Education Act. In higher education the number of universities had doubled overnight in 1992/93 and student numbers had been increased in all post-compulsory sectors.

Looking only at strengths rather than weaknesses, it would be possible to view all this in a fairly favourable light (as the Conservatives attempted to do in the May 1997 election campaign). Yet, as all the *Learning Age* documents have illustrated, the system was confused, patchy, socially exclusive and still failing learners who were most disadvantaged. Access to HE has indeed increased dramatically in the last decade, but students from social class V still make up only 2% of the university population (Wojtas, 1999). As in the FE sector, it seems that access and participation have been increased and expanded but not widened. The state of PCET in general also leaves much to be desired. Hillman, for instance, refers to 'deficiencies in education and training' which have been a 'cause for concern for policy-makers for 150 years' (p.30), and Young describes the post-compulsory sector as 'sharply divided' with 'vocational provision that carries little credibility' (p.190). The latter criticism is most significant for the present analysis since VET in general was in a chaotic state following a spate of misdirected reforms and experiments, and the status of vocational studies was lower than ever after a decade of failure and incoherence due mainly to the discredited NCVQ experiment. In 1999 we are still trying to achieve a national system of high quality VET which can match those of our Continental competitors.

In dealing with this legacy of failure the New Deal and lifelong learning policy has, arguably, started a process of reform which might address the central and persistent problems and weaknesses. At this stage the achievements are modest and there is nothing radical enough to suggest that the New Deal will bring about a new educational settlement along the lines discussed throughout this book. Indeed, in spite of their passionate advocacy of humanistic rather than scientific economic analysis and strategy, 'new economists' such as Solow (1999) are ultimately dubious about whether *any* 'workfare' programmes can solve all the problems of contemporary global capitalism. Certainly, in terms of social, political and economic objectives, the New Deal cannot really compare with the USA New Deal of the 1930s, though perhaps this comparison is unfair since the 1930s New Deal was seeking to rescue America from, in FDR's words, 'this dark hour of our national life' (Commager, 1963, p.240) following the economic collapse after the 1929 Wall St Crash. In 1997, New Labour had inherited a reasonably successful economy and was planning to implement policies to improve education and training, employment and general social life. However, in spite of these obvious historical differences, it seems feasible to try to offer an analysis of Labour's New Deal in terms of the key slogan of the original New Deal: 'Relief, Recovery and Reform' (Johnson, 1966).

Relief

It seems clear that the key New Deal scheme for individuals, in the form of the WTW and related projects designed to overcome barriers preventing people from returning to employment, has short-term objectives with relief predominantly in mind. Any system designed to deal with the problems of unemployment cannot but have such a short-termist, temporary foundation. Indeed, the work-relief aspects of Roosevelt's New Deal, realised through the great public works programmes of the so-called 'alphabet agencies' (Sauvain, 1989, pp.170ff.) such as the Civil Works Administration, the Federal Emergency Relief Administration and the National Recovery Administration, were, by definition, also short-term, though their long-term consequences were far-reaching.

However, even if the 'third way' is bound to be somewhat less radical than the FDR's Public Works Administration, the short-term relief consequences of the New Deal WTW and related initiatives are still welcome, significant and carry much potential for the future development of VET programmes for unemployed and disadvantaged groups. Finn (1997) is highly critical of the 'revolving door' approach which has characterised past job training schemes, and is quite right to argue that the 'New Deal will quickly fail if it just recycles the unemployed through short-term placements' (p.255). The evidence thus far demonstrating the prioritising of finding unsubsidised jobs for WTW participants is highly promising in this respect.

Recovery

The recovery relevant here is, not primarily from economic recession, but from a system of educational exclusion, under-achievement by citizens and under-investment in VET by employers and the state. In general educational terms it could also be described as a recovery from an elitist system dominated by overly-academic values, a credentialist diploma disease, a second-rate and low status VET system and a regime which completely fails about half of its participants. The new emphases on partnership and social inclusion in this area are welcome and necessary ingredients of a moral framework within which PCET can be reformed in the interests of all stakeholders.

At the level of rhetoric and macro-policy the government's lifelong learning objectives are difficult to fault in this respect, since the New Deal 'relief' schemes are all embedded in a wider framework which is designed to encourage continuity and progression of learning throughout life. In terms of micro-policy and practical implementation, however, there is a now an urgent need to balance short-term employability objectives with longer-term general VET objectives so as to transform attitudes and foster a learning culture. The learning processes associated with studentship, and the vital values framework within which they are located, need to be foregrounded so that New Deal welfare programmes can be reconstructed as New Deal VET programmes.

Reform

In the area of reform the two years of New Labour education policy could never really bear comparison with the spate of ground-breaking legislation enacted by Roosevelt, which included fifteen messages sent to Congress, fifteen major new laws enacted and revlutionary reforms in banking, agriculture, industry and work-relief (Hofstadter, 1959), during the early years of the American New Deal. However, the New Labour educational reform programme in its first two years is still impressive; reforms in the PCET sector have come thick and fast and the following list is not meant to be exhaustive:

- *Learning Age* paper published committed to expanding post-school numbers by 500,000 by 2002 (later increased to 700,000)

PCET sector have come thick and fast and the following list is not meant to be exhaustive:

- *Learning Age* paper published committed to expanding post-school numbers by 500,000 by 2002 (later increased to 700,000)
- Individual Learning Accounts introduced
- UfI pilot scheme launched and developed
- New DEAL WTW for 18-24 year olds implemented
- New Deals for older unemployed, disabled and homeless launched
- Learning Direct helpline established
- Changes in organisation and governance of FE sector

Starting 1999 in a decidedly upbeat and buoyant mood, the outgoing Associate Director of NIACE for the last fourteen years, Stephen McNair (1999), declared in his editorial for *Adults Learning* that the:

> last few years have been astonishing. Twenty years ago policymakers saw adult learning as worthy but dull. Ten years ago it was possibly not worthy, and certainly too expensive. Now it is seen as one of the engines of economic and social renewal (p.3).

McNair goes on to 'pick a few initiatives at random' and observes that:

> the last few months have seen the launch of the Trade Union Learning Fund, 700,000 new students in FE (most of them mature), the HE funding council planned to spend £30M a year on widening participation, a national telephone information service on adult learning, and the University for Industry offering the first radically new kind of institution since the OU (ibid.).

All such measures (and more could have been mentioned, such as the extra £720 million for FE and additional £120 million for work-based training for 18-24 year olds; THES, 1999c, p.2) can, quite legitimately and justifiably, be described in terms of a committed and forthright determination to reform post-school learning and to extend and widen access to education and training to include all those people who formerly have gained little from the system. It is not, of course (since it hardly ever is!) all good news. There is evidence that the introduction of tuition fees for HE students has resulted in a drop in applications from mature students for the second year running, prompting government to offer additional greater demand (Field, 1998). It is also vital to take note of the fact that, since VET reform must necessarily connect with (if not follow) wider economic reform, New Deal educational reformism must always be incomplete. As Ormerod (1999) has argued recently, however laudable New Deal policies are it might ultimately be the case that the 'market mechanism is incapable of creating sufficient jobs for the number of unqualified workers that exists' (p.24).

However, in spite of all the necessary caveats, I would still want to agree with McNair that the achievements thus far are impressive and, if we look at the reform programme as a system in transition, it has to be said that the PCET system looks a lot healthier than it did just a few years ago. Given all this, what is the state of vocational studies in the wake of this period of reform? It seems reasonable to suggest that the system shows signs of improvement and allows for the possibility of establishing a high status VET route in the future but there are a number of weaknesses and areas for improvement. Of course, at the level of policy and theory rather than that of implementation and practice, it is always easier to present critical analyses and to construct alternative programmes. Fully admitting this, the present investigation and evaluation would be sadly incomplete without such speculation and prescription.

I would offer the following list of issues and recommendations which, on the basis of the analysis and discussion of vocational studies conducted throughout the book, seem to be areas worth attending to if long-term lifelong learning aims are to be achieved and a high quality/high status national VET system established in the future.

Apprenticeships

There is some evidence of progression by participants from the New Deal WTW options to MA schemes. This movement should be positively encouraged so that, as suggested in the LSE Centre For Economic Performance report (Hart, 1998), the current 10% participation in the relevant age groups is expanded to 30-40%. The de-skilling of vocational studies and downgrading of VET in favour of academic pursuits has, as the historical analysis in Chapter 2 demonstrated, gone hand in hand with the decline of the apprenticeship system. It is now time to halt and reverse this process by re-asserting the importance of the concept of apprenticeship, reconstructed through the 'learning at work' and 'learning for work' models underpinned by general foundations and a common core of learning (examined at the end of Chapter 4), and re-positioning appenticeship so that it becomes (instead of shallow NVQ-type occupationalism) the cornerstone of a high quality national VET system. In this respect, upgraded MA schemes (uncoupled from NVQs) offer a way forward, and the recent decision by the Construction Industry Training Board to launch (though perhaps 're-establish' would be the correct term, considering the history of training in this sphere) new apprenticeships in collaboration with the Confederation of Master Builders is very encouraging in this respect (Read, 1998). As Gospel (1998a) passionately argues, the reform of apprenticeship and related VET utilising the MA programme (suitably revised and modified) as a basic minimum foundation may just be:

> ...the last opportunity to get work-based training in Britain on the right lines, and to enjoy the gains which a successful scheme could bring, and which many of Britain's competitors have enjoyed for so long (p.23).

Common Core, General Diploma and Unified Curriculum

Along with those supporting a Baccalaureate and general education diploma approach to post-16 qualifications, I would endorse the abolition of A-levels (along with the abolition of NVQs/GNVQs) and the establishment of a General Education diploma in which academic and vocational pursuits are given equal emphasis. As mentioned in Chapter 3, a unified curriculum seems to be a necessary corollary of upgrading VET and, accepting Hodgson & Spours' (1997) views on the gradualist and incrementalist trends in this area, the debate should now be concerned with the design of a unified curriculum and questions of when, not if, such a curriculum is introduced into the system. The so-called A-level 'gold standard' is a convenient myth which serves to mask deep-seated prejudices which have nothing to do with questions of education and training and everything to do with social stratification (Gleeson & Hodkinson, 1999). Employers, in this and many other areas of VET, must share responsibility here for, whilst criticising academic values as sterile and anti-industrial, they have, cynically and with systematic ambiguity, consistently maintained the use of A-levels and degrees as screening mechanisms for selecting employees. In this and many other spheres such as their roles in constructing VET curricula and participating in the governance of post-school institutions, it is high time for employer involvement (not to say, dominance) to be appropriately curbed and restricted.

The establishment of a unified curriculum will need to be informed by the common knowledge and *culture generale* approach which characterises Continental systems, and to be linked with learning programmes characteristic of the studentship strategies discussed in the last chapter. In this area it is difficult to better the aguments of Skilbeck et al. (1994) that:

> The idea of a core of common, fundamental learnings for working life, and their definition, organisation and delivery to students in appropriate settings, provides a means of interrelating the traditionally, and dysfunctionally, separated domains of general and vocational education. What is needed is to free the core idea from its older academic, subject-based connections and to treat it afresh in a redefined context (p.60).

Vocational Studies and NVQs

A consequence of adopting a unified curriculum model will, naturally, be the long overdue scrapping of NVQs/GNVQs and the behaviourist functional analysis approach which underpins them. As demonstrated in Chapter 3 this system has failed on just about every measure and criterion imaginable, and it has downgraded vocational studies and given VET a very bad name. In view of all this, the support given to the NVQ system, in terms of its use in equivalence tables and descriptions of MAs and other training programmes, in *The Learning Age* (DfEE, 1998a, pp.63-7) is as disgraceful and indefensible as the recent aborted schemes attempting to export the disecredited NVQ system to overseas countries (Hyland, 1998d). It is time to stop tinkering with unsuitable and unsatisfactory CBET strategies and to direct our energies instead to the construction of worthwhile vocational curricula. The Secretary of State would do well to take the advice of the head of the QCA in this sphere and give backing to vocational qualifications 'other' than NVQs, especially in view of the fact that such 'traditional' qualifications are clearly preferred by the vast majority of employers, trainers, trainees, VET tutors and learners.

Knowledge and Capability rather than Skill Certification

The diploma disease is still with us and there remains an undue emphasis on targets expressed in terms of 'recognised qualifications' (NACETT,

1998, p.13). This strategy is both misleading and dangerous, first, because these qualifications are generally seen in terms of NVQ or equivalents (thus unduly relying on a failed and discredited system) and, second, because such an approach emphasises mere certification at the expense of the needs and requirements of learners and employers.

In a similar way, the obsession with various forms of skill-talk (criticised in Chapter 3) radically distorts VET aims and objectives by reducing them to simplistic bits of pyscho-motor activity. As was recommended in the earlier discussion, since skill-talk, especially that concerned with key, core, or generic skills, is confused, vacuous and of dubious logical or empirical status, it should be abandoned in favour of prescriptions of content and processes for learning programmes. Sometimes, as with the discussion of 'generic, vocational and job-specific' employability skills by the National Skills Task Force (DfEE, 1998j, p.15), skill-talk seems to be simply a short-hand way of attempting to describe what employers, employees, trainees and learners actually need for contemporary working conditions and the changing labour market. Such terminology is, however, both inadequate and confusing and leaves everything to be done in terms of designing and implementing quality VET programmes.

National strategies need to move beyond such fatuous terminology and seek to specify, clearly and precisely, exactly what content, processes and assessment techniques should be used to design and structure learning for work and learning at work programmes. Of even greater urgency and significance is the need to (re-)construct such programmes in the light of general educational foundations informed by core learning and knowledge components. As Green (1997a) has pointed out, the core skills approach to providing educational foundations is woefully inadequate and should be replaced by a common core of knowledge similar to those which underpin Continental VET systems. Fowler (1998) puts this well in his obervation that:

> Vocational training requires general studies. Quality training demands the inclusion of a general element; as technological developments supersede technological developments, so the proportion of time devoted to general education needs to rise. Trainees need to learn things which job-specific technical education is not good at teaching: notably the need to develop the capacity to go on learning, almost regardless of the context of that learning (p.243).

Social Values and Vocational Learning

In addition to all this, the values dimension of vocational studies needs to be emphasised and, connected with a social theory of lifelong learning emphasised throughout the foregoing analysis, needs to be centrally located in the core of common learnings if VET is to achieve high status and quality in the future. Economistic, technicist and individualistic strategies need to be replaced by approaches which stress experience, learning style, studentship and the importance of the social/community dimension of all learning activity. As Ranson (1998a) rightly observes:

> There is no solitary learning: we can only create our worlds together. The unfolding agency of the self always grows out of the interaction with others. It is *inescapably a social creation* (p.20; original italics).

New Labour policy on PCET, incorporating New Deal and related lifelong learning initiaitives, can only, in 1999, be seen in terms of a system in transition. However, even at this early stage the transitional signs are modestly positive and optimistic in terms of the key issues discussed throughout this book: the upgrading of vocational studies and the re-assertion of the values dimension of VET located within a social theory of lifelong learning. It seems reasonable to speculate that we might be about one-third of the way along the (necessarily very long!) royal road to a 'new educational settlement'. It would be difficult to better Gleeson's (1996) inspirational description of such a settlement in the argument that:

> Real and lasting educational reform cannot be subordinated to the causal determinants of economy, or traditions of hierarchy and social exclusion. Genuine alternatives must embrace an active view of citizenship which links partnership and empowerment in personal education and economic relations, beyond market, qualification and employer-led considerations. This demands recognition that the driving force of reform is the quality *of teaching and learning* in school and post-compulsory education. It also involves realisation that education, learning, society and work are synonymous, not separate entitities. Principles of democracy and social justice are involved here, in terms of how education and training helps shape, rather than passively reflect on, the future of industrial society (p.15; original italics).

Bibliography

Adams, Sir John (1933): *Modern Developments in Educational Practice* (London: University of London Press).

Adams, J. (1996): *Apprenticeship: A Comparative Study of the Traditional and The Modern Apprenticeship* (University of Warwick: Dept of Continuing Education) Unpublished MA thesis.

ADAPT (1998): *Adapt News* (Birmingham : Adapt News).

Ainley, P. (1988): *From School to YTS: Education and Training in England and Wales 1944-1987* (Milton Keynes: Open University Press).

Ainley, P. (1990): *Vocational Education and Training* (London: Cassell).

Ainley, P. (1993): *Class and Skill* (London: Cassell).

Ainley, P. (1996): 'The Eternal Return of the Same: Dearing's Latest Review'; *Forum*, 38 (3), pp.90-92.

Ainley, P. & Corney, M. (1990): *Training for the Future: The Rise and Fall of the Manpower Services Commission* (London: Cassell).

ALBSU (1987): *Literacy, Numeracy and Adults* (London: Adult Literacy and Basic Skills Unit).

ALBSU (1989): *A Nation's Neglect* (London: Adult Literacy and Basic Skills Unit).

Alfino, M., Caputo, J.S. & Wynyard, R. (Eds) (1998): *McDonaldization Revisited: Essays on Consumer Culture* (London: Praeger).

Anderson, C.A. (1965): 'Literacy and Schooling on the Development Threshold'; in Anderson, C.A. & Bowman, M.J. (Eds): *Education and Economic Development* (Chicago, Illinois: Aldine Pub.Co.).

Annett, J. & Sparrow, J. (1985): *Transfer of Learning and Training* (Sheffield: Manpower Services Commission).

Argryis, C. & Schon, D. (1974): *Theory in Practice: Increasing Professional Effectiveness* (San Francisco: Jossey-Bass).

Armstrong, S., Thompson, G. & Brown, S. (Eds) (1997): *Facing up to Radical Changes in Universities and Colleges* (London: Kogan Page).

Arthur, J. (1998): 'Communitarianism: what are the implications for education?'; *Educational Studies*; 24(3), pp.353-368.

Ashby, E. (1958): *Technology and the Academics* (London: Macmillan).

Ashworth, P.D. (1992): 'Being competent and having "competencies"'; *Journal of Further & Higher Education,* 16(3), pp.8-17.

Ashworth, P.D. & Saxton, J. (1990): 'On Competence'; *Journal of Further & Higher Education*, 14 (2), pp.3-25.

Atkinson, T. (1996): 'Why do Britain's have-nots have less?'; *Times Higher*

Education Supplement, April 12.

Audit Commission/HMI (1993): *Unfinished Business: Full-Time Courses for 16-19 Year Olds* (London: HMSO).

Aviram, A. (1992): 'The Nature of University Education Reconsidered'; *Journal of Philosophy of Education*, 26 (2),'pp.183-200.

Avis, J. (1996): 'The Myth of the Post-Fordist Society'; in Avis, J., et al. (1996); op.cit.

Avis, J., Bloomer, M., Esland, G., Gleeson, D. & Hodkinson, P. (1996): *Knowledge And Nationhood* (London: Cassell).

Bailey, C. (1984): *Beyond the Present and the Particular* (London: Routledge & Kegan Paul).

Ball, C. (1991): *Learning Pays : The Role of Post-Compulsory Education and Training* (London: Royal Society of Arts).

Ball, C. (1995): *Achieving Quality in Guidance:Conference Report* (Staffordshire: Staffs Training and Enterprise Council).

Ball, S.J. (1990): *Politics and Policy Making in Education* (London: Routledge).

Barnard, H.C. (1961): *A History of English Education from 1760* (London: University of London Press).

Barnett, C. (1986): *The Audit of War* (London: Macmillan).

Barnett, R. (1990): *The Idea of Higher Education* (Buckingham: Open University Press).

Barnett, R. (1994): *The Limits of Competence* (Buckingham: Open University Press).

Barnett, R. (1998): '"In" or "For" the Learning Society?'; *Higher Education Quarterly*, 52 (1), pp.7-21.

Barrow, R. (1987): 'Skill Talk'; *Journal of Philosophy of Education*, 21(2), pp.187-199.

Bates, I. (1998): *The Competence and Outcomes Movement: The Landscape of Research* (Leeds: University of Leeds School of Education).

Bates, I. & Dutson, J. (1995): 'A Bermuda Triangle?; A case study of the disappearance of competence-based vocational training policy in the context of practice'; *British Journal of Education and Work*, 8(2), pp.41-59.

Baty, P. (1997a): 'DfEE called to account'; *Times Higher Education Supplement,* March 14.

Baty, P. (1997b): 'Big vision of bosses' champion'; *Times Higher Education Supplement*, December 5.

Baty, P. (1998a): 'Special funds to tackle FE weaknesses'; *Times Higher Education Supplement*, October 9.

Baty, P. (1998b): 'Blunkett angers principals with get-tough stance'; *Times Higher Educational Supplement*, December 4.

Baty, P. & Tysome, T. (1998): 'Tighter rules on title use'; *Times Higher Education Supplement*, June 12.

BCC (1998a): *Small Firms Survey - Skills*   (London: British Chambers of Commerce).

BCC (1998b): *Skills for Competitiveness* (London: British Chambers of Commerce).

Beaumont, G. (1996): *Review of 100 NVQs and SVQs* (London: Dept for Education and Employment).

Becker, G.S. (1964): *Human Capital: A Theoretical and Empirical Analysis with special reference to Education* (Princeton, New Jersey: Princeton University Press).

Bees, M. & Swords, M. (Eds) (1990): *National Vocational Qualifications and Further Education* (London: Kogan Page/NCVQ).

Beinart, S. & Smith, P. (1998): *National Adult Learning Survey 1997: Summary* (London: Dept for Education and Employment).

Bell, C. (1996): *Some Key Facts About G/NVQs Awarded* (London: Article 26).

Bell, G.H. (1981): 'Industrial Culture and the School'; *Journal of Philosophy of Education*, 15(2), pp.175-190.

Benjamin, H. (1939/75): 'The Saber-Tooth Curriculum'; in Golby, M., Greenwald, J. & West, W. (Eds) (1975): *Curriculum Design* (London: Croom Helm).

Benn, C. & Fairley, J.(Eds) (1986): *Challenging the MSC on Jobs, Training and Education* (London: Pluto).

Berg, L. (1992): 'Vocationalism in Norwegian Higher Education'; *European Journal of Education*, 28 (1/2), pp.79-88.

Biggs, J.B. (1987): *Student Approaches to Learning and Studying* (Victoria: Australian Council for Educational Research).

Biggs, J.B. (1988): 'Approaches to learning and to essay-writing'; in Schmeck, R.R. (Ed): *Learning Strategies and Learning Styles* (New York: Plenum).

Bloom, B.S. (1956): *Taxonomy of Educational Objectives* (London: Longmans).

Bloomer, M. (1996): 'Education for Studentship'; in Avis et al. (1996); op.cit.

Bloomer, M. (1997): *Curriculum Making in Post-16 Education* (London: Routledge).

Blunkett, D. (1998): 'Opportunities to live and learn'; *Times Higher Education Supplement*, February 27.

Booth, A. & Snower, D. (1996): *Acquiring Skills: market failures, their symptoms and policy responses* (Cambridge: Cambridge University Press).

Bowles, S. & Gintis, H. (1976): *Schooling in Capitalist America* (London: Routledge & Kegan Paul).

Braverman, H. (1974): *Labour and Monopoly Capital - The Degradation of work in the Twentieth Century* (New York: Monthly Press).

Brivati, B. (1998): 'Anyone got an A-Z?'; *Times Higher Education Supplement* May 22.

Brookfield, S. (1986): *Understanding and Facilitating Adult Learning* (Milton Keynes: Open University Press).

Brown, P. (1987): *Schooling Ordinary Kids: Inequality, Unemployment and the New Vocationalism* (London: Tavistock).

Brown, P. & Lauder, H. (Eds) (1992): *Education for Economic Survival: From Fordism to Post-Fordism?* (London: Routledge).

Brown, A.S., Collins, A. & Duguid, P. (1989): 'Situated Cognition and the Culture of Learning'; *Educational Researcher*, 18 (1), pp.32-42.

Bryson, A., Ford, R. & White, M. (1997): *Making Work Pay : Lone Mothers, Employment and Well-Being* (York: Joseph Rowntree Foundation).

BTEC (1993): *Implementing BTEC GNVQs : A Guide for Centres* (London: Business & Technology Education Council).

Buckman, P. (Ed) (1973): *Education Without Schools* (London: Souvenir Press).

Budge, D. (1998): 'Public pain, student gain?'; *Times Educational Supplement*, May 22.

Burke, J. (Ed) (1989): *Competency Based Education and Training* (Lewes: Falmer).

Burke, J. (Ed) (1995): *Outcomes, Learning and the Curriculum* (London: Falmer).

Burroughs, G. 1971): *Design and Analysis in Education Research* (Birmingham: University of Birmingham School of Education).

Burstall, E. (1996): 'Second chance stifled'; *Times Educational Supplement*, March 22.

Callender, C. (1992): *Will NVQs Work? Evidence from the Construction Industry* (University of Sussex: Institute of Manpower Studies).

Canning, R. (1998): 'The failure of competence-based qualifications:an analysis of work-based vocational education policy in Scotland'; *Journal of Education Policy*, 13(5), pp.625-639.

Cantor, L., Roberts, I.F. & Pratley, B. (1995): *A Guide to Further Education in England and Wales* (London: Cassell).

Capey, J. (1995): *GNVQ Assessment Review* (London: National Council for Vocational Qualifications).

Carr, W. (1997): 'Professing Education in a Post-Modern Age'; *Journal of Philosophy of Education*, 31(2), pp.309-327.

Carr, W. & Hartnett, A. (1996): *Education and the Struggle for Democracy* (Buckingham: Open University Press).

Castle, E.B. (1967): *Ancient Education and Today* (Harmondsworth: Penguin).

CBI (1989): *Towards a Skills Revolution* (London: Confederation of British Industry).

Chi, M., Glaser, R. & Farr, N. (1988): *The Nature of Expertise* (Hillsdale,New Jersey: Lawrence Erlbaum Associates).

Child, D. (1981): *Psychology and the Teacher* (London: Holt, Rinehart & Winston).

Chomsky, N. (1991): 'Towards a Humanistic Conception of Education and Work'; in Corson, D. (Ed) (1991); op.cit.

Clarke, J. & Willis, P. (1984): 'Introduction'; in Bates, I., Clarke, J., Cohen, P., Finn, D., Moore, R. & Willis, P. (Eds): *Schooling for the Dole? The New Vocationalism* (Basingstoke: Macmillan).

Coates, P. (1991): 'The 16-19 Core Skills Initiative'; *The Curriculum Journal*, (1), pp.43-53.

Cobban, A. (1988): *The Medieval English University* (London: Scolar Press).

Cockett, M. (1996): 'Chaos or Coherence, Progression and Continuity'; in Halsall, R. & Cockett, M. (Eds) (1996); op.cit.

Coffey, D. (1992): *Schools and Work: Developments in Vocational Education* (London:Cassell).

Coffield, F. (1998): 'Going Into Labour, But Giving Birth to a Tory Child?'; *Parliamentary Brief*, May, pp.25-6.

Cole, G. (1998): 'Biggest classroom in the world'; *TES Online Education - Times Educational Supplement*, May 15.

Collins, M.(1991): *Adult Education as Vocation* (London: Routledge).

Commager, H.S. (1963): *Documents of American History* (New York: Meredith).

Corney, M. (1997): 'Beauty contest to woo the favour of small businesses'; *Times Educational Supplement*, February 28.

Corson, D. (Ed) (1991): *Education For Work* (Clevedon: Multilingual Matters).

COVTEC (1992): *An Introduction to NVQs* (Coventry: Coventry and Warwickshire Training and Enterprise Council).

CPRS (Central Policy Review Staff) (1980): *Education, Training and Industrial Performance* (London: HMSO).

Crick, B. (1998): 'Lessons to make citizens of us all'; *Times Educational Supplement*, March 27.

Crequer, N. (1998): 'Squeezed in trap of debt and hardship'; *Times Educational Supplement*, December 4.

Curtis, S.J. & Boultwood, M.E.A. (1970): *A Short History of Educational Ideas* (London: University Tutorial Press).

Dahrendorf, R. (1982): *On Britain* (London: British Broadcasting Corporation).

Dave, R.H. (Ed) (1976): *Foundations of Lifelong Education* (London: Pergamon).

Davies, P. & Parry, G. (1993): *Recognising Access* (Leicester: National Institute of Adult Continuing Education).

Dawn, T. (1995): *Fifty Years of Further Education - Celebration or Wake* (Oxford: Oxford Brookes University School of Education).

Dearden, R.F. (1972): 'Happiness and Education'; in Dearden, R.F., Hirst, P.H. & Peters, R.S. (Eds): *Education and the Development of Reason* (London: Routledge & Kegan Paul).

Dearden, R.F. (1984): *Theory and Practice in Education* (London: Routledge & Kegan Paul).

Dearden, R.F. (1990): 'Education and Training'; in Esland, G. (Ed) (1990); op.cit.

Dearing, Sir Ron (1996): *Review of Qualifications for 16-19 Year Olds* (Hayes:

School Curriculum and Assessment Authority).

Dearing, Sir Ron (1997): *Higher Education in the Learning Society* (London: Dept for Education and Employment).

De Bono, E. (1978): *Teaching Thinking* (Harmondsworth: Penguin).

Deissinger, T. (1997): 'The German dual system - a model for Europe?'; *Education + Training*, 39(8), pp.297-302.

Dent, H.C. (1968): *The Education Act 1944* (London:University of London Press).

DES (1973): *Adult Education : A Plan for Development (Russell Report)* (London: HMSO).

DES (1977): *Education in Schools: A Consultative Document* (London:HMSO).

DES (1985a): *Better Schools: A Summary* (London: Dept of Education and Science/Welsh Office).

DES (1985b): *The Curriculum 5 to 16* (London:HMSO).

DES (1991): *Education and Training for the 21st Century* (London: HMSO).

Dewey, J. (1915): *The School and Society* (Chicago: University of Chicago Press) [originally published in 1900].

Dewey, J. (1963): *Experience and Education* (London: Collier-Macmillan) [originally published in 1938].

Dewey, J. (1966): *Democracy and Education* (New York: Free Press) [originally published in 1916].

DfEE (1995): *Skills and Enterprise Briefing 8/95* (London: Dept for Education and Employment).

DfEE (1996): *The Qualifications and National Curriculum Authority* (London: Dept for Education and Employment).

DfEE (1997a): *First Steps in Upgrading NVQs - 248/97* (London: Dept for Education and Employment).

DfEE (1997b): *Design of the New Deal for 18-24 Year Olds* (London: Dept for Education and Employment.

DfEE (1997c): *Incentives and Barriers to Take-Up of NVQs/SVQs by Individuals* (London: Dept for Education and Employment).

DfEE (1998a): *The Learning Age : A Renaissance for a New Britain* (London: The Stationery Office).

DfEE (1998b): *Skills and Enterprise Briefing 2/98* (London: Dept for Education and Employment).

DfEE (1998c): *University for Industry: Pathfinder Prospectus* (London: Dept for Education and Employment).

DfEE (1998d): *A Study of Employers' Use of NVQs and SVQs Across Industrial Sectors* (London: Dept for Education and Employment).

DfEE (1998e): *Skills and Enterprise Briefing 4/98* (London: Dept for Education and Employment).

DfEE (1998f): *Further Education for the New Millennium* (London: Dept for Education and Employment).

DfEE (1998g): *Sunderland University Head to Lead Ufl* (London: Dept for Education and Employment).

DfEE (1998h): *Learning Direct : A Guide* (London: Dept for Education and Employment).

DfEE (1998i): *Accountability in Further Education* (London: Dept for Education and Employment).

DfEE (1998j): *Towards a National Skills Agenda* (London: Dept for Education and Employment).

DfEE (1998k): *New Deal News* (London: Dept for Education and Employment) 575/98.

DfEE (1999a): *DfEE News* (London: Dept for Education and Emplyment) 17/99.

DfEE (1999b): *New Deal for Young People and Long-Term Unemployed People Aged 25+: Statistics* (London: Dept for Education and Employment) 38/99.

DOE (1981): *A New Training Initiative - A Programme for Action* (London: HMSO).

DOE, DES (1984): *Training for Jobs* (London: HMSO).

DOE, DES (1985): *Education and Training for Young People* (London: HMSO).

DOE, DES (1986): *Working Together - Education and Training* (London: HMSO).

Dore, R. (1976): *The Diploma Disease* (London: Allen & Unwin).

Dore, R. (1997): 'Reflections on the Diploma Disease Twenty Years Later'; *Assessment in Education*, 4(1), pp.189-205.

Downey, M. & Kelly, A.V. (1978): *Moral Education: Theory and Practice* (London: Harper & Row).

DTI (1994): *Competitiveness: helping business to win* (London: HMSO).

DTI (1995): *Competitiveness: forging ahead* (London: HMSO).

Duke, C. (1992): *The Learning University* (Milton Keynes: Open University Press).

Dyson, K. (1990): *Small and Medium Enterprises* (London: Routledge).

Ecclestone, K. (1998): 'Euston Road and the ivory towers : the impact of the GNVQ research industry'; *Journal of Education Policy*, 13(6), pp.679-697.

EDAP (1992): *A Unique Initiative in British Industry* (Basildon, Essex: Ford Employee Development and Assistance Programme).

ED (1993a): *Development of Transferable Skills in Learners* (Sheffield: Employment Dept Methods Strategy Unit).

ED (1993b): *Systems and Procedures of Certification of Qualifications in the United Kingdom* (Sheffield: Employment Dept Methods Strategy Group).

ED (1994): *Individual Commitment: NVQ Case Studies* (Sheffield: Employment Dept).

Educa (1997a): 'NCVQ –RIP'; *Educa*, No.176, October.

Educa (1997b): 'Standards in FE'; *Educa*, No.178, December.

Educa (1998a): 'Modern Apprenticeships'; *Educa*, No.186, October.

Educa (1998b): 'New Deal News'; *Educa*, No.185,'September.

Edwards, R. (1993): 'The Inevitable Future? Post-Fordism in Work and Learning';

in Edwards, R., Sieminski, S. & Zeldin, D. (Eds): *Adult Learners, Education and Training* (London: Routledge/Open University Press).

Edwards, R. (1994): 'From a distance: globalisation, space-time compression and distance education'; *Open Learning*, 9(3), pp.9-17.

Edwards, R. (1997): *Changing Places ?: flexibility, lifelong learning and a learning society* (London: Routledge).

Edwards, R., Sieminski, S. & Zeldin, D. (Eds) (1993): *Adult Learners, Education and Training* (London: Routledge/Open University Press).

Elliott, J.(1993): *Reconstructing Teacher Education* (London:Falmer).

Engestrom, Y. (1994): *Training for Change* (Geneva: International Labour Organisation).

EPI (1995): *The Skills Mirage* (London: Employment Policy Institute).

Ernst & Young (1995): *The Evaluation of Modern Apprenticeship Prototypes: Final Report* (University of Sheffield: Centre for the Study of Post-16 Developments).

Esland, G. (Ed) (1990): *Education, Training and Employment* (Wokingham: Addison-Wesley Pub.Co./Open University Press).

Esland, G. (1996a): 'Knowledge and Nationhood: the New Right, Education and the Global Market'; in Avis, J et al. (1996); op.cit.

Esland, G. (1996b): 'Education, Training and Nation-State Capitalism: Britain's Failing Strategy'; in Avis, J et al. (1996); op.cit.

Esland, G., Flude, M. & Sieminski, S. (1999): 'Introduction'; in Flude, M. & Sieminksi, S. (Eds) (1999); op.cit.

Etzioni, A. (1995): *The Spirit of Community* (Glasgow: Harper Collins).

Etzioni, A. (1997): *The New Golden Rule: community and morality in a democratic society* (New York: Basic Books).

Evans, B. (1992): *The Politics of the Training Market* (London: Routledge).

Evans, K., Brown, A. & Oates, T. (1987): *Developing Work-Based Learning: an evaluative review of the YTS core skills project* (Sheffield: Manpower Services Commission/University of Surrey).

Evans, K. & Malcolm, H. (1985): *Analysis of the Curriculum in Foundation Training* (Sheffield: Manpower Services Commission/University of Surrey).

Farley, M. (1983): 'Trends and Structural Changes in English Vocational Education'; in Watson, K. (Ed): *Youth, Education and Employment: International Perspectives* (London: Croom Helm).

Fay, P. (1988): 'Stalling between fools : contradictions in the structure and processes of YTS'; *Journal of Further & Higher Education*, 12(2), pp.23-50.

FEFC (1993): *Recurrent Funding Methodology* (Coventry: Further Education Funding Council).

FEFC (1994a): *General National Vocational Qualifications in the Further Education Sector in England* (Coventry: Further Education Funding Council).

FEFC (1994b): *NVQs in the Further Education Sector in England* (Coventry:

Further Education Funding Council).

FEFC (1994c): *Guidance on the Recurrent Funding Methodology* (Coventry: Further Education Funding Council).

FEU (1982): *Basic Skills* (London: Further Education Unit).

FEU (1992): *Flexible Colleges* (London: Further Education Unit).

FEU (1993): *Learner Support Services in Further Education* (London: Further Education Unit).

FEU (1995): *A Framework for Credit : A Common Framework for Post-14 Education and Training for the 21st Century* (London: Further Education Unit).

FEU/Nuffield (1994): *GNVQs 1993-94: A National Survey Report* (London: Further Education Unit/The Nuffield Foundation).

Field, J. (1995): 'Reality testing in the workplace: are NVQs employment led?'; in Hodkinson, P. & Issitt, M. (Eds) (1995); op.cit.

Field, J. (1998): 'The Silent Explosion – Living in the Learning Society'; *Adults Learning*; 10(4), pp.6-8.

Finegold, D. & Soskice, D. (1988): 'The Failure of Training in Britain: analysis and prescription'; *Oxford Review of Economic Policy*, 4(3), pp.21-53.

Finegold, D., Keep, E., Miliband, D., Raffe, D., Spours, K. & Young, M. (1990): *A British Baccalaureate: Overcoming Divisions between Education and Training* (London: Institute for Public Policy Research).

Finegold, D. & Irvine, D.I. (1997): 'Institutional Incentives for Employer Training'; *Journal of Education and Work*, 10(2), pp.109-127.

Finn, D. (1986): 'YTS, the jewel in the MSC's crown?'; in Benn, C. & Fairley, J. (Eds): *Challenging the MSC on Jobs, Training and Education* (London: Pluto).

Finn, D. (1990): 'The great debate on education, youth employment and the MSC'; in Esland, G. (Ed) (1990); op.cit.

Finn, D. (1997): 'Labour's New Deal for the Unemployed'; *Local Economy*, November, pp.247-258.

Fish, D. (1993): 'Uncertainty in a certain world : values, competency-based training and the reflective practitioner'; *Journal of the National Association for Values in Education and Training*, VIII, pp.7-12.

Fisher, S. & Hicks, D. (1985): *World Studies* (Edinburgh: Oliver & Boyd).

Fitzpatrick, M. (1998): 'Reform call to end civil turmoil'; *Times Educational Supplement*, June 26.

Fletcher, S. (1991): *NVQs, Standards and Competence* (London: Kogan Page).

Flude, M. & Sieminski, S. (Eds) (1999): *Education, Training and the Future of Work II: Developments in Vocational Education and Training* (London: Routledge/Open University).

Forster, K. (1996): 'Competencies and the Curriculum: Can schooling contribute to the reconstruction of work?'; *Educational Philosophy and Theory*, 28(1), pp.24- 39.

Foster, P.(1977): 'The Vocational School Fallacy'; in Karabel, J. & Halsey, A. (Eds): *Power and Ideology in Education* (Oxford: Oxford University Press).

Fowler, G. (1998): 'Improving vocational training'; *Education + Training*,40 (6/7), pp.242-243.

Fryer, R.H. (1997): *Learning for the Twenty-First Century* (London: National Advisory group for Continuing Education and Lifelong Learning).

Gallie, W.B. (1964): *Philosophy and Historical Understanding* (London: Unwin).

Gardner, J. (1979): *People and Communication* (London: Cassell).

Gardner, P. & Johnson, S. (1996): 'Thinking critically about critical thinking'; *Journal of Philosophy of Education*, 30 (3), pp.441-456.

Gay, L.R. (1987): *Educational Research* (London: Merrill Publishing Co.).

Geach, P. (1971): *Mental Acts* (London: Routledge & Kegan Paul).

Geiger, G.R. (1958): *John Dewey in Perspective* (New York: Oxford University Press).

Gellert, C. & Rau, E. (1992): 'Diversification and Integration: the Vocationalization of the German higher education system; *European Journal of Education*, 28(1/2), pp.89-100.

Gibbs, G. (1990): *Improving Student Learning Project* (Oxford: Oxford Centre for Staff Development).

Gibbs, G. (1992): 'Improving the Quality of Student Learning through Course Design'; in Barnett, R. (Ed): *Learning To Effect* (Buckingham: Open University).

Giddens, A. (1998): *The Third Way: The Renewal of Social Democracy* (London: Polity Press).

Gleeson, D. (1996): 'Continuity and Change in Post-Compulsory Education and Training'; in Halsall, R. & Cockett, M. (Eds) (1996); op.cit.

Gleeson, D. & Hodkinson, P. (1999): 'Ideology and Curriculum Policy: GNVQ and mass post-compulsory education in England and Wales'; in Flude, M. & Sieminski, S. (Eds) (1999); op.cit.

Goddard, A. & Thomson, A. (1999): 'Ministers act as poor jump ship'; *Times Higher Education Supplement*, January 29.

Gokulsing, K., Ainley, P. & Tysome, T. (1996): *Beyond Competence: The NCVQ And the Challenge to Higher Education in the Millennium* (Aldershot: Avebury).

Gordon, P. & White, J. (1979): *Philosophers as Educational Reformers* (London: Rouledge & Kegan Paul).

Gospel, H. (1995): 'The Decline of Apprenticeship Training in Britain'; *Industrial Relations Journal*, 26(1), pp.32-44.

Gospel, H. (1998a): 'The Revival of Apprenticeship Training in Britain'; *British Journal of Industrial Relations*, 36(3), pp.435-457.

Gospel, H. (1998b): 'Reinventing Apprenticeship'; *CentrePiece* , 3(3), pp.19-23.

Goss, D. (1991): *Small Business and Society* (London: Routledge).

Great Britain Statutes (1992): *Further and Higher Education Act 1992* (London: HMSO).

Green, A. (1990): *Education and State Formation* (London: Macmillan).

Green, A. (1995): 'The European Challenge to British Vocational Education and Training'; in Hodkinson, P. & Issitt, M. (Eds) (1995); op.cit.

Green, A. (1997a): 'Core Skills, General Education and Unification in Post-16 Education'; in Hodgson, A. & Spours, K. (Eds) (1997); op.cit.

Green, A. (1997b): *Education, Globalization and the Nation State* (London: Macmillan Press).

Green, T.F. (1968): *Work, Leisure and the American School* (New York: Random House).

Gribble, J. (1969): *Introduction to Philosophy of Education* (Boston, Mass: Allyn & Bacon Inc.).

Griffiths, M. (1987): 'The teaching of skills and the skills of teaching: a reply to Robin Barrow'; *Journal of Philosophy of Education*, 21(2), pp.203-214.

Hackett, G. (1998): 'Browsing around for the right courses'; *Times Educational Supplement*, February 27.

Hague, H. (1998): 'University for a new age'; *Times Educational Supplement*, January 16.

Halliday, J. (1990): *Markets, Managers and Theory in Education* (Lewes: Falmer).

Halpin, D. & Troyna, B. (Eds) (1994): *Researching Educational Policy: ethical and methodological issues* (London: Falmer).

Halsall, R. (1996): 'Core Skills - the Continuing Debate'; in Halsall, R. & Cockett, M.(Eds) (1996); op.cit.

Halsall, R. & Cockett, M. (Eds) (1996): *Education and Training 14-19: Chaos or Coherence?* (London: David Fulton).

Halsey, A., Heath, A. & Ridge, J. (1980): *Origins and Destinations: Family, Class and Education in Modern Britain* (Oxford: Oxford University Press).

Handy, C. (1989): *The Age of Unreason* (Boston: Harvard Business School).

Hargreaves, D. (1982): *The Challenge for the Comprehensive School* (London: Routledge & Kegan Paul).

Hart, J. (1998): 'Report urges training overhaul'; *Times Educational Supplement*, October 30.

Hart, W.A. (1978):'Against Skills'; *Oxford Review of Education*, 4(2), pp.205-216.

Hartley, D. (1995): 'The McDonaldisation of Higher Education: food for thought?'; *Oxford Review of Education*, 21 (4), pp.409-423.

Hartley, J., Trueman, M. & Lapping, C. (1997): 'The performance of mature and younger students at Keele University: analysis of archival data'; *Journal of Access Studies*, 12 (1), pp.98-112.

Harris, S. & Hyland, T. (1995): 'Basic Skills and Learning Support in Further Education'; *Journal of Further & Higher Education*, 19(2), pp.42-48.

Hazell, R. (1934): 'Education in the Printing Industry'; *Industrial Welfare and*

Personnel Management, XVI(183), pp.24-28.

Heaney, S. (1990): *New Collected Poems: 1966-1987* (London: Faber & Faber).

Heater, D. (1980): *World Studies: Education for International Understanding in Britain* (London: Harrap).

HEC (1997): *Key Skills in Higher Education?* (London: Higher Education for Capability).

Heelas, P. & Morris, P. (Eds) (1992): *The Values of the Enterprise Culture* (London: Routledge).

Herbst, P. (1973): 'Work, Labour and University Education'; in Peters, R.S. (Ed); *The Philosophy of Education* (Oxford: Oxford University Press).

Higham, J., Sharp, P. & Yeomans, D. (1996): *The Emerging 16-19 Curriculum: Policy and Provision* (London: David Fulton).

Higgins, T. & Megson, C. (1995): 'GNVQs are good for you: it's official; *Education*, November 24.

Hillman, J. (1997): *University for Industry: Creating a National Learning Network* (London: Institute for Public Policy Research).

Hillman, J. (1998): 'Mission to find latent skills'; *Times Educational Supplement*, July 31.

Hills, G. (1989): 'Put your money on the doers'; *Times Educational Supplement*, January 20.

Hills, G. (1990): 'The pursuit of judgement'; *The Guardian*, September 18.

Hirschhorn, L. (1984): *Beyond Mechanisation: Work and Technology in a Post-Industrial Age* (Cambridge, MA: MIT Press).

Hirst, P.H. (1974): *Knowledge and the Curriculum* (London: Routledge & Kegan Paul).

HMC (1995): *The [1995] Education 14-19 Conference* (Leicester: Headmasters' Conference).

HMI (1989): *Post-16 Education and Training - Core Skills* (London: Dept of Education and Science).

Hodgson, A. & Spours, K. (Eds) (1997): *Dearing and Beyond: 14-19 Qualifications, Frameworks and Systems* (London: Kogan Page).

Hodkinson, P. (1992): 'Alternative Models of Competence in Vocational Education and Training'; *Journal of Further & Higher Education*, 16(2), pp.30-9.

Hodkinson, P. (1996): 'Careership: The Individual, Choices and Markets in the Transition into Work'; in Avis, J. et al. (Eds) (1996); op.cit.

Hodkinson, P. (1997): 'A lethal cocktail: NVQs, small employers and payment by results'; *Educa*, No.169, p.7.

Hodkinson, P. & Issitt, M. (Eds) (1995): *The Challenge of Competence: Professionalism through Vocational Education and Training* (London: Cassell).

Hodkinson, P. & Sparkes, A. (1993): 'Young people's choices and careers guidance action planning'; *British Journal of Guidance and Counselling*, 21(2), pp.246-261.

Hodkinson, P. & Sparkes, A. (1995): 'Markets and Vouchers: the inadequacy of individualist policies for vocational education and training in England and Wales'; *Journal of Educational Policy*, 10(2), pp.198-207.

Hodkinson, P., Sparkes, A. & Hodkinson, H. (1996): *Triumphs and Tears: Young People, Markets and the Transition from School to Work* (London: David Fulton).

Hofstadter, R. (1959): *The Age of Reform* (New York: Knopf Books).

Holland, R.F. (1980): *Against Empiricism : On Education, Epistemology and Value* (Oxford: Basil Blackwell).

Holt, J. (1977): *Instead of Education* (Harmondsworth: Penguin).

Holt, M. (Ed) (1987): *Skills and Vocationalism: The Easy Answer* (Milton Keynes: Open University Press).

Houghton, V. & Richardson, K. (Eds) (1974): *Recurrent Education: A Plea for Lifelong Learning* (London: Ward Lock Educational).

Hounsell, D. (1985): 'Learning and essay-writing'; *Higher Education Research and Development*, 3(1), pp.13-31.

Hughes, C. & Tight, M. (1998): 'The Myth of the Learning Society'; in Ranson, S. (Ed) (1998); op.cit.

Husen, T. (1974): *The Learning Society* (London: Methuen).

Hutchinson, F.P. (1996): *Educating Beyond Violent Futures* (London: Routledge).

Hutton, W. (1995): *The State We're In* (London: Jonathan Cape).

Hyland, T. (1980): 'Integration and Cross-Modular Activity on BEC Courses'; *Journal of Further & Higher Education*, 4(3), pp.70-77.

Hyland, T. (1986): 'In Defence of World Studies'; *Multicultural Teaching*, 5 (1), pp.25-27.

Hyland, T. (1991): 'Taking Care of Business: Vocationalism, Competence, and the Enterprise Culture'; *Educational Studies*, 17 (1), pp.77-87.

Hyland, T. (1992a): 'Moral Vocationalism'; *Journal of Moral Education*, 21 (2), pp.139-150.

Hyland, T. (1992b): 'Expertise and Competence in Further and Adult Education'; *British Journal of In-Service Education*, 18(1), pp.23-28.

Hyland, T. (1993): 'Vocational Reconstruction and Dewey's Instrumentalism'; *Oxford Review of Education*, 19 (1), pp.89-100.

Hyland, T. (1994a): *Competence, Education and NVQs: Dissenting Perspectives* (London: Cassell).

Hyland, T. (1994b): 'Silk Purses and Sows' Ears: NVQs,GNVQs and Experiential Learning'; *Cambridge Journal of Education*, 24(2), pp.233-243.

Hyland, T. (1994c): 'Tilting At Windmills: the problems of challenging the NCVQ'; *Educational Studies*, 20 (2), pp.251-265.

Hyland, T. (1995a): 'Morality,Work and Employment:towards a values dimension in vocational education and training'; *Journal of Moral Education*, 24(4), pp.445-456.

Hyland, T. (1995b): 'Behaviourism and the Meaning of Competence'; in Hodkinson, P. & Issitt, M. (Eds) (1995); op.cit.

Hyland, T. (1996a): 'Credits and Debits: CATS and the Commodification of Learning'; *Education Today*, 46 (2), pp.31-35.

Hyland, T. (1996b): 'Through a Glass Darkly: A Critique of the NCVQ Visions of Higher Level Vocational Qualifications'; *Oxford Review of Education*, 22 (3), pp.357-362.

Hyland, T. (1996c): 'Access, Credit and the Learning Society'; *Journal of Access Studies*, 11(2), pp.153-164.

Hyland, T. (1996d): 'NVQs, Skills Training and Employers' Needs: Beyond Beaumont and Dearing'; *Journal of Vocational Education and Training*, 48(4), pp.349-365.

Hyland, T. (1996e): 'Professionalism, Ethics and Work-Based Learning'; *British Journal of Educational Studies*, 44 (2), pp.168-180.

Hyland, T. (1997a): 'Reconsidering Competence'; *Journal of Philosophy of Education*, 31 (3), pp.491-503.

Hyland, T. (1997b): 'The skills that fail to travel'; *Times Higher Education Supplement*, May 2.

Hyland, T. (1998a): 'Work-Based Experience and Higher Professional Learning in British Universities'; in Forest, J. (Ed): *University Teaching: International Perspectives* (New York: Garland).

Hyland, T. (1998b): 'Morality and Further Education'; *Journal of Moral Education*, 27(3), pp.333-344.

Hyland, T. (1998c): 'Skill Scam'; *Guardian Higher Education*, July 14.

Hyland, T. (1998d): 'Exporting Failure: the strange case of NVQs and overseas markets'; *Educational Studies*, 24 (3), pp.369-380.

Hyland, T. & Johnson, S. (1998): 'Of Cabbages and Key Skills: Exploding the Mythology of Core Transferable Skills in Post-School Education'; *Journal of Further & Higher Education*, 22 (2), pp.163-172.

Hyland, T. & Matlay, H. (1997): 'Small Businesses, Training Needs and VET Provision'; *Journal of Education and Work*, 10 (2), pp.129-139.

Hyland, T. & Matlay, H. (1998): 'Lifelong Learning and New Deal Vocationalism'; *British Journal of Educational Studies*, 46 (4), pp.399-414.

Hyland, T. & Weller, P. (1994): *Implementing NVQs in FE Colleges* (University of Warwick: Dept of Continuing Education).

IES (1995): *Employers' Use of the NVQ System* (University of Sussex: Institute of Employment Studies).

IFS (1998): *Higher Education, Employment and Earnings in Britain* (London: Institute of Fiscal Studies).

IIE (1996): *Towards Employability* (London: Industry in Education).

IJLE (1998): 'Editorial'; *International Journal of Lifelong Education*, 17 (2), p.69.

Illich, I. (1973): *Deschooling Society* (Harmondsworth: Penguin Books).

IMS (1982): *Skills Needed for Young People's Jobs* (London: Institute of Manpower Studies).

Jarrett, J.L. (1991): *The Teaching of Values: caring and appreciation* (London: Routledge).

Jenkins, S. (1995): *Accountable to None: The Tory Nationalisation of Britain* (London: Hamish Hamilton).

Jessup, G. (1990): 'National Vocational Qualifications: Implications for Further Education'; in Bees, M. & Swords, M. (Eds) (1990); op.cit.

Jessup, G. (1991): *Outcomes: NVQs and the Emerging Model of Education and Training* (London: Falmer).

Johnson, S. (1998): 'Skills, Socrates and the Sophists: Learning from History'; *British Journal of Educational Studies*, 46 (2), pp.201-213.

Johnson, T.H. (1966): *The Oxford Companion to American History* (Oxford: Oxford University Press).

Jonathan, R. 1987): 'The Youth Training Scheme and Core Skills: an educational analysis'; in Holt, M. (Ed) (1987); op.cit.

Jonathan, R. (1997): *Illusory Freedoms: Liberalism, Education and the Market* (Oxford: Blackwell).

Jones, D. (1997): *Further Education and Guidance* (University of Warwick: Dept of Continuing Education) Unpublished MA Dissertation.

Joseph, Sir Keith (1984): 'View from the top'; *Times Educational Supplement*, January 13.

Kamenka, E. (1969): Marxism *and Ethics* (London: Macmillan).

Kellner, P. (1998): 'Our mutual friends'; *Times Educational Supplement*, June 19.

Kennedy, H. (1997): *Learning Works: Widening Participation in Further Education* (Coventry: Further Education Funding Council).

Kenneth Richmond, W. (1945): *Education in England* (Harmondsworth: Penguin).

Kenway, J., Bigum, C. & Fitzclarence, L. (1993): 'Marketing education in the postmodern age'; *Journal of Education Policy*, 8 (2), pp.105-122.

Knowles, M. (1970): *The Modern Practice of Adult Education: Andragogy versus Pedagogy* (New York: Association Press).

Kolb, D.A. (1993): 'The process of experiential learning'; in Thorpe, M., Edwards, R. & Hanson, A .(Eds): *Culture and Processes of Adult Learning* (London: Routledge).

Labour Party (1997): *Labour Party Manifesto* (London: The Labour Party).

Lamoure, J. & Rontopoulou, L. (1992): 'The Vocationalization of Higher Education in France'; *European Journal of Education*, 28 (1/2), pp.45-56.

Langford, G. (1985): *Education, Persons and Society: A Philosophical Inquiry* (Basingstoke: Macmillan).

Larkin, J.H. (1989): 'What kind of knowledge transfers?'; in Resnick, L.B. (Ed):

Knowing, Learning and Instruction (Hillside, New Jersey: Lawrence Erlbaum Associates).

Lave, J. & Wenger, E. (1991): *Situated Learning : Legitimate Peripheral Participation* (Cambridge: Cambridge University Press).

Lawson, K.H. (1975): *A Critique of Recurrent Education* (Nottingham: Association of Recurrent Education) Discussion Paper No.1.

Lawson, K.H. (1998): *Philosophical Issues in the Education of Adults* (Nottingham: University of Nottingham Continuing Education Press).

Lawson, T. (1992): 'Core Skills 16-19'; in Whiteside, T., Sutton, A. & Everton, T. (Eds) (1992); op.cit.

Lawson, J. & Silver, H. (1978): *A Social History of Education in England* (London: Methuen).

Lawton, D. (1989): *Education, Culture and the National Curriculum* (London: Hodder & Stoughton).

Leach, A.F. (1904): *The Schools of Medieval England* (London: The Antiquary's Books).

Leadbetter, C. (1998): 'Head breaks the mould'; *Times Educational Supplement*, June 26.

Lee, D., Marsden, D., Rickman, P. & Duncombe, J. (1990): *Scheming for Work: A Study of the YTS in the Enterprise Cutlure* (Milton Keynes: Open University Press).

Lees, D. & Chiplin, R. (1970): 'The economics of industrial training'; *Lloyds Bank Review*, April, pp.35-41.

Legge, D. (1982): *The Education of Adults in Britain* (Milton Keynes: Open University Press).

Lengrand, P. (1975): *An Introduction to Lifelong Education* (London: Croom Helm).

Leroux, J. & Lafleur, S. (1995): 'Employability Skills: the demands of the workplace'; *The Vocational Aspect of Education*, 47 (2), pp. 67-89.

Lester Smith, W.O. (1966): *Education: An Introductory Survey* (Harmondsworth: Penguin).

Lewis, T. (1991): 'Difficulties attending the new vocationalism in the USA'; *Journal of Philosophy of Education*, 25 (1), pp.95-108.

Lewis, T. (1997): 'Towards a Liberal Vocational Education'; *Journal of Philosophy of Education*, 31 (3), pp.477-489.

Levi, P. (1988): *The Wrench* (London: Abacus).

Liepmann, K. (1960): *Apprenticeship : An Enquiry into its Adequacy under Modern Conditions* (London: Routledge & Kegan Paul).

Low-Beer, A. (1969): *Spencer* (New York: Collier-Macmillan).

Lucas, B. (1998): 'Salute the joined-up learning revolution'; *Times Educational Supplement*, June 5.

Lyotard, J.-F. (1984): *The Postmodern Condition : A Report on Knowledge*

(Minneapolis: University of Minnesota Press).

Macfarlane, E. (1993): *Education 16-19 In Transition* (London: Routledge).

MacIntyre, A. (1981): *After Virtue* (London: Duckworth).

Maclure, S. (1973): *Educational Documents* (London: Methuen).

Maclure, S. (1989): *Education Re-Formed* (London: Hodder & Stoughton).

Maclure, S. (1991): *Missing Links : the challenge to further education* (London: Policy Studies Institute).

Maclure, S. (1998): 'Through the Revolution and Out the Other Side'; *Oxford Review of Education*, 24 (1), pp.5-24.

Macpherson, C.B. (1964): *The Political Theory of Possessive Individualism* (Oxford: Oxford University Press).

Marcuse, H. (1964): *One Dimensional Man* (London: Routledge).

Marks, J. (1996): *Vocational Education, Training and Qualifications in Britain* (London: Institute of Economic Affairs).

Marton, F., Hounsell, D. & Entwistle, N. (Eds) (1984): *The Experience of Learning* (Edinburgh: Scottish Acadamic Press).

Mason, C. (1998): 'New Deal with marked cards'; *Local Economy*, August, pp.176-186.

Matlay, H. (1996): *Paradox Resolved? Owner/manager attitudes to and actual provision of training in the small business sector* (University of Birmingham: paper presented at the 19th Institute for Small Business Association Conference).

Matlay, H. & Hyland, T. (1997): 'NVQs in the Small Business Sector: A critical overview'; *Education + Training*, 39 (9), pp.325-332.

Matlay, H. & Hyland, T. (1999): 'Small Firms and the University for Industry: An Appraisal'; *Educational Studies*, 25 (2), forthcoming.

McCulloch, G. (1986): 'Policy, Politics and Education - TVEI'; *Journal of Educational Policy*, 1 (1), pp.35-52.

McGavin, H. (1998a): 'TEC blight diagnosed'; *Times Educational Supplement*, July 31.

McGavin, H. (1998b): 'New Deal welcomed but not so lucrative'; *Times Educational Supplement*, October 2.

McGill, P. (1997): 'New Deal threat to young women'; *Times Educational Supplement*, December 5.

McGivney, V. (1990): *Education's for Other People* (Leicester: National Institute for Adult Continuing Education).

McGivney, V. (1993): 'Participation and Non-Participation: a review of the literature'; in Edwards, R., Sieminski, S. & Zeldin, D. (Eds) (1993); op.cit.

McGivney, V. (1996): *Staying or Leaving the Course : non-completion and retention of mature students in further and higher education* (Leicester: National Institute for Adult Continuing Education).

McMaster, G. (1991): 'Japan's secret of success'; *Times Educational Supplement*,

June 7.

McNair, S. (1999): 'From Worthy Margin to Lively Mainstream'; *Adults Learning,* 10 (5), p.3.

Meighan, R. (1981): *A Sociology of Educating* (London: Holt, Rinehart & Winston).

Merrick, N. (1994): 'Stores split over value of NVQs'; *Times Educational Supplement,* June 3.

Merson, M. (1996): 'Education,Training and the Flexible Labour Market'; *British Journal of Education and Work,* 9 (2), pp.79-91.

Miles, S. (1998): 'McDonaldization and the Global Sports Store'; in Alfino, M., Caputo, J.S. & Wynyard, R. (Eds) (1998); op.cit.

Milner, H. (1998): 'The Broker and the Catalyst'; *Adults Learning,* 9 (5), pp.15-17.

Mitchell, L .(1989): 'The Definition of Standards and Their Assessment'; in Burke, J. (Ed) (1989); op.cit.

MSC (1977): *Training for Skills* (Sheffield: Manpower Services Commission).

Munn, P. & MacDonald, C. (1988): *Adult Participation in Education and Training* (Edinburgh: Scottish Council for Research in Education).

Murphy, J. (1993): 'A Degree of Waste: the economic benefits of educational expansion'; *Oxford Review of Education,* 19 (1), pp.9-31.

Musgrave, P.W. (1964): 'The Definition of Technical Education,1860-1910'; *The Vocational Aspect of Secondary and Further Education,* 34 (1), pp.105-111.

Musgrave, P.W. (1966): 'Constant Factors in the Demand for Technical Education'; in Musgrave, P.W. (Ed): *Sociology,History and Education* (London: Methuen).

NACETT (1995): *Report on Progress Towards the National Targets* (London: National Advisory Council for Education and Training Targets).

NACETT (1998): *Fast Forward fo Skills* (London: National Advisory Council for Education and Training Targets).

Nash, I. (1995): 'Colleges' council to tighten up on ethics'; *Times Educational Supplement,* January 6.

Nash, I. (1997a): 'Relaunch in spring to defuse critics'; *Times Educational Supplement,* January 24.

Nash, I. (1997b): 'University for Industry plans are revealed'; *Times Educational Supplement,* April 18.

Nash, I. (1997c): 'Cut dropping out or lose New Deal cash'; *Times Educational Supplement,* December 12.

Nash, I., Crequer, N. & Slater, J. (1998): 'Door opens for excluded groups'; *Times Educational Supplement,* December 4.

NCC (1990a): *Education for Citizenship* (York: National Curriculum Council).

NCC (1990b): *Core Skills 16-19* (London: HMSO).

NCC (1992): *Education for Work : a guide for industry and commerce* (York: National Curriculum Council).

NCE (1993): *Learning To Succeed: Report of the National Commission on Education* (London: Heinemann).

NCVQ (1989): *Initial Criteria and Guidelines for Staff Development* (London: National Council for Vocational Qualifications).

NCVQ (1991): *Criteria for National Vocational Qualifications* (London: National Council for Vocational Qualifications).

NCVQ (1992a): *Response to Consultation on GNVQs* (London: National Council for Vocational Qualifications).

NCVQ (1992b): *NVQ Monitor* (London: National Council for Vocational Qualifications).

NCVQ (1993a): *GNVQs : Core Skill Units* (London: National Council for Vocational Qualifications).

NCVQ (1993b): *GNVQ Information Note* (London: National Council for Vocational Qualifications).

Neave, G. (1992): 'On Instantly Consumable Knowledge and Snake Oil'; *European Journal of Education*, 28 (1/2), pp.5-28.

Nelson-Jones, R. (1989): *Human Relationship Skills* (London: Cassell).

NIACE (1998): *Reaching Adult Learners* (Leicester: National Institute of Adult Continuing Education).

Nicholls, A. (1995): *Schools and Colleges: collaborators or competitors in the education system* (London: Schools Guidance Council).

Nichols, A. (1998): 'Too much fuss and bother?'; *Times Educational Supplement* June 19.

Norman, R. (1983): *The Moral Philosophers* (Oxford: Clarendon Press).

OECD (1996): *Best Practice Policies for Small and Medium-Sized Enterprises* (Paris: Organisation for Economic Co-operation and Development).

OECD (1998): *Pathways and Participation in Vocational and Technical Education and Training* (Paris: Organisation for Economic Co-operation and Development).

Ofsted (1992): *GNVQs in Schools : The Introduction of General National Vocational Qualifications* (London: HMSO).

Ofsted (1994): *GNVQs in Schools 1993-94* (London: HMSO).

Opinion Leader Research (1997): *Young People's Attitudes Towards New Deal and the Employment Service* (London: Opinion Leader Research).

Ormerod, P. (1994): *The Death of Economics* (London: Faber & Faber).

Ormerod, P. (1999): 'A shrug at the dole queue'; *Times Higher Education Supplement*, February 12.

Otter, S. (1995): 'Learning Outcomes in Higher Education'; in Burke, J. (Ed) (1995); op cit.

Papanoutsos, E.P. (1978): 'The Gift of Art'; *Journal of Aesthetic Education*, 12 (4), pp.87-94.

Parker, M. (1998): 'Nostalgia and Mass Culture: MacDonaldization and Cultural

Elitism'; in Alfino, M., Caputo, J.S. & Wynyard, R. (Eds) (1998); op.cit.

Parkin, N. (1978): 'Apprenticeships: Outmoded or Undervalued?'; *Personnel Management*, 10 (5), pp.22-46.

Patel, K. (1998): 'Degree boosts earning power'; *Times Higher Education Supplement*, February 2.

Peters, R.S. (1966): *Ethics and Education* (London: Allen & Unwin).

Peters, R.S. (Ed) (1977): *John Dewey Reconsidered* (London: Routledge & Kegan Paul).

Peters, R.S. (1978): 'Ambiguities in Liberal Education and the Problem of its Content'; in Strike, K.A. & Egan, K. (Eds): *Ethics and Educational Policy* (London: Routledge & Kegan Paul).

Pettigrew, A., Arthur, M. & Hendry, C. (1990): *Training and Human Resource Management in SMEs: A Critical Review of the Literature and a Model for Future Research* (Sheffield: Training Agency).

Phillips Griffiths, A. (1965): 'A Deduction of Universities'; in Archambault, R.D. (Ed); *Philosophical Analysis and Education* (London: Routledge & Kegan Paul).

Pickard, J. (1985): 'The Technical and Vocational Education Initiative'; *Times Educational Supplement*, May 3.

Piore, M.J. & Sabel, C.F. (1984): *The Second Industrial Divide* (New York: Basic Books).

Pirsig, R.M. (1974): *Zen and the Art of Motorcycle Maintenance* (London: Corgi).

Plumb, J.H. (1961): *England in the Eighteenth Century* (Harmondsworth: Penguin).

Pollard, A., Purvis, J. & Walford, G. (Eds) (1988): *Education, Training and the New Vocationalism* (Milton Keynes: Open University Press).

Poole, R. (1990): 'Morality, Masculinity and the Market'; in Sayers, S. & Osborne, P. (Eds): *Socialism, Feminism and Philosophy* (London: Routledge).

Pound, T. (1998): 'Forty Years On: the issue of breadth in the post-16 curriculum'; *Oxford Review of Education*, 24 (2), pp.167-179.

Powell, J.P. (1968): 'On learning to be original, witty, flexible, resourceful, etc.'; *Proceedings of the Philosophy of Education Society of Great Britain* II, pp.43-9.

Prais, S. (1991): 'Vocational Qualifications in Britain and Europe: Theory and Practice'; *National Institute Economic Review*, May, pp.86-92.

Prais, S. (1995): *Productivity, Education and Training: an international perspective* (Cambridge: Cambridge University Press).

Prasad, R. (1998): 'A New Deal for the Young – but not if you're black'; *The Big Issue*, April 6-12, pp.4-5.

Prestage, M. (1992): 'Academe amid the production lines'; *Times Educational Supplement*, May 15.

Pring, R. (1976): *Knowledge and Schooling* (London: Open Books).

Pring, R. (1995): *Closing the Gap: Liberal Education and Vocational Preparation*

(London: Hodder & Stoughton).

Pring, R. (1997): 'Aims, Values and the Curriculum'; in Tomlinson, S. (Ed) (1997); op.cit.

Prosser, M. & Millar, R. (1989): 'The "how" and "why" of learning physics'; *European Journal of Psychology of Education*, 4 (3), pp.513-528.

Psacharopoulos, G. (1981): 'Returns to education : an updated international comparison'; *Comparative Education*, 17 (2), pp.321-341.

Pye, D. (1968): *The Nature and Art of Workmanship* (Cambridge: Cambridge University Press).

Raffe, D. (1993): 'Tracks and Pathways; Differentiation in Education and Training Systems and their Relation to the Labour Market'; paper presented at the *First Conference of the European Research Network on Transitions in Youth* (Barcelona: Spain).

Raggatt, P. (1994): 'Implementing NVQs in colleges: progress, perceptions and issues'; *Journal of Further & Higher Education*, 18 (1), pp.59-74.

Ramsden, P. (1992): *Learning to Teach in Higher Education* (London: Routledge).

Ramsden, P., Beswick, D. & Bowden, J.A. (1986): 'Effects of learning skills intervention on first-year university students' learning'; *Human Learning*, 5 (2), pp.151-164.

Ranson, S. (1984): 'Towards a teriary tripartism: new codes of social control and the 17+'; in Broadfoot, P. (Ed): *Selection, Certification and Control: Social Issues in Educational Assessment* (Lewes: Falmer).

Ranson, S. (1994): *Towards the Learning Society* (London: Cassell).

Ranson, S. (Ed) (1998): *Inside the Learning Society* (London: Cassell).

Ranson, S. (1998a): 'Lineages of the Learning Society'; in Ranson, S. (Ed) (1998); op.cit.

Ranson, S., Martin, J., McKeown, P. & Nixon, J. (1996): 'Towards a Theory of Learning'; *British Journal of Educational Studies*, 44 (1), pp.9-26.

Ranson, S. & Stewart, J. (1998): 'The Learning Democracy'; in Ranson, S.'(Ed) (1998); op.cit.

Rawls, J. (1972): *A Theory of Justice* (Oxford: Oxford University Press).

Read, J. (1998): 'Building trade upgrades training packages'; *Times Educational Supplement*, August 8.

Reeves, F. (1995): *The Modernity of Further Education* (Wolverhampton: Bilston College Publications/Education Now).

Reich, R. (1991): *The Work of Nations: A Blueprint for the Future* (New York: Vintage).

Reid, E. (1980): 'Young People and Employment (1): Employers' Use of Educational Qualifications'; *Education Policy Bulletin*, 8 (1), pp.16-23.

Reisenberger, A., Hughes, M. & Green, M. (1994): *Managing the Delivery of Guidance in Colleges* (Dorset: Blackmore Further Education Unit).

Revell, P. (1997): 'Training too dear for many firms'; *Times Educational*

Supplement, January 31.

Richardson, J.T.E. (1994) : 'Mature students in higher education - academic performance and intellectual ability'; *Higher Education*, 28 (3), pp.373-386.

Rifkin, J. (1995): *The End of Work: The Decline of the global Labour Force and the Dawn of the Post-Market Era* (New York: G.P. Putnam's & Sons).

Rikowski, G.(1998a): 'Only Charbydis: The Learning Society Through Idealism'; in Ranson, S. (Ed) (1998); op.cit.

Rikowski, G. (1998b): *Education for Industry: A Complex Technicism* (Birmingham: University of Birmingham School of Education).

Rikowski, G. (1998c): *Three Types of Apprenticeship, Three Forms of Mastery: Nietzsche, Marx, Self and Capital* (Birmingham: University of Birmingham School of Education).

Rikowski, G. (1998d): *Nietzsche's School? The Roots of Educational Postmodernism* (Birmingham: University of Birmingham School of Education).

Rikowski, G. (1999): 'Education, Capital and the Transhuman'; in Hill, D., McLaren, P., Cole, M. & Rikowski, G. (Eds); *Postmodern Excess in Educational Theory: Education and the Politics of Human Resistance* (London: Tufnell Press) in press.

Ritzer, G. (1993): *The McDonaldisation of Society* (London: Pine Forge Press).

Robbins, L. (1963): *Higher Education: Report of the Committee* (London: HMSO).

Robinson, K. (1998): 'Creativity knows no stereotypes'; *Times Educational Supplement*, March 13.

Robinson, P. (1996): *Rhetoric and Reality: Britain's new vocational Qualifications* (London School of Economics: Centre for Economic Performance).

Roderick, G. & Stephens, M. (Eds) (1982): *The British Malaise: Industrial Performance,Education and Training in Britain Today* (Lewes: Falmer).

Rosenbaum, J. & Binder, A. (1997): 'Do Employers really Need More Educated Youth?'; *Sociology of Education*, 70 (1), pp.15-27.

RSA (1998): *Redefining Work* (London: Royal Society of Arts).

Russell, B. (1946): *History of Western Philosophy* (London: Allen & Unwin).

Russell, B. (1997a): 'Adult classes hit twice by cuts'; *Times Educational Supplement*, July 14.

Russell, B. (1997b): 'Vocational A-level has failed'; *Times Educational Supplement*, June 6.

Russell, C. (1997): 'Power and the Market'; *Times Higher Education Supplement*, December 5.

Ryle, G. (1972): 'A rational animal'; in Dearden, R.F., Hirst, P.H. & Peters, R.S. (Eds); *Education and the Development of Reason* (London: Routledge & Kegan Paul).

Ryle, G. (1973): *The Concept of Mind* (Harmondsworth: Penguin) [originally published in 1949].

Sandel, M. (1992): 'The procedural republic and the unencumbered self'; in Avineri, S. & De-Shelit, A. (Eds); *Communitarianism and Individualism* (Oxford: Oxford University Press).

Sauvain, P. (1989): *The Modern World 1914-1980* (Cheltenham: Stanley Thornes).

Schaefer, S. (1998): 'Blair's vision to reform Britain'; *The Guardian*, September 30.

Scheffler, I. (1960): *The Language of Education* (Springfield, Illinois: Charles C.Thomas).

Scheffler, I. (1965): *Conditions of Knowledge* (Chicago: Scott,Foresman & Co.).

Schmeck, R.R. (1983): 'Learning Styles of College Students'; in Dillon, R. & Schmeck, R.R. (Eds); *Individual Differences in Cognition* (New York : Academic Press).

Schofield, H. (1972): *The Philosophy of Education: An Introduction* (London: Allen & Unwin).

Schofield, P. (1923): 'Training and the Young Worker'; *Welfare Work*,Vol.IV, No.46, pp.15-21.

Schuller, T. & McGarry, J. (Eds) (1979): *Recurrent Education and Lifelong Learning* (London: Kogan Page).

Schuller, T. & Field, J. (1998): 'Social capital, human capital and the learning society'; *International Journal of Lifelong Education*, 17 (4), pp.226-235.

Schulz, T.W. (Ed) (1961): *Investment in Human Beings* (Chicago:University of Chicago Press).

Searle, C. (1987): 'Policy-Makers and the Youth Training Scheme: concepts of education and training'; in Holt, M. (Ed) (1987); op.cit.

Sharp, P. (1997): *The Development of the Vocational Curriculum for 16-19 Year Olds in Colleges and Schools,1979-1995* (Leeds: University of Leeds School of Education).

Sheldrake, J. & Vickerstaff, S. (1987): *The History of Industrial Training in Britain* (Godstone,Surrey: Avebury).

Shilling, C. (1989): *Schooling for Work in Capitalist Britain* (Lewes: Falmer Press).

Shirley, I. (1991): 'State Policy and Employment'; in Corson, D. (Ed) (1991); op.cit.

Short, C. (1986): 'The MSC and Special Measures for Unemployment'; in Benn, C. & Fairley, J. (Eds) (1986); op.cit.

Sieminski, S. (1993): 'The "flexible" solution to economic decline'; *Journal of Further & Higher Education*, 17 (1), pp.92-100.

Silver, H. & Brennan, J. (1988): *A Liberal Vocationalism* (London: Methuen).

Simon, B. (1974): *Education and the Labour Movement,1870-1920* (London: Lawrence & Wishart).

Sinclair, T.A. (Trans.) (1962): *Aristotle - The Politics* (Harmondsworth: Penguin).

Singer, P. (1982): *Practical Ethics* (Cambridge: Cambridge University Press).

Singley, M.K. & Anderson, J.R. (1989): *The Transfer of Cognitive Skill* (Cambridge, MA: Harvard University Press).

Skilbeck, M. (1987): 'Three Educational Ideologies'; in Horton, T. & Raggatt, P. (Eds); *Challenge and Change in the Curriculum* (London: Hodder & Stoughton).

Skilbeck, M., Connell, H., Lowe, N. & Tait, K. (1994): *The Vocational Quest* (London: Routledge).

Skills & Enterprise Network (1997): *Modern Apprenticeships - A Success Story* (London: Dept for Education and Employment) Issue 3/97.

Skills & Enterprise Network (1998a): *Soft Skills Matter* (London: Dept for Education and Employment) Issue 1/98.

Skills & Enterprise Network (1998b): *Labour Market and Skill Trends 1998/ 1999* (London: Dept for Education and Employment).

Smith, D. (1996): 'Do markets work?'; *Social Sciences* (London: Economic and Social Research Council).

Smith, M. (1984): 'Mental Skills: some critical reflections'; *Journal of Philosophy of Education*, 16 (3), pp.225-232.

Smith, R. (1987): 'Skills - the middle way'; *Journal of Philosophy of Education*, 21 (2), pp.197-201.

Smith, R. (1997): 'The education of autonomous citizens'; in Bridges, D. (Ed); *Education, Autonomy and Democratic Citizenship* (London: Routledge).

Smithers, A. (1993): *All Our Futures: Britain's education revolution* (London: Channel 4 Television 'Dispatches' Report in Education).

Smithers, A. (1996): *Comments on the Beaumont Report* (London: Institute of Commercial Management).

Smithers, A. (1999): 'A Critique of NVQs and GNVQs'; in Flude, M. & Sieminski, S. (Eds) (1999); op.cit.

Snelling, J.(1987): *The Buddhist Handbook* (London: Rider).

Social Exclusion Unit (1998): *Bringing Britain Together: a national strategy for neighbourhood renewal* (London: The Stationery Office).

Solow, R.M. (1999): *Work and Welfare* (Princeton, N.J.: Princeton University Press).

Spours, K. (1997): 'GNVQs and the Future of Broad Vocational Qualifications'; in Hodgson, A. & Spours, K. (Eds) (1997); op.cit.

Spours, K. & Young, M. (1997a): 'Not overarching enough'; *Times Educational Supplement*, November 21.

Spours, K. & Young, M. (1997b): 'Towards a Unified Qualifications System for Post-Compulsory Education : Barriers and Strategies'; in Hodgson, A. & Spours, K. (Eds) (1997); op.cit.

Spours, K. & Young, M. (1998): '14-19 Education: legacy,opportunities and challenges'; *Oxford Review of Education*, 24 (1), pp.83-97.

Standish, P. (1997): 'Heidegger and the Technology of Further Education'; *Journal of Philosophy of Education*, 31 (3), pp.439-459.

Stephens, M.D. (1990): *Adult Education* (London: Cassell).

Stewart, J. & Sambrook, S. (1995): 'The role of functional analysis in NVQs: a critical appraisal'; *British Journal of Education and Work*, 8 (2), pp.93-106.

Storey, D. (1994): *Understanding the Small Business Sector* (London: Routledge).

Strain, M. (1998): 'Towards an Economy of Lifelong Learning: Reconceptualising Relations between Learning and Life'; *British Journal of Educational Studies*, 46 (3), pp.264-277.

Strain, M. & Field, J. (1998): 'On the Myth of the Learning Society'; in Ranson, S. (Ed) (1998); op.cit.

Stronach, I. (1990): 'Education, Vocationalism and Economic Recovery: the case against witchcraft'; in Esland, G. (Ed) (1990); op.cit.

Sullivan, K. (1990): 'Japan-ease universities'; *The Guardian*, October 2.

Swain, H. (1998): 'Blunkett puts £38m behind skills boost'; *Times Higher Education Supplement*, September 18.

Targett, S. (1993): 'Advertising money doubled'; *Times Educational Supplement*, November 12.

Targett, S. (1995): 'NCVQ goes to market'; *Times Educational Supplement*, January 6.

Tennant, M. (1991): 'Expertise as a Dimension of Adult Development'; *New Education*, 13 (1), pp.49-55.

TES (1996): 'High price of NVQs assessed at work'; *Times Educational Supplement*, October 4.

TES (1998): 'Not worth the paper...'; *Times Educational Supplement*, March 27.

THES (1998a): 'Brown brainchild blighted at birth'; *Times Higher Education Supplement*, April 3.

THES (1998b): 'NVQ failure "triumph for the market"'; *Times Higher Education Supplement*, December 11.

THES (1999a): 'New Deal extends to college placements'; *Times Higher Education Supplement*, January 15.

THES (1999b): 'FE calls top helpline figures'; *Times Higher Education Supplement*, January 29.

THES (1999c): 'Workplace training receives cash boost'; *Times Higher Education Supplement*, January 22.

Thomas, D. (Ed) (1995): *Flexible Learning Strategies in Higher and Further Education* (London: Cassell).

Thomson, A. (1997): 'Student numbers in FE grow by 16%'; *Times Higher Education Supplement*, August 1.

Thomson, A. (1998): 'Alarm at shift in FE expansion targets'; *Times Educational Supplement*, December 4.

Tight, M. (1998a): 'Lifelong Learning: Opportunity or Compulsion?'; *British Journal of Educational Studies*, 46 (3), pp.251-263.

Tight, M. (1998b): 'Education, Education, Education! The vision of lifelong Learning in the Kennedy, Dearing and Fryer reports'; *Oxford Review of Education*, 24 (4), pp.473-485.

Tomlinson, J. (1996): *Inclusive Learning : principles and recommendations* (Coventry: Further Education Funding Council).

Tomlinson, S. (Ed) (1997): *Education 14-19: Critical Perspectives* (London: The Athlone Press).

Tooley, J. (1995): *Disestablishing the School* (Aldershot: Avebury).

Tooley, J. (1998): 'The neo-liberal critique of state intervention in education: a reply to Winch'; *Journal of Philosophy of Education*, 32 (2), pp.107-121.

Training Agency (1990): *Enterprise in Higher Education: key features of EHE proposals* (Sheffield: Training Agency).

Training & Employment Network (1997): *Target 2000 Briefing and Consultation* (London: Training & Employment Network).

Truelove, S. (Ed) (1991): *Handbook of Training and Development* (Oxford: Blackwell)

Trusted, J. (1987): *Moral Principles and Social Values* (London: Routledge & Kegan Paul).

Tuckett, A. & Sargant, N. (1996): 'Headline Findings on Lifelong Learning from the NIACE/Gallup Survey 1996'; *Adults Learning*, 7 (9), pp.219-223.

Tuckett, A. (1997): ' For the Many, Not the Few'; *Adults Learning*, 9 (4), p.3.

Tuxworth, E. (1989): 'Competence based education and training: background and origins'; in Burke, J. (Ed) (1989); op.cit.

Twining, J. (1997): 'The National Grid for Learning'; *Educa*, No.177, pp.10-11.

Twining, J. (1998): 'The turn of the NTOs'; *Educa*, No.179, pp.8-9.

UDACE (1989): *Understanding Competence* (Leicester : Unit for the Development of Adult Continuing Education).

University of Sussex (1996): *The Assessment of NVQs* (University of Sussex: Institute of Education).

Unwin, L. (1997): 'Reforming the Work-Based Route: Problems and Potential for Change'; in Hodgson, A. & Spours, K. (Eds) (1997); op.cit.

Wadd, K. (1988): 'Chicken or egg?'; *Times Educational Supplement*, September 30.

Wall, G.I. (1968): 'The Concept of Vocational Education'; *Proceedings of the Philosophy of Education Society of Great Britain*, 1967-68, pp.51-65.

Ward, L. (1995a): 'NVQs get "do know,don't care" response'; *Times Educational Supplement*, December 29.

Ward, L. (1995b): 'Catering to raining needs'; *Times Educational Supplement,* October 13.

Ward, L. (1996): 'Awards improperly claimed by college'; *Times Educational Supplement*, May 17.

Ward, C. (1997): 'More about the New Deal'; *Educa*, No. 177, pp.8-9.

Ward, C. (1998): 'The resurgence of "other" qualifications and their place in the National Framework'; *Educa*, No. 182, pp.8-10.

Wardle, D. (1976): *English Popular Education, 1780-1975* (Cambridge: Cambridge University Press).

Warnock, G.J. (1967): *Contemporary Moral Philsophy* (London: Macmillan).

Warnock, M. (1977): *Schools of Thought* (London: Faber & Faber).

Watkins, D.A. & Hattie, J. (1981): 'The learning processes of Australian university students'; *British Journal of Educational Psychology*, 51 (3), pp.384-393.

Weinstock, A. (1976): 'I blame the teachers'; *Times Educational Supplement*, January 23.

Wellington, J. (1987): 'Skills for the Future? Vocational Education and New Technology'; in Holt, M. (Ed) (1987); op.cit.

Wellington, J. (1994): 'How far should the post-16 curriculum be determined by the needs of employers?'; *The Curriculum Journal*, 5 (3), pp.229-247.

White, J. (1973): *Towards a Compulsory Curriculum* (London: Routledge & Kegan Paul).

White, J. (1997): *Education and the End of Work: A New Philosophy of Work and Learning* (London: Cassell).

Whitehead, A.N. (1962): *The Aims of Education* (London : Ernest Benn) [originally published in 1932].

Whiteside, T., Sutton, A. & Everton, T. (Eds) (1992): *16-19 Changes in Education and Training* (London: David Fulton).

Whittaker, M. (1998): 'Quick off the mark with their partners'; *Times Educational Supplement*, December 4.

Whitty, G. (1985): *Sociology and School Knowledge* (London: Methuen).

Wiener, M. (1981): *English Culture and the Decline of the Industrial Spirit, 1850-1980* (Cambridge: Cambridge University Press).

Wilds, E.H. & Lottich, K.V. (1970): *The Foundations of Modern Education* (New York: Holt, Rinehart & Winston).

Wilkinson, E. (1931): 'Co-operation between Education and Industry'; *Labour Management*, Vol.XIII (133), pp.240-248.

Wilkinson, R.H. (1970): 'The Gentleman Ideal and the Maintenance of a Political Elite'; in Musgrave, P.W. (Ed); *Sociology, History and Education* (London: Methuen).

Williams, G. (1963): *Apprenticeship in Europe: The Lesson for Britain* (London: Chapman & Hall).

Williams, R. (1971): *The Long Revolution* (Harmondsworth: Penguin).

Willis, P.(1977): *Learning to Labour* (London: Saxon House).

Wilson, J. (1972): *Philosophy and Educational Research* (Slough: National Foundation for Educational Research).

Winch, C. (1995): 'Education Needs Training'; *Oxford Review of Education*,

21 (3), pp.315-325.

Winch, C. (1998): 'Markets, Educational Opportunities and Education: Reply to Tooley'; *Journal of Philosophy Education*, 32 (3), pp.429-436.

Wojtas, O. (1999): 'Scots class myth debunked'; *Times Higher Education Supplement*, January 29.

Wolf, A. (1995): *Competence-Based Assessment* (Buckingham: Open University Press).

Wolf, A. (1997a): 'Growth stocks and lemons: diplomas in the English market-place,1976-1996'; *Assessment in Education*, 4 (1), pp.33-49.

Wolf, A. (1997b): *Evaluation of GNVQs* (London: Nuffield Foundation/Further Education Development Agency).

Wolf, A. & Silver, R. (1995): *Measuring Broad Skills: the prediction of skill retention and transfer over time* (London: Dept for Education and Employment).

Woodhall, M. (1990): 'Human Capital Concepts'; in Esland, G. (Ed) (1990); op.cit.

Wragg, T. (1998): 'Dalek dogma is a bitter pill'; *Times Educational Supplement*, May 15.

Wright, D. (1989): *Moral Competence* (London: Further Education Unit).

Wringe, C. (1991): 'Education, schooling and the world of work'; in Corson, D. (Ed) (1991); op.cit.

Wyatt, J. (1990): *Commitment to Higher Education* (Buckingham: Open University Press).

Young, M. (1997): ' The Dearing Review of 16-19 Qualifications: A Step Towards a Unified System?'; in Hodgson, A. & Spours, K. (Eds) (1997); op.cit.

Young, M. (1998): 'Post-Compulsory Education for a Learning Society'; in Ranson, S. (Ed) (1998); op.cit.

Young, M. & Leney, T. (1997): 'From A-Levels to an Advanced Level Curriculum for the Future'; in Hodgson, A. & Spours, K. (Eds) (1997); op.cit.

Young, M. & Spours, K. (1998): '14-19: legacy, opportunities and challenges'; *Oxford Review of Education*, 24 (1), pp.83-97.

Zuboff, S. (1988): *In the Age of the Smart Machine* (New York: Basic Books).

Index